Scott

Villa El Arsen

David + Susie Scott
Home James, Culmington
Ludlow SY8 2DB
Tél/Fax : 01584 861 325
susiescott451@hotmail.com

RICHARD KNIGHT is an award-winning travel writer. Currently the editor of the *Gapyear* magazine and website, he has written for the *Daily* and *Sunday Telegraph*, the *Times*, the *Financial Times*, the *Guardian*, the *Observer*, the *Daily Mail*, the *Independent* and many other publications in Britain and abroad. He is the author of *The Millennium Guide* (also from Trailblazer) and has written or contributed to several other travel books. He is a Fellow of the Royal Geographical Society.

Wanderlust overtook Richard at an early age and he has since travelled at every opportunity. His most recent visit to Morocco was to research this guide, which he did with the help of a flatulent mule.

Trekking in the Moroccan Atlas
First edition 2001

Publisher
Trailblazer Publications
The Old Manse, Tower Rd, Hindhead, Surrey GU26 6SU, UK
Fax (+44) 01428-607571
info@trailblazer-guides.com
www.trailblazer-guides.com

British Library Cataloguing in Publication Data
A catalogue record for this book is available from the British Library

ISBN 1-873756-35-6

Editor: Patricia Major
Typesetting: Anna Jacomb-Hood
Layout: Bryn Thomas and Anna Jacomb-Hood
Town plans and illustrations: Nick Hill
Trail maps and index: Jane Thomas

Printed on chlorine-free paper from farmed forests by
Star Standard (☎ +65-8613866), Singapore

TREKKING
IN THE
MOROCCAN
ATLAS

RICHARD KNIGHT

WITH ADDITIONAL MATERIAL AND RESEARCH
ON THE JBEL SIRWA & JBEL SAHRO REGIONS BY
PATRICK MAGUIRE

TRAILBLAZER PUBLICATIONS

For Mum and Dad

Patrick Maguire dedicates his contribution to this book
to the memory of his father, Michael

Acknowledgements

I am particularly grateful to Patrick Maguire for the hard work he put into this book
and for the good humour with which he tackled some of Morocco's more testing
treks. (Congratulations to Patrick on winning the Skylines 2000 Travel Photographer
of the Year Award). I am indebted to GB Airways for its generous support, Dr
Stephen Jury and Ronald Rutherford of Reading University's School of Plant
Sciences for their help with the flora section of this book and to Sir John Baird, former Surgeon General of the Ministry of Defence, for his help with the health section.
Many thanks also to Mr El Kasmi and his colleagues at the Moroccan National
Tourist Board offices in London and Marrakesh.

Sincere thanks also to all the trekkers I met on the trail for their advice and
encouragement and to the many local people who showed me such kindness while I
was in the mountains. Rupert Evers deserves special mention, if not an OBE, for
trekking with me for those first hilarious weeks in Morocco. Researching this guide
was made easier and more enjoyable by the company I kept in the mountains: Amina
Aït Brahim Hamou, the best guide in the Atlas; the two Brahims and Mohammed,
muleteers of distinction; and, of course, the mules.

All at Trailblazer Publications have once more proved themselves to be a great
team to work for. Sincere thanks to Bryn Thomas for his sorely-tested patience,
Patricia Major, my editor, and Jane Thomas for creating the maps and index with
such care.

Finally, thanks to all my friends and family who put up with me at various stages
of this book's conception and completion and without whom it would not have been
written.

A request

The author and publisher have tried to ensure that this guide is as accurate and up to
date as possible. Nevertheless things change: prices rise, new hotels are built and
trails are rerouted. If you notice any changes or omissions that should be included in
the next edition of this book, please write to Richard Knight at Trailblazer (address
on p2) or email him on richk@trailblazer-guides.com. A free copy of the next edition
will be sent to persons making a significant contribution.

Updated information will shortly be available on the Internet at
www.trailblazer-guides.com

Cover photo: Trekking in Jbel Sahro © Patrick Maguire

CONTENTS

INTRODUCTION

In buying this book you have taken a first step towards an unforgettable adventure. If you are still in the bookshop browsing, dig out your wallet and proceed to the till; take that first step now!

The Moroccan Atlas is a mountain range of exceptional beauty and cultural interest but it is still relatively little visited, a fact which makes the Atlas, to my mind, a far more exciting proposition than the European ranges. Add to that the extraordinary hospitality of the local Berber people, the rich texture of North African life and the exotic allure of Marrakesh and other Moroccan centres, and you will begin to see why a growing number of trekkers are choosing to explore this great range which the ancient Greeks thought to be the home of Atlas.

About this book
This guidebook is as practically useful and up to date as possible; it has been written with both the experienced and novice trekker in mind. The routes described are challenging but accessible. Regular hikers might find they cover ground more quickly than the route notes suggest but the book has been designed to allow readers to tackle as much or as little as they please at any one time. It also contains detailed information on Marrakesh, an exploration of which is a fascinating part of the Atlas experience, and on all other relevant towns and trailheads. There's practical information on every aspect of planning, arranging and enjoying an Atlas trek – from what to pack to what to say in French, Arabic and Berber. There are also sections on the flora and fauna of the Atlas, including a field guide to bird life and a section on minimum impact trekking to help visitors help locals to maintain the unspoilt state of the Atlas mountains.

The routes
This book can suggest and describe only a fraction of the treks available in the Atlas mountains, a range which spans some 1200 miles across Morocco, Algeria and Tunisia. But the routes reported here form a representative and exciting selection which is sure to satisfy newcomers and past visitors alike. Each route offers some distinct or unique draw which qualifies it for inclusion in the guide: the Toubkal area is the highest in the Atlas; M'goun is arguably the most classically beautiful; Sirwa is remote and challenging; and Sahro is the Atlas at its weird and striking best.

I sincerely hope you find this book useful and that you will have as much enjoyment as I did trekking in the Moroccan Atlas. *Inshallah!*

Richard Knight, London

*The design featured at the start of each part of this book is a
Berber tattoo motif, used to ward off the evil eye,
from the Middle Atlas mountains.*

With a group or on your own?

Time, Moroccans say, is the one coin each may spend as he thinks best, and no one may complain because another has more than his fair share.
André Launay *Morocco*

In comparison with ranges such as the Alps or the Pyrenees tourism in the Atlas mountains is relatively undeveloped, so trekkers seeking solitude need not explore far beyond the more-established routes; 'established' is a comparative word and indeed one meets few fellow trekkers even on the better-known routes. An exception is the Toubkal circuit. The Atlas walker can decide between travelling with an organised group, trekking with a guide or trekking completely alone without feeling under pressure to escape the crowds as one might in more exploited mountain ranges.

INDEPENDENT TREKKING

Kipling said 'he travels the fastest who travels alone' but he had never navigated his way across the Atlas mountains. It's not easy. There are no route markers and the routes themselves can be very indistinct. Apart from the danger of getting lost, it would be ecologically damaging for each trekker to carve a new path through the mountains. For these reasons, all but the most competent trekkers and map readers should consider employing a local guide rather than travelling solo.

TREKKING WITH A GUIDE AND MULE

Guides

Morocco has a well-organised programme for training **mountain guides** which is now used for guides from a number of other African countries. Would-be guides must pass a demanding three-day selection test before being accepted. They are then given one year's training at a centre near Tabant.

There are only 200 or so trained guides in the country. Qualified guides live in all Atlas trailheads so finding one is simple. They are given a badge which you should always ask to see before signing up to their services. It's also important to take a guide with whom you can develop a friendly relationship; go for tea with your prospective guide and try to gauge whether you will get on well together in the mountains. Most guides speak Berber and French but some also speak English. Expect to pay around £16/US$27 per day for a trained guide.

There are several very good reasons to use a guide:
● **Safety** A guide will help prevent you from getting lost and will be ready to help find a way out of the mountains in an emergency.
● **Communication** The Atlas Berbers have only recently begun to welcome visitors to their previously hidden world. Few speak French and fewer still know English. A guide will act as interpreter so you can talk to local people; apart from the cultural insight such an exchange might offer, this could be critical in an emergency situation.
● **Understanding** If you form a good relationship with your guide, which is likely over the course of a trek, you will benefit enormously from the chance this gives you to find out more about Moroccan life. When trekkers make friends of their guides, they are able to ask questions and gain understanding which otherwise would be denied to an outsider.
● **Enjoyment** Finding your own way through the mountains will take some effort. Admittedly, it is this very challenge which appeals to some. But if your guide is leading the way, you are left free to concentrate on trekking rather than map-reading.

Mules and *muleteers*

Groups of more than two people, or those trekking for an extended period, should consider taking a mule to carry their gear. This is the normal procedure in the Atlas and locals will think it bizarre if you prefer to carry your own pack. A mule, accompanied by a *muleteer* (mule-driver), will cost about £5/US$8 per day. Each mule carries about 100 kilos which usually equates to four backpacks. The muleteer will stack what appears to be an enormous amount of kit onto his mule but, if you fear for its safety, remember that to the muleteer this one animal provides an entire livelihood. He will look after it. Using a mule means you put money straight into local pockets. It also makes your trek safer since evacuation by mule is often the fastest way out of the Atlas in an emergency (see p39). The muleteer will organise food for the mule.

Even the fittest trekker will struggle to maintain the same pace as a muleteer and his animal. Mountain Berbers have spent their whole lives at altitude and they don't expect visitors to match their speed. They will wait every 40 minutes or so for the group to catch up.

While it's certainly true that most muleteers know their way round the mountains almost as well as trained guides, attempting to use a muleteer to act as a guide (which, admittedly, would save a lot of money) is frowned upon and most will refuse. Equally, never suggest paying a little extra for your guide to carry your pack. A guide would find such a proposal insulting.

Cuisinier

Your guide and muleteer will expect you to pay for their food while trekking. Usually this means employing a muleteer who doubles as a *cuisinier* (cook), although you could take a separate cuisinier. The cuisinier will then help you budget for and buy food for the entire trip (see p76) and he will race ahead each evening to prepare the meal in time for your arrival. Again, this is the accepted way things are done in the Atlas and, though it might sound rather decadent to employ a cook, you should consider going along with it. You will eat well if you do. If you plan to cook yourself, you will need to provide enough for the hearty appetite of your muleteer and guide.

Gîtes d'étape, refuges and camping

Despite a large number of villages in the Atlas, most of which provide accommodation either in a gîte d'étape (lodge) or private house, trekkers will almost certainly find it necessary to camp. In fact, it would be very difficult to plan a trek of any length with a gîte d'étape at the end of each stage.

If you do find yourself invited to stay in a private house, which is quite likely, don't expect more than a fairly primitive dwelling. Locals ask around £2/US$3 per night to put someone up. It's well worth it for a glimpse of domestic Berber life.

In summer, when temperatures soar, many trekkers choose to sleep under the stars or in bivvy-bags. On the higher slopes, however, nights can become very cold, even in summer; take a lightweight trekking tent. In winter, of course, overnight temperatures plummet well below freezing, so appropriate camping equipment must be taken. Remember to ask permission to camp whenever possible and tidy up afterwards (see p81).

There are a number of refuges (mountain huts) in the High Atlas, some managed by Club Alpin Français (CAF), which can be used for £2-4/US$3-6 per night. The CAF huts provide mattresses and a cooker and most refuges sell water and soft drinks. Only the Neltner refuge under Jbel Toubkal offers food. While there are plans to extend the refuge system, at present it is very limited. Refuges, like gîtes, are clearly marked in the relevant trekking section of this book.

GROUP TOURS

Convenience is the main reason why people join organised treks but there are other advantages: you might find yourself in a group of friendly, like-minded people and your guide will probably speak your language. If you've travelled to Morocco alone, joining a group is one way to avoid trekking solo. Several agencies combine trekking with other Moroccan 'highlights' or other mountain activities. Another advantage, of course, is that the better agencies offer a higher degree of comfort than you might achieve for yourself. And if you book through a company in your own country, you will probably find a representative on hand in Morocco to help smooth the way for you.

On the downside, group tours are relatively expensive. It's cheaper to organise the whole thing yourself. (Don't be put off by the thought that arranging a guide and muleteer is in some way difficult. It's not.) Another drawback is the fact that group tours follow a fixed itinerary. You might also find that a group trek proceeds at a different pace to yours. Groups tend to find their 'mean speed' which can be rather slow. It's also true that trekking with a large group of the same nationality makes it difficult to engage with local culture as fully as one might while trekking independently.

If you do decide to take the group option, however, you will find that several international adventure travel companies offer Atlas itineraries (see below). Then there are a number of Morocco specialists and, of course, a host of trekking agencies based in Morocco itself. Many of these companies, which tend to be based in Marrakesh, are slightly cheaper than their overseas competitors. It can be difficult arranging a trek through a Moroccan agency from home; it might be worth persevering, however, since a number of overseas-based agencies simply use Morocco-based companies anyway.

TREKKING AGENCIES

Trekking agencies in Britain
There are quite a number of British-based travel companies which offer Atlas treks. Some of these are combined with other popular Moroccan itineraries such as the 'kasbah trail', the 'imperial cities' or the 'oases route' into the Sahara. Most trek-only tour prices don't include airfares. A two-week High Atlas traverse will cost from £350 without flights or £700 with. Prices increase from there depending on the level of comfort offered and the exact itinerary. Jbel Toubkal treks (with flights) combined with Marrakesh are usually around the £650 mark.

● **Acacia Expeditions** (☎ 020-7706 4700; 🖷 020-7706 4686; 🖵 acacia @africa.demon.co.uk), Lower Ground Floor, 23a Craven Terrace, Lancaster Gate, London W2 3QH, offers a 15-day High Atlas trek.
● **Best of Morocco** (☎ 01380-828533; 🖷 01380-828630; 🖵 morocco @morocco-travel.com), Seend Park, Seend, Wilts SN12 6NZ, has tailor-made trekking and horse-trekking trips.
● **Destinations Educational Study Tours and Group Travel** (☎ 01494-792184; 🖷 01494-773576; 🖵 pzeyss@destinations-travel.com), 3 Sycamore Dene, Chesham, Bucks HP5 3JT, provides specialist travel to Morocco, including the High Atlas, for schools, universities and societies.
● **Discover Ltd** (☎ 01883-744392; 🖷 01883-744913; 🖵 info@dis cover.ltd.uk), Timbers, Oxted Rd, Godstone, Surrey RH9 8AD, also offers Atlas trekking and study tours to schools and universities. Discover Ltd owns the recently-restored Toubkal Kasbah at Imlil (see p129).
● **Exodus Travels** (☎ 020-8675 5550; 🖷 020-8673 0779; 🖵 sales@exod ustravels), 9 Weir Rd, London SW12 0LT, has a wide range of Atlas treks in the High, Central and Anti Atlas regions.

● **Explore Worldwide** (☎ 01252-760000; 📠 01252-760001; 💻 info @explore.co.uk), 1 Frederick St, Aldershot, Hants GU11 1LQ, offers a Jbel Sahro trek.

● **Far Frontiers** (☎/📠 01985-850926; 💻 cbhshort@aol.com), The Cottage, West Farm House, Corton, Wilts BA12 0SY, devises Jbel Toubkal and High Atlas traverse treks as well as camel trekking and Sahara safaris.

● **Guerba Expeditions** (☎ 01373-826611; 📠 01373-858351), Wessex House, 40 Station Rd, Westbury, Wilts BA13 3JN, has a 15-day High Atlas trek.

● **Marrakesh Express** (☎ 0141-332 1991; 📠 0141-332 1881; 💻 info @marrakesh-express.com), 133 Hill St, Glasgow G3 6JA, provides tailor-made trekking itineraries in the High Atlas as well as a number of other more general interest trips around Morocco.

● **Morocco Made to Measure** (☎ 020-7235 0123; 📠 020-7235 3851; 💻 clmltd@aol.com), First Floor, 69 Knightsbridge, London SW1X 7RA, has an extensive range of Moroccan tours available, including a number of Atlas treks on foot or horseback.

● **Mountain Treks and Training** (☎/📠 0121-680 3507), 125 Coombes Lane, Longbridge, Birmingham B31 4QU, organises school and youth group treks around Jbel Toubkal, Jbel Sahro, the M'goun massif and Jbel Sirwa.

● **Naturetrek** (☎ 01962-733051; 📠 01962-736426; 💻 info@nature trek.co.uk), The Cadcam Centre, Bighton, Nr Alresford, Hants SO24 9RE, offers a 17-day High Atlas trek.

● **Ramblers Holidays** (☎ 01707-331133; 📠 01707-333276; 💻 ramhols@dial.pipex.com), Box 43, Welwyn Garden City, Herts AL8 6PQ, has treks in the Middle Atlas.

● **Sherpa Expeditions** (☎ 020-8577 2717; 📠 020-8572 9788; 💻 sherp a.sales@dial.pipex.com), 131a Heston Rd, Hounslow, Middlesex TW5 0RD, has three 15-day treks around Jbel Toubkal, Jbel Sahro and the M'goun massif.

● **Steppes East** (☎ 01285-810267; 📠 01285-810693; 💻 sales@steppes east.co.uk), Castle Easton, Cricklade, Wilts SN6 6JU, claims to arrange tailor-made travel 'for individuals' including trekking in the Atlas.

● **The Imaginative Traveller** (☎ 020-8742 8612; 📠 020-8742 3045; 💻 info@imaginative-traveller.com), 14 Barley Mow Passage, Chiswick, London W4 4PH, organises 10- to 15-day adventure tours in Morocco, including trekking.

● **Travelbag Adventures** (☎ 01420-541007; 📠 01420-541022; 💻 sales @travelbag-adventures.co.uk), 15 Turk St, Alton, Hants GU34 1AG, offers Jbel Toubkal and Jbel Sirwa treks.

● **Walks Worldwide** (☎ 01332-230883; 📠 01332-360851; 💻 sales @walks-ww.co.uk), 25 Mount Carmel St, Derby DE23 6TB, High Atlas treks including Jbel Sahro.

- **Worldwide Adventures Abroad** (☎ 0114-247 3400; 🖹 0114-251 3210; 💻 abroad@infoserve.net), 7 Delamere Close, Beighton, Sheffield S20 2QE, has an 'Atlas adventure trek'.
- **Worldwide Journeys & Expeditions** (☎ 020-7381 8638; 🖹 020-7381 0836; 💻 wwj@journexdemon.co.uk), 8 Comeragh Rd, London W14 9HP, offers High Atlas treks among its extensive range of African tours.
- **Other companies** with interesting Atlas mountains itineraries, though not necessarily trekking, include **Abercrombie & Kent** (☎ 020-7730 9600; 🖹 020-7720 9376; 💻 info@abercrombiekent.co.uk), **British Airways Holidays** (☎ 0870-242 4249; 🖹 01293-722803), which offers a 'Berbers and Kasbahs' trip, **Headwater** (☎ 01606-813333; 🖹 01666-813334; 💻 info@headwater.com) with a 'Secrets of the Berbers' tour and **Tribes Travel** (☎ 01728-685971; 🖹 01728-685973; 💻 info@tribes.co.uk) which takes travellers to the *moussem* festival at Imilchil in the Middle Atlas.

Trekking agencies in Continental Europe

France Allibert (☎ 04-76.45.22.26; 🖹 04-76.45.27.28) offers treks in the Toubkal, Sirwa and Sahro regions.
- **Atalante** (☎ 04-72.53.24.80; 🖹 04-72.53.24.81) has an Atlas traverse and shorter treks to Jbel Toubkal, Sirwa and Sahro.
- **Club Aventure** (🖹 01-44.32.09.59, 💻 info@clubaventure.fr) takes trekkers to all the major walking regions in the Atlas.
- **Explorator** (☎ 01-53.45.85.85) specialises in the Sirwa and Sahro areas.
- **Fram** (☎ 01-40.26.20.00; 🖹 01-40.26.26.32) has Atlas walking tours.
- **Terres d'Aventure** (☎ 01-53.73.77.73) operates in most popular areas in the Atlas including M'goun.
- Other relevant tour operators include: **Argane**; **Horizons Nomades**; **Nouvelles Frontiers**; **Odysée Montagnes** and **Zig-Zag**.

Germany Baumeler Travel (☎ 0761-380 570, 🖹 0761-380 5730, 💻 www.baumeler.de) J Baumeler Wanderreisen GmbH, Engelbergerstr 21, 79106 Freiburg, leads walking tours in Morocco.
- **Wikinger Reisen GmbH** (☎ 02331-9046, 🖹 02331-904875, 💻 mail @www.wikinger.de, www.wikinger.de) Kölner Str. 20, D-58135 Hagen. Wikinger offers walking tours in the Atlas.

Netherlands Adventure World (☎ 023-5382 954, 💻 023-5384 744, atc@euronet.nl), Muiderslotweg 112, 2026AS Haarlem, offers a High Atlas trek.

Portugal Rotas do Vento (☎ 213-64.94.52, 🖹 213-64.98.43, 💻 rotas@rotasdovento.pt) R dos Lusiadas 5, 40k, 1300-365 Lisbon, Portugal, provides organised trekking opportunities in the M'goun region.

Switzerland Atlas Sahara Trekking (☎/🖹 026-323 43 60, 💻 jmaa@swissonline.ch), Rue du Simplon 4, 1700 Freiburg, can arrange camel and mule trekking in several Atlas areas.

Trekking agencies in USA

Escapade tours (☎ 602-473 7222; ☎ 800-356 2405); **Exodus** (☎ 914-666 4417; ☎ 800-692 5495); **Explorers Travel** (☎ 732-870 0223; ☎ 800-631 5650); **Himalayan Travel** (☎ 203-359 3711; ☎ 800-225 2380); **Imilchil Morocco Travel** (☎ 303-399 1953); **Morocco Travel International** (☎ 703-998 0100; ☎ 800-428 5550); **Mountain Travel** (☎ 510-527 8100; ☎ 800-227 2384); **Odysseys Unlimited** (☎ 781-370 3600; ☎ 888-370 6765); **Oussaden Tours** (☎ 212-685 4654; ☎ 800-206 5049); **Overseas Adventure Travel** (☎ 617-876 0533; ☎ 800-221 0814); **Travcoa** (☎ 714-476 2800; ☎ 800-992 2003); **Travel Bound** (☎ 212-334 1350; ☎ 800-456 8656); **Turtle Tours** (☎ 602-488 3688); **Wilderness Travel** (☎ 510-548 0420; ☎ 800-368 2794).

Trekking agencies in Canada

Butterfield & Robinson (☎ 416-864 1354; 🖹 416-864 0541); **Club Adventures Inc** (☎ 514-699 7784; 🖹 514-699 8758); **Evasion Tours** (☎ 514-284 5550; 🖹 514-264 0666); **Exotik Tours** (☎ 514-284 3324; 🖹 514-643 5493); **GM Tours** (☎ 416-598 2428); **Tours Escapade** (819-771 5331; 🖹 819-771 4782); **Travel Cuts** (☎ 416-979 8608); **Trek Holidays** (☎ 416-922 7584); **Worldwide Adventures Inc** (☎ 416-963 9163).

Trekking agencies in Australia

Adventure World (☎ 02-9956 7766; 🖹 02-9956 7707); **Exotic Destinations** (☎ 03-9886 4955; 🖹 03-9886 3644); **Exodus Expeditions** (☎ 02-9552 6317); **Explore Holidays** (☎ 02-9857 6200; 🖹 02-9857 6257; 🖳 info@exploreholidays.com.au); **IB Tours International** (☎ 02-9560 6722; 🖹 02-9560 6044); **Outdoor Travel** (☎ 03-9670 7252); **Timeless Tours and Travel** (☎ 02-9904.1239; 🖹 02-9904 1809; 🖳 travtour@timeless.com.au); **World Expeditions** (☎ 02-9264 3366); **Ya'lla Tours** (☎ 03-9510 2844; 🖹: 03-9510 8425; 🖳 yallamel@yallatours.com.au).

Trekking agencies in Morocco

● **Marrakesh** See p106 for trekking agencies in Marrakesh
● **Ouarzazate** See p122 for trekking agencies in Ouarzazate
● Otherwise try: **Agence Tigouga Aventure** (☎ 08-85.35.01) in Agadir; **Dynamic Tours** (☎ 02-20.26.82; 🖹 02-26.48.51), **Fantastic Tours** (☎ 02-20.11.37; 🖹 02-20.11.39) and **Randonnées Voyages** (☎ 02-26.63.65; 🖹 02-47.25.13) in Casablanca; **Ame d'Aventure** (☎/🖹 03-45.92.26) in Azilal; **Apple Tours** (☎ 07-70.12.42), **Lazer Tours** (☎ 07-20.70.34; 🖹 07-77.50.74), **Ribat Tours** (☎ 07-70.03.95; 🖹 07-70.75.35) and **Yasmine Travel** (☎ 07-67.54.57; 🖹 07-67.54.59) in Rabat; and **Tigouga Aventure** (☎ 08-85.31.22) in Taroudant.

Getting to Morocco

Morocco can be reached by road and rail from Europe and by air from Britain, France, Spain and North America. Information in this section is particularly vulnerable to change so check the details carefully.

BY AIR

Air travel remains the most efficient way to reach Morocco. Prices are relatively low and flight-times from Europe are short. Morocco is served by GB Airways, Royal Air Maroc (RAM), Air France and Iberia. There are a number of international airports in Morocco including those at Rabat, Casablanca, Fes, Agadir, Marrakesh and Ouarzazate. Marrakesh and Ouarzazate are the most convenient for getting to the High Atlas mountains but Casablanca, which is connected to Marrakesh by train, bus and internal RAM flights, is normally cheaper to reach from Continental Europe.

From Britain
GB Airways (☎ 0845-7733377), which operates British Airways aircraft, offers the best service from London with flights from Gatwick to: Casablanca (daily, from £230); Tangier (twice weekly, from £200); and Marrakesh (twice weekly, from £275). The flight time is approximately three and a half hours but might include a stop in Gibraltar. **Royal Air Maroc** (☎ 020-7439 4361) fly daily from London Heathrow to: Agadir (from £275); Casablanca (from £230); Tangier (from £200); Marrakesh (from £275); and Fes (from £350). See below for Air France flights via Paris and Iberia flights via Madrid.

From Continental Europe
Air France (☎ 0845-0845 111 in the UK or 0802-0802 802 in France) fly daily to Casablanca, Rabat and Marrakesh from Paris and Marseille. A return fare from Paris to Marrakesh will cost from £280 or 2855FF. **Royal Air Maroc** (☎ 020-7439 4361 in the UK or 01.44.94.13.10 in France) fly daily direct from Paris-Orly Airport to: Casablanca (from £315 or 3190FF); and Marrakesh (from £320 or 3265FF). **Iberia** (☎ 020-7830 0011 in the UK or 91-587 8787 in Spain) fly from Madrid to Marrakesh via Casablanca every Sunday, Wednesday and Thursday. A return fare from Madrid to Marrakesh will cost from £260 or 66,731ptas.

From USA
Royal Air Maroc (☎ 212-750 6071) fly five times a week from New York-JFK to Casablanca (from about US$1000) and Marrakesh (from about US$1050).

BY ROAD

European coaches and cars can get to Morocco by crossing on a ferry from southern Spain (see below). **Eurolines** (☎ 01582-404511) runs coaches from London to Marrakesh via Casablanca. French travellers board the same bus which stops in Paris on the way. The journey takes at least 36 hours, leaving London Victoria coach station on a Friday evening and arriving in Morocco on the following Sunday morning. At £225 from London it's not good value; you might as well fly.

BY RAIL

Train services, like coaches, offer questionable value to British and French travellers. It is possible to travel by train from London Waterloo to Algeciras from where a ferry crosses to Tangier (see below). But the journey costs over £300 from London and takes at least 24 hours including stops in Irun and Madrid. From Spain, however, the train is more competitively priced. If you feel like taking your time getting from Britain to Morocco, an Inter-rail pass represents reasonable value. A two-zone card (£209 for travellers aged under 26 and £279 for anyone older) lasts one calendar month and allows almost unlimited rail travel in Europe including Morocco. Contact **European Rail** (☎ 020-7387 0444) in London.

BY FERRY

Road and rail users will need to cross to Africa by ferry from southern Spain. The most commonly-used route is Algeciras-Tangier. The crossing takes two hours and costs £30 return for a foot passenger or £94 for a medium-sized car. Coach passengers will have paid the cost of the ferry in the price of their ticket. In the UK, **Sea-France Southern Ferries** (☎ 020-7491 4968) are ticket agents for this route. There are nine or ten crossings each day. It's also possible to cross to the Spanish enclave of Melilla from Màlaga. This is potentially a cheap option for British travellers who could fly from London Stansted to Màlaga with **Go** (☎ 0845-605 4321; ⌨ www.go-fly.com) for as little as £120.

Visas

Most visitors to Morocco, including British, French and American tourists, require a passport (valid for at least six months from time of entry) but no visa in order to stay in Morocco for up to 90 days. Exceptions include residents of New Zealand, South Africa and

❏ FURTHER INFORMATION

Travel advice

For up-to-date advice on travel in Morocco or, indeed, anywhere in the world, contact:

● **The Foreign and Commonwealth Office** (UK)
☎ 020-7238 4503/4; 🖳 www.fco.gov.uk

● **Department of State** (USA)
🖳 www.travel.state.gov

● **Department of Foreign Affairs and International Trade** (Canada)
☎ 1 800-267 6788; 🖳 www.dfait-maeci.gc.ca

● **Department of Foreign Affairs and Trade** (Australia)
☎ 06-261 9111; 🖳 www.dfat.gov.au

National tourist offices

Most major Moroccan towns have a tourist office (Office National Marocain de Tourisme) where you will find town plans and accommodation lists. See p107 for details of the Marrakesh office and p123 for Ouarzazate, the office in Rabat is at 31 angle rue Oued Fes, avenue Abtal, Rabat, ☎ 07-751 171 or 07-777 449; ▤ 07-777 437). But it's a good idea to contact the Moroccan National Tourist Office in your own capital before leaving home; these international branches normally have supplies of the latest literature, including the highly useful *Great Trek through the Atlas Mountains* booklet, as well as staff who speak your language. The GTAM booklet, updated most years, includes lists of qualified mountain guides and a good deal more information besides.

Australia
11 West St North
Sydney, NSW 2060
☎ 02-9922 4999

Canada
Suite 2450, 1870 Ave McGill College
Quebec H3A 3G6
☎ 514-842 8111

France
161 rue Saint Honoré
place du Théâtre Français
Paris 75001
☎ 01-42.60.63.50

Italy
23 Via Larga
20122 Milano
☎ 02-5830 3633

Spain
Calle Quintana 2
28008 Madrid
☎ 91-541 2995

UK
Second Floor,
205 Regent St
London
W1R 7DE
☎ 020-7437 0073

USA
Suite 1201,
20 East 46th St
New York,
NY 10017
☎ 212-557 2520

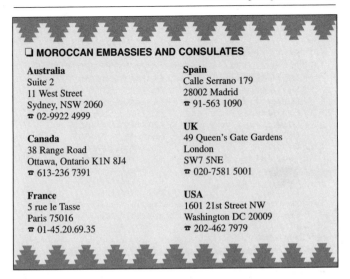

❏ **MOROCCAN EMBASSIES AND CONSULATES**

Australia
Suite 2
11 West Street
Sydney, NSW 2060
☎ 02-9922 4999

Canada
38 Range Road
Ottawa, Ontario K1N 8J4
☎ 613-236 7391

France
5 rue le Tasse
Paris 75016
☎ 01-45.20.69.35

Spain
Calle Serrano 179
28002 Madrid
☎ 91-563 1090

UK
49 Queen's Gate Gardens
London
SW7 5NE
☎ 020-7581 5001

USA
1601 21st Street NW
Washington DC 20009
☎ 202-462 7979

Zimbabwe. Nationals from these countries will need visas which can be applied for in advance and last for one month. They cost US$25. Apply to your nearest Moroccan embassy well before you plan to travel (the documents are sent to Rabat for official approval so might take some time to reappear).

All visitors are required to fill out a form on entering the country. It's best to keep your answers as dull as possible to avoid being made to explain the purpose of your visit to some suspicious immigration official. You can apply for an extension to your 90-day limit at any police headquarters. In practice, however, it's probably quicker to leave the country and come back in again in order to gain a new 90-day stamp.

No trekking permits are required for any of the routes described in this guide.

Budgeting and costs

ACCOMMODATION AND MEALS

Western travellers will find Morocco to be a fairly inexpensive destination. Accommodation can be very cheap; prices start at around 30dh (£1.90; US$3.20) per person for a room in an unclassified, bottom-of-the-range hotel. If you allow 150dh (£9.60; US$15.80) for a double room,

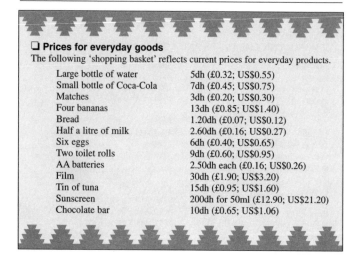

❏ **Prices for everyday goods**

The following 'shopping basket' reflects current prices for everyday products.

Large bottle of water	5dh (£0.32; US$0.55)
Small bottle of Coca-Cola	7dh (£0.45; US$0.75)
Matches	3dh (£0.20; US$0.30)
Four bananas	13dh (£0.85; US$1.40)
Bread	1.20dh (£0.07; US$0.12)
Half a litre of milk	2.60dh (£0.16; US$0.27)
Six eggs	6dh (£0.40; US$0.65)
Two toilet rolls	9dh (£0.60; US$0.95)
AA batteries	2.50dh each (£0.16; US$0.26)
Film	30dh (£1.90; US$3.20)
Tin of tuna	15dh (£0.95; US$1.60)
Sunscreen	200dh for 50ml (£12.90; US$21.20)
Chocolate bar	10dh (£0.65; US$1.06)

however, you should find something quite reasonable. Food can also be cheap. One could eat a full meal from a stall for as little as 20dh (£1.20; US$2.15) but the average main course in a restaurant is closer to 40dh (£2.50; US$4).

That said, Morocco is a land of extremes. While it's possible to spend very little on food and shelter, it's just as easy to spend huge sums. The best hotels and restaurants have prices to match their European equivalents. On the other hand, gîtes d'étape will cost no more than 30dh (£1.90; US$3.20) per person per night although CAF huts can charge twice that.

GUIDES AND TRANSPORT

The Atlas mountains demand few major expenses: a guide and muleteer will be the largest single costs; expect to pay 250dh (£16; US$27) per day for a guide and 75dh (£5; US$8) per day for a muleteer and his mule.

Transport costs will add up but, generally, travel in Morocco is still much cheaper than anywhere in Europe. A long-distance bus or train ticket will cost about 80dh (£5.20; US$8.50) and even internal flights are relatively good value. Keep in mind, however, that it might cost more to get to certain trailheads in the High Atlas in a *grand taxi* (long-distance taxi) than it would to cover long, inter-city routes by train or bus. Still, if you try, you can spend very little. Shared grands taxis can take you a long way for 15dh (£0.95; US$1.60) or so and *camions* (trucks) provide an even cheaper alternative.

YOUR OVERALL BUDGET

If you really tighten your belt you could get by on £10 (US$16.50) a day in most parts of Morocco. In the Atlas, you will have little need to spend money other than on provisions, transport to and from the trailhead and your guide and muleteer (see above for a breakdown of costs). A week-long trek, therefore, might cost £250 (US$415) including a guide, mule-teer, food, transport and a couple of nights in a gîte. That cost could be shared by up to four trekkers before you would need to employ an extra mule and muleteer.

Goods in Atlas villages can be twice the price of those in Marrakesh because of supply problems. There is nothing worse, however, than watching the almost fanatical fervour with which some 'budget travellers' try to eek out their finances. Keep things in perspective. If you haggle your night's accommodation down from 50 to 30dh, for example, you have saved yourself only the price of a Sunday newspaper.

Take some extra money or a credit card for emergencies and remember to leave enough cash to tip your guide and muleteer. See p72 for guidelines.

When to go

CLIMATE

Marrakesh sits in the foothills of the High Atlas but shares the predominantly Mediterranean climate of north-east Morocco. Summers are very hot and dry with little rainfall and temperatures soaring to 40°C. Winter temperatures hover around 20°C with rainfall seldom above 25mm in any one month but the influence of the Sahara can make nights cold.

The Atlas can be trekked all year though winters are cold and snowy; the highest peaks, including Jbel Toubkal, can be under snow from November to June and inexperienced trekkers may be limited to walking below the snow-line between November and May.

It can be very cold on the higher peaks at night, even in summer; although altitude usually prevents summer temperatures from becoming unbearable, it does get uncomfortably hot in the valleys. Summers in the Atlas are very dry; indeed, rivers and other watercourses (*wadis*), powerful in winter, become trickles or disappear completely in high summer.

The Moroccan rainy season lasts from October to April and the mountains can become very wet during these months, while swollen rivers, flooding their banks, can be dangerous in February. Spring is the really best time to visit; since some snow remains to make trekking more com-

❏ Temperature and rainfall

Marrakesh

	Jan	Feb	Mar	Apr	May	Jun	Jul	Aug	Sep	Oct	Nov	Dec
Max °C	18	20	22	25	28	33	38	37	33	27	23	19
Min °C	5	8	9	11	14	17	21	20	19	15	10	8
Rain (mm)	29	30	31	33	20	8	2	2	10	17	27	33

Rabat

	Jan	Feb	Mar	Apr	May	Jun	Jul	Aug	Sep	Oct	Nov	Dec
Max °C	17	19	20	20	23	25	28	27	27	24	21	18
Min °C	8	8	10	11	15	16	18	18	17	16	12	9
Rain (mm)	85	64	68	49	22	8	2	2	8	34	90	102

fortable underfoot, and days and nights are relatively warm, dry and pleasant. Some trekkers, however, may welcome the challenge of the other seasons.

RAMADAN

While Ramadan, described in more detail on p70, is in some respects a particularly interesting time to visit Morocco, it is a bad time to go trekking since guides and muleteers won't want to work and some gîtes will be closed.

Route options

The Atlas mountains form one of the world's great trekking ranges. Here one finds diversity and challenge, beauty and adventure. But the route you decide to pursue will depend on a number of factors: the season and your level of fitness will affect your choice; so, too, will your particular reasons for visiting the Atlas. If you want to reach the roof of North Africa, make for Toubkal; if you want to drink tea in an ancient Berber village go to M'goun. Trekkers hoping to find solitude will meet few other travellers on the ascent to Jbel Sirwa while the Sahro region offers striking land-scapes and isolated communities.

PLANNING YOUR ROUTE

Decide what you hope to get from your Atlas trek and plan a route accordingly. Don't try to pack in too much; the most memorable treks are those taken slowly enough to enjoy fully the environment through which one is walking. You will need to leave time to get from Marrakesh or Ouarzazate to the trailhead; details are included in the relevant sections but be aware that patience is often required when using Moroccan public transport and it makes sense to leave ample time to get down from the mountains. You might also plan to leave two or three days to explore Marrakesh which is itself one of the highlights of travelling to the Atlas mountains.

JBEL TOUBKAL   pp125-39

This well-known section of the High Atlas range is by far the most popular part of the Atlas mountains because of Jbel Toubkal (4167m/13,667ft), the highest peak in North Africa. You have the choice between bagging the summit in two or three days from Imlil or completing an extended circuit over six or seven days.

Circuit

To get to Jbel Toubkal one needs to travel from Marrakesh to Asni and then on to Imlil. From Imlil there is a trail to the Neltner Refuge, which sits at 3207m/10,518ft, and then up to the summit. The extended circuit covers remote and dramatic terrain, the stunning Lac d'Ifni, several Berber villages and a number of high-altitude passes.

Pros and cons No one should trek in the Atlas without conquering its greatest mountain. And the views from this high-altitude circuit are breathtaking. You will also meet more fellow trekkers on this route which can add to the enjoyment though, for some, the presence of other trekkers might detract from the pleasure of the trek.

Toubkal is a harsh and unforgiving landscape which, though beautiful, surprises those visitors who expect a relatively easy time and there are great changes in altitude and long, dry periods during which water is scarce.

M'GOUN MASSIF   pp149-74

The M'goun massif in the High Atlas range is a more lush and friendly area than Toubkal; the landscape is very different and, accordingly, offers a very different experience. The highest peak, M'goun, stands at 4068m/13,343ft and is the tallest outside the Toubkal area. There are bright, densely-populated valleys around M'goun and deeply-carved gorges along the higher sections of the trek, parts of which are quite isolated. The trailhead for these treks is Tabant; to get there from Marrakesh travel to Azilal and then on to Tabant.

Circuit

The six- or seven-day circuit described in this guide leads from Tabant to the vast Tarkeddid plateau (2900m/9512ft), then up to the summit (4068m/13,343ft) before running alongside the Ouililimt river to a series of charming Berber villages. From there the trail crosses a 2905m/9528ft-high col to descend back to Tabant in the Aït Bou Guemez valley.

Pros and cons Few could argue that the views from this trek are among the finest in Morocco. The trek itself is diverse with long stretches at high altitude and periods of isolation combined with village visits and popular routes on which one is bound to pass other trekkers.

Traverse

This low-altitude six-day traverse is relatively easy both to trek and navigate. It gives walkers a chance to spend time in High Atlas villages including that of Megdaz, perhaps the most attractive in the range. From Tabant the trail leads through the villages of Abachkou, Ifira, Amerzi, Aït Ali n'Ito, Megdaz and Aït Tamlil. Transport is available from Aït Tamlil to Demnate and Azilal.

Pros and cons Trekkers in search of a physical challenge might find this stage too easy, though others might find the relatively benign terrain a blessed relief after the demands of Jbel Toubkal or the M'goun summit. Perhaps the most obvious advantage to this route is the chance it offers to spend time in Berber villages. Berber hospitality is deservedly famous and meeting local people is an essential ingredient in a great Atlas trek.

JBEL SIRWA   pp175-99

The Sirwa region bridges the Anti and High Atlas ranges. It is a vast, harsh and magnificent expanse of weird rock formations, isolated communities and volcanic peaks. Trekking Sirwa is exciting, challenging and unforgettable. However, it can be difficult to navigate across this at times intimidating moonscape and less experienced trekkers should employ the help of a local guide. The route notes given in this book for Sirwa are particularly detailed because of the indistinct nature of the trail. Taliouine is the place to start a Sirwa adventure.

Circuit

The trailhead is at Taliouine but the circuit proper starts from Akhfamane. From there, the trail climbs steeply past Ti n'Iddr to reach Jbel Sirwa (3305m/10,840ft) after two or three days' trekking. After the

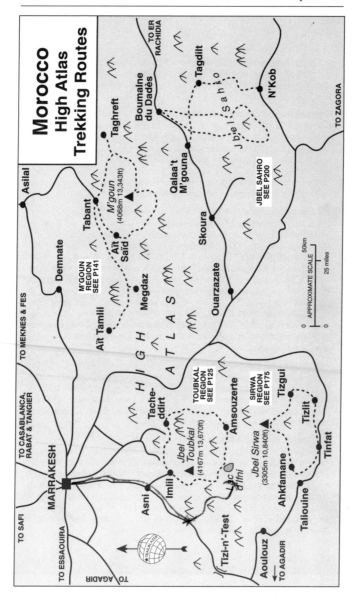

❑ AFTER YOUR TREK

While the Atlas mountains arguably form Morocco's most impressive feature, there is a lot more to see besides. It would be a pity to leave Morocco without tasting some of its other delights. A few of these are outlined in this brief section.

Marrakesh and the Imperial cities

Marrakesh, described in Part 4 of this book, is one of the most exciting cities in Morocco. Trekkers will almost certainly pass through Marrakesh on their way to the Atlas. It is well worth planning your itinerary to allow time to spend here either before or after your trek. Other ancient imperial cities such as Fes and Meknes are also worth exploring. Fes, particularly, is an important Moroccan cultural centre. As the oldest of the imperial cities, Fes probably ranks higher than Marrakesh for cultural importance.

Aït Benhaddou and the Drâa Valley to Zagora and Tinfou

For a real cross-section of what inland Morocco has to offer, hire a car in Marrakesh (see p89) and drive from there to M'Hamid or Tinfou via Ouarzazate along the Drâa Valley. The winding road takes you up into the Atlas before dropping to the Kasbah-strewn, sandy valley floor on its way through Zagora towards the Sahara desert. The road ends in M'Hamid, just 40km from Algeria, but Tinfou, which is itself no more than a couple of small kasbahs, is nestled in the pre-Saharan dunes. The views here are fantastic, although this is not the Sahara proper. For that you need to get to Merzouga (see below). On the way back, try to visit the giant kasbah of Aït Benhaddou which is about 30km from Ouarzazate. This is the best-maintained kasbah in the Atlas, mainly as a result of restoration for use in films such as *Lawrence of Arabia*, and it is a fascinating place.

Merzouga and the Saharan dunes

To see Saharan dunes as you might imagine them, a sweeping, drifting expanse of ever-changing colour, travel past Erfoud to the village of Merzouga. It's a long journey from Marrakesh but this is the only place in Morocco to see the sort of dunes which typify the Algerian Sahara. The dunes at Tinfou are impressive but cannot compete with this.

Essaouira and the Atlantic coast

If the bustle of Marrakesh gets too much, or you need a rest after your exertions in the Atlas, head for Essaouira on the Atlantic coast. The town is generally thought to be the most laid-back in Morocco, although that term is, of course, relative, and there is certainly an appealing coastal calm here which stands in stark contrast to the dusty streets of Marrakesh. Jimi Hendrix used to hang out here and the old fortified Portuguese centre still attracts a fair number of sandal-wearing, chilled-out travellers, many of whom look as though they might have been around to welcome Jimi personally.

summit, the route snakes down through several tiny, remote communities, including Tizgui, Tagouyam, Tinfat and Miggarn, to whom trekkers are a rarity.

Pros and cons This is a fairly difficult trek. Intense heat can make things harder and navigation is tricky. Sometimes water is scarce and trekkers have to be fairly self-sufficient; read the route notes before setting off in order to plan what you need to take with you. Nevertheless, trekking Sirwa is a wonderfully rewarding experience; while much of Morocco is growing tame in order to attract tourists, Sirwa remains completely wild.

JBEL SAHRO   pp200-29

Like Sirwa, Sahro is more remote than Toubkal and M'goun. While the trekking is lower and, perhaps, easier, navigating here can be difficult. The striking landscape of Sahro is punctuated by bright oases, twisted peaks and abandoned *kasbahs (*self-contained, fortified communities*)*. In fact, Sahro is like the surface of another planet and trekkers will be amazed by the strange beauty of the place. As with Sirwa, it is important that you read the route notes before setting off. Again, the route notes given in this guide are very detailed since there are no obvious reference points or tracks for orientation. Head to N'Kob for the Jbel Sahro traverse or Tassouit, the end-point for the traverse, for the circular trek.

Traverse
N'Kob (sometimes Nekob) is the trailhead for this traverse although the trek proper starts from Tifdassine. The six- or seven-day route meanders across an at times barren wilderness which is framed by weird peaks and scarred by sheer gorges. Head from Tifdassine through Boilouz, over Tizi n'Ouarg (2592m/8501ft) to Tagdilt and on to Tassouit.

Pros and cons This is a hard but rewarding trek across vast tracts of the Sahro region. There are few communities and no supplies so trekkers will need to be able to look after themselves. A guide might be needed since the trail is hard to follow. On the more positive side, there is no other area quite like Sahro which offers some of the most remarkable trekking in Africa. This is a challenge worth accepting.

Circuit
The circuit starts from Tassouit, where the traverse ends, and takes about six days. From Tassiout the circuit leads past Assaka n'Aït Ouzzine, over Tizi n'Tagmout and Tizi n'Tmirchct (2378m/7799ft) to Boumalne du Dadès, just a short distance from Tassiout and Qalaa't M'gouna. Frequent transport links both to Ouarzazate.

Pros and cons

There are fewer trekkers here than one might expect to meet around Toubkal or M'goun which means the trails across Sahro can be hard to follow and the local communities have few facilities. This is a slightly easier trek than the traverse but equally representative of the great diversity Sahro has to offer with its long ascents and descents, glimpses of nomads, remote Berber hamlets and local architecture.

What to take

In London, an expert traveller had pointed out that weight could be saved by carrying only one spare sock. Thus equipped with a total of three socks, the professional circulates them on the principle of crop rotation.
Nicholas Crane, *Clear Waters Rising*

Most Atlas trekkers will allow themselves more than three socks but the principle still applies: don't take too much. What you do decide to pack will, however, depend on how and when you decide to travel. If you travel in a tour group, for example, tents and accommodation might be organised for you. If you plan to hire a mule, you will be able to transport more bulk than you would on your back. Remember that it can get very cold at altitude at any time of year, particularly at night, while the sun can be strong during the day. Remember, too, that if you trek alone you will not always be able to find overnight shelter; most of the treks in this guide assume readers in this category have their own tents.

This kit list is extensive and you will want to tailor it to your own needs; if you collect everything from the list, your backpack will be enormous. It is, however, very important to prepare properly for a trek. Supplies are limited in the Atlas mountains, and even Marrakesh has very little in the way of trekking equipment, so you will need to collect all the gear you need before travelling to Morocco.

WHAT TO PACK IT ALL IN

A comfortable **backpack** is better than a **holdall**, though you might want to take the latter as well for leaving a change of clothes or spare kit in your hotel in Marrakesh or Ouarzazate. Even if you decide not to carry your bag yourself on your trek but to strap it to the back of a mule, there may be other times when you need to carry it.

The best backpack to buy is not necessarily the most expensive. Comfort is the main quality you need from your backpack, so take time to try different packs to see which suits you. While there are a number of theories about which style of backpack is best, and you will probably find this to be a hot topic of conversation at the Toubkal refuge most evenings, I recommend one with an **internal adjustable frame** and expandable side pockets. You must make sure that the weight of the pack is carried on your hips, not your shoulders.

Load the pack before leaving home and practise walking with it; this will give you a chance to get the various straps and adjustable parts just right. It's worth taking a bigger backpack than you think you need because you are almost bound to accumulate things on your travels and anyway you don't want to compress your gear too much. A 75-litre pack should do, although some trekkers will consider that size to be luxurious.

Another essential piece of kit is a small **daypack** to carry with you everywhere. This should be big enough for your camera, snacks, a water bottle and other essentials which you might not want to be separated from during the day. A 20-litre pack should be adequate; and, luckily, this is also about the right size for airline hand-baggage.

SLEEPING-BAG

A sleeping-bag is essential for campers and non-campers; gîtes d'étape don't always provide bedding. The warmth of the bag you take will depend on the time of year you plan to travel. A four-season bag should suffice over the winter; a one- or two-season bag will do in summer. For greater flexibility in winter and summer, take a light **fleece sleeping-bag liner** as this will allow you to add an extra season when necessary. (It's also a good idea to take a **cotton sleeping-bag liner**, just a sheet sewn together, to use all the time; this can then be washed and dried easily). Choose a synthetic bag over one which is down-filled; there are now a number of very small, light and effective synthetic bags which can be rolled up tightly. More importantly, once a down-filled bag gets wet, it stays wet for a long time.

Campers will need to take a **sleeping-mat**. This will help keep you warm and will also take some of the sting out of the hard ground. A three-quarter-length lightweight foam mat will prove adequate.

FOOTWEAR AND FOOT CARE

One of the most common complaints suffered by any trekker is the blister. This seemingly minor problem could seriously diminish your enjoyment of a trek or even force you to stop walking altogether; so it's very important to get the right boots and socks and to look after your feet. Ignore the fact that local muleteers will skip past you in sandals and make sure you keep your feet dry, well-supported and blister-free.

Boots

Trainers won't do; buy proper walking boots. Your first decision is whether to buy leather or fabric boots. Fabric boots are probably better;

they require less wearing in and less maintenance (Brasher is a good brand). Leather boots are considered more durable but you must make sure they're well worn in before you set off for Morocco. If you take leather boots, remember to take Nikwax or some similar product to treat them. It's definitely worth buying boots with a Goretex or Sympatex lining to make them waterproof. If you're taking a favourite pair of old boots, make sure they're in reasonable condition. If you're taking new boots, go for long walks to wear them in and identify potential problem areas on your feet. Take a small tube of superglue and some tape for emergency boot repairs; much of the terrain in the Atlas is sharp and rocky and your boots might suffer nicks. Also take spare laces.

Socks
Very important – buy good ones. Wear thin silk inner socks under thicker hiking socks. Anti-blister inner socks (such as Bridgedale) can be very effective. Close-fitting fabric boots might not require two pairs of socks but take some inners anyway; they're useful to wear alone for short periods if your feet get too hot.

Other footwear
Take either a pair of trainers or a pair of rafting sandals (Reef are good) to wear in the evenings after you've finished trekking for the day. Sandals are also useful for wearing while washing or wading through streams.

Foot care
Keep your feet dry, take your boots off during long breaks, wash your feet regularly and change socks often. Some trekkers believe in coating their feet and toes with anti-fungal foot powder (such as Mycil) every evening and morning as a preventative measure. See p244 for advice on dealing with blisters.

CLOTHES

The temperature varies greatly during any single day in the Atlas mountains. When the summits are cold and icy, the valleys may be scorching; even in summer, when the days can become almost unbearably hot, the nights are often bitterly cold. Trekkers will need to take a sensible range of clothes to deal with extremes of temperature. Several thin layers of clothes will keep you warmer than one or two bulky garments. The sun can be as dangerous as the cold; make sure you carry ample protection.

Waterproof jacket
Not essential depending on when you visit. In summer rain is unlikely but winters can be very wet. Take full waterproofs between November and May and make sure they are lightweight and breathable. Think twice before buying a very expensive jacket; they can be over-priced and, in the Atlas, an average-quality jacket should suffice.

Fleece jacket
A very warm fleece is essential for the evenings, mornings and, sometimes, nights. Try to find one which will roll up tightly.

Trousers/skirt
Take two pairs of medium-weight, quick-drying 'Rohan'-style walking trousers (the best available Rohans are expensive but there are a number of adequate alternatives). These are comfortable and practical for trekking; they will protect your legs from the sun or cold and won't offend local people (see p73-4). Choose subdued colours for the same reason. Local Bèrber-style trousers are a good alternative; they're light-weight, cheap and will amuse the locals you meet on your way. Women might prefer to take long skirts which are easy to walk in and, again, are much more acceptable to Berber people than shorts.

Shorts
On hot days you will probably want to change into shorts. In more remote Berber villages, however, shorts might offend. This applies particularly to women who should never wear really short shorts.

Shirts/T-shirts
Take long-sleeved cotton shirts. They protect from the sun, dry quickly and look respectable. T-shirts are also useful to wear underneath on cold days or to sleep in.

Underwear
Loose-fitting cotton underwear is best. Bring thermal underwear for the colder months or to sleep in.

Hat
A wide-brimmed hat will protect you from the sun. A baseball cap won't. Floppy hats are preferable; you can cram them into your backpack. Take a woolly hat for cold evenings.

Gloves
Thin fleece gloves are worth taking for cold nights.

Swimming costume
Men should take respectable swimming trunks and women should wear only one-piece suits. Men and women should also wear a sarong if bathing in a public place.

Neck-scarf
A useful item for sun protection.

Towel
These can be bulky so take a small one. A sarong can work just as well and has other uses.

TOILETRIES

Basic supplies are available in Marrakesh but it's better to bring toiletries from home if you are at all fussy about what you use. Take as little as possible. Washing opportunities are limited in the Atlas so you will use far less than you might expect to at home.

Shampoo and **shower gel** are best carried in small sample-size bottles. Better still, take a biodegradable all-purpose washing concentrate like **Mountain Suds. Shaving** can be difficult in the Atlas if you don't like shaving in cold water. To save space, however, consider taking **shaving oil** rather than gel or foam. **Tampons**, expensive in Morocco, are available in Marrakesh and some larger villages but it's safer to bring a supply from home. Similarly, you should carry adequate supplies of any **contraceptives** which you normally use.

Sunscreen is essential; the sun can be very strong in Morocco so take a high factor. Total block is useful for lips, ears and nose. Despite the expense, you should bring good-quality water-resistant cream. **Lip-balm** will help prevent chapping from general exposure.

Toilet paper is on sale in some larger villages but, since the locals use water and their left hands, you can't rely on finding any; stock up in Marrakesh. You will need to take a lighter to burn the paper you use. More up-market trekkers use **Wet Ones** but pink Moroccan loo rolls are good enough for most.

MEDICAL AND FIRST-AID KITS

Putting together an adequate medical kit for trekking can be surprisingly expensive. Don't automatically take everything on these lists; strike a balance between being well prepared and lugging over-stocked kits around the mountains. Think carefully about which products you are most likely to need.

If you plan to trek independently or for an extended period, consider taking a course in basic first-aid before you go so that you could, if called upon, deal with potentially dangerous situations. Access to medical help in the Atlas can be slow. That said, the Atlas are fairly densely populated and help will find you. Self-diagnosis should always be a last resort. If you join an organised trek, the leaders should have a well-stocked medical kit so you need only take personal supplies of day-to-day products. For a detailed guide to potential **health hazards** in the Atlas, see p241. Suggested brands are given in brackets.

(Opposite) Stark peaks and lunar landscape of the Jbel Sahro Region (see p200). (Photo © Patrick Maguire).

Medical kit
- **Oral re-hydration sachets** (Dialoryte) Take three or four sachets in case of diarrhoea or dehydration.
- **Antiseptic cream or iodine drops** For immediate treatment of cuts.
- **Paracetamol** To treat headaches.
- **Antibiotics** You might consider taking a course of antibiotics obtained from your doctor at home, but only use these if really necessary. Norfloxacin is the usual treatment for bacterial diarrhoea (see p244); it may be worth taking a course with you if you're going on a long trek.
- **Tinidazole/Flagyl** For the treatment of Giardia (see p244).
- **Diamox** Can help against altitude sickness. Some doctors claim this drug to be dangerous because it can hide symptoms of AMS (see p242).
- **Imodium** For diarrhoea but deals with the symptom not the cause so best used when you need to be blocked up (ie if you have a long bus trip ahead of you and you have diarrhoea).
- **Tweezers** For splinter and thorn removal.
- **Nail clippers** Keep your toe-nails neat to avoid problems.
- **Waterproof plasters** Take a long strip.
- **Zinc-oxide tape** Excellent stuff for preventing blisters.
- **Blister plasters** (Second Skin) Also helpful in the war against blisters.
- **Vaseline** Always useful for sore lips, hands and feet.
- **Antihistamine tablets** (Clarityn) Can be used to tackle an allergic reaction.
- **Anti-fungal foot powder** (Mycil) Can help prevent blisters.
- **Water purification tablets or drops** (See p242).
- **Personal medication** Take a supply to last the length of your stay.

First-aid kit
These are the basic components of a first-aid kit. If you have no idea how to use these things, however, you should ask your doctor or chemist to explain. Better still, take a short first-aid course.
- **Non-adhesive dressing** (Melolin)
- **One triangular bandage**
- **One crepe bandage**
- **One medium-large bandage**
- **Small scissors**
- **Safety pins**
- **Sterilised needle pack**
- Winter ice-trekkers should consider taking an **inflatable splint**

General items
Every trekker has a catalogue of items which they wouldn't leave home without. This list is designed to help you decide what to take. You don't

---

(Opposite) Trekking with a guide and mule is the most enjoyable way to explore the High Atlas. (Photos © Patrick Maguire).

necessarily need all these things. Good-quality **sunglasses**, however, are essential. Make sure they block out ultra-violet light. Take a **torch** (flashlight) and spare batteries as well as a **penknife**, **compass** and **lighter**. In winter, an **ice-axe** and **crampons** might be necessary for the higher peaks. Crampons can be rented in Imlil for the ascent of Jbel Toubkal. A waterproof **map-case** is handy if only to hold letters, pens and any sketchbook or notebook you might want to take. Take a plastic **backpack liner** to make sure you keep your gear dry. You will need a **water bottle**, preferably one litre. Other items to consider taking include: a **sewing kit** for running repairs; **washing liquid** for clothes (make sure it's biodegradable); **travel games** or a pack of cards; a **shortwave radio** for news-junkies; and, of course, a **camera** and **film**. It is essential to have a reliable **watch** since, in the route guides, average trekking times between villages and landmarks are given.

Provisions

Apart from a stash of fruit and nuts and some chocolate bars, there's not much you'll need to take into the mountains if you're going on an organised trek. Otherwise you might try to devise a route which takes you to gîtes where you often be able to buy meals. However, you will need to take cooking gear as a fall-back. If you're trekking independently you will need to stock up with food, preferably in Marrakesh, Azilal or Ouarzazate. In villages and even towns the size of Azilal, however, you will need to wait for the weekly *souq* (market, see p67 for market days) before you can get everything you need.

If you decide to take a cook (cuisinier), he should mastermind the buying of supplies based on what he plans to cook. Since the cuisinier will cut far better deals in the souq, this often works out cheaper than feeding yourself. Remember that any guide or muleteer you take with you will

---

❏ **Cooking gear**

If you go on an organised trek, or employ a cuisinier to cook for your group, you will have no call for cooking gear. If you travel alone, you will need to take a cooking kit.

The most effective stove is a Trangia which uses methylated spirits. Methylated spirits can be hard to find in the mountains so bring fuel bottles (Sigg are best) with you and fill them whenever you can. Trangia stoves can cook for long periods with relatively little fuel.

The gas cylinders most commonly found in the Atlas are large Butagaz types which won't fit most camping stoves. You can, however, buy an attachment to fit these cylinders in Marrakesh. It is worth buying an attachment anyway (they are inexpensive) to take with you as a back-up plan.

expect to be fed well. There's little need to bring supplies from home since most things are available in Marrakesh. One exception to that is dried trekking food.

MONEY

Cash is the only option in the Atlas mountains. Gîtes d'étape won't accept cards, cheques or foreign currencies and, if you find a place to buy a Coke, only dirhams will do. That said, once you've organised supplies and, if you choose, a guide and mule, there are few expenses left (see p20 for a guide to costs). ATM machines, money exchange and money transfers are available in Marrakesh and Ouarzazate. See p71 for more information about money in Morocco and exchange rates.

PHOTOGRAPHIC EQUIPMENT

The Atlas region is a rich destination for the photographer; colourful people and places provide exciting opportunities to experiment with different types of picture. You should, however, always ask permission before taking a picture of a person – or, indeed, a camel, mule, home or market stall. Berber women will often be particularly reluctant to be photo-graphed; don't push the point if you are faced with this reaction. Many Moroccans will expect a tip of 5dh or so for being in a picture or allowing you to film their property.

Well-known film brands such as Kodak and Fuji are easy to find in towns and cities but, not surprisingly, film is almost impossible to find in the Atlas mountains. Take plenty with you. Generally bright conditions make 100 ISO film the best speed to use.

Also bring spare camera batteries. Note that after a cold night on a mountain you may find that yours appear to be flat. Take them out and warm them up in your hands to get them going again. Some people even keep them in their sleeping bag at night.

RECOMMENDED READING

Reading other people's accounts of the Atlas will help you to gain more from the experience. Many writers on Morocco are French, but there are a number of English-language books which are also worth reading as well as a host of Moroccan texts which have been translated.

General guidebooks
Lonely Planet publish a good all-round Morocco guide, as does Rough Guides. The *Cadogan Guide to Morocco* by Barnaby Rogerson is probably the best general guide to the country. The *Footprint Guide to Morocco* is strong on cultural information and the French-language *Le Guide du Routard Maroc* is useful for phone numbers and prices but is thin on detail.

Walking guides

There are few English-language walking guides since it was the French who pioneered the Atlas as a trekking destination. Those that do exist, at the risk of appearing to denigrate the opposition, are either out dated or lack useful detail. Karl Smith's *The Atlas Mountains*, published by the Cicerone Press, suggests a number of itineraries while Michael Peyron's *Great Atlas Traverse* (published in two volumes) is a 'grand design' for traversing the range. A third book is Robin Collomb's *Atlas Mountains*.

A useful guide to the M'goun area is *Randonnées Pedestres dans le Massif du Mgoun* published by the GTAM organisation. Two other French-language books on the Atlas mountains which are worth reading, though not specifically walking guides, are *Le Haut Atlas Central Guide Alpin* by André Fougerolles and *Le Massif du Toubkal* by Jean Dresch and Jacques de Lépiney.

Guides to flora and fauna

The Collins field guide to *Birds of Britain and Europe with North Africa and the Middle East* by Heinzel, Fitter and Parslow is a fairly portable edition. Also try Lars Johnsson's *Birds of Europe with North Africa and the Middle East* and Alan Snook's *Birdwatching Guide to Morocco*.

Other books

American author Paul Bowles is perhaps the best-known Western writer to document North Africa through his work. From his home in Tangier, Bowles chronicled Moroccans and Moroccan life in books such as *The Sheltering Sky* and *The Spider's House*. While not specifically about the Atlas, both books reveal much about Morocco.

Elias Canetti's *The Voices of Marrakesh* and Peter Mayne's *Year in Marrakesh* provide enjoyable pictures of that city. Esther Freud's *Hideous Kinky*, the true story of a hippy mother who drags her daughters to Marrakesh on a journey of self-discovery, enjoyed a new lease of life in 1999 when it was made into a film. The film itself, shot on location in Marrakesh and the Atlas, is quite entertaining for anyone who has spent any time there.

More relevant, perhaps, is Richard Hughes's *In the Lap of the Atlas* which relates traditional myths and describes the author's travels to the Atlas. Hamish Brown's *The Great Walking Adventure* is a personal account of the mountain range in which he has spent a great deal of his life.

Three other books which might be rather more difficult to track down are: *Berber Village*, an account of an Oxford University expedition to the High Atlas in 1959; *Journal of a tour in Morocco and the Great Atlas* by Joseph Dalton Hooker and John Ball which describes the authors' exploration of the High Atlas in 1871; and Joseph Thomson's *Travels in the Atlas and southern Morocco* which is a personal travelogue published in

1889. For the best Moroccan fiction translated into French and English, look out for the works of Mohammed Mrabet, Ben Jalloun and Driss Chraibi.

MAPS

Much of the Atlas has been mapped at 1:100,000 scale with the Toubkal area also mapped at 1:50,000. These maps are slightly inaccurate but at least they are not restricted to military use. The maps which complement the treks in this book are named as follows: Jbel Toubkal (1:50,000); Amezmiz, Oukaimeden, Tizi-n'-Test and Taliwine (all 1:100,000) which cover the Toubkal massif including Taliwine which is the trailhead for Jbel Sirwa; Tazenakht (1:100,000) which extends the Taliwine map to the east; Azilal (NW), Zawyat Ahancal (NE), Qalaa't M'gouna (SE) and Skoura (SW) (all 1:100,000) which overlap to cover the M'goun area; and Tazzarine and Boumalne (both 1:100,000) for Jbel Sahro.

There are two problems with these maps: firstly, they are not very clear and place names change wildly from one edition to the next; secondly, they are extremely difficult to find and fairly expensive (perhaps 150dh per sheet). The only way to be sure to find all the maps you need is to go personally to the Map Division of the appropriate ministry in Rabat (see box below)

The *Bureau des Guides* in Imlil can sometimes supply the 1:50,000 Toubkal map (or, if they can't, there is normally someone in the trailhead who can). Hôtel Ali in Marrakesh can also supply maps sometimes. Stanfords (☎ 020-7836 1321; 🖹 020-7836 0189; 🖳 sales@stanfords.co.uk) 12-14 Long Acre, Covent Garden, London WC2E 9LP, sells the set of four 1:100,000 maps covering the Toubkal Massif and an air map of Morocco which might help one to get an overall picture of the range. Interesting though they may be, by the time you've tracked down all these maps and paid for them, you might as well have hired a mountain guide.

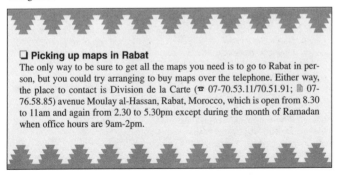

❑ **Picking up maps in Rabat**
The only way to be sure to get all the maps you need is to go to Rabat in person, but you could try arranging to buy maps over the telephone. Either way, the place to contact is Division de la Carte (☎ 07-70.53.11/70.51.91; 🖹 07-76.58.85) avenue Moulay al-Hassan, Rabat, Morocco, which is open from 8.30 to 11am and again from 2.30 to 5.30pm except during the month of Ramadan when office hours are 9am-2pm.

Mountain safety

Any mountain environment can be dangerous and it goes without saying that concern for one's own safety is paramount. The High Atlas, like any mountain system, is liable to rapid weather changes. Ensure you are fully prepared for extremes of weather and make certain you keep one set of spare clothes completely dry. Look after yourself as you trek; tend to problems as they crop up. Don't try to cover more ground than you can comfortably manage. You are, after all, on holiday and you should feel no pressure to race ahead. Indeed, the real beauty of trekking is the very fact that you see the country around you at a slow pace, allowing you fully to appreciate it. Of course, it's also important that you prepare for your trek. Get into the rhythm of walking for extended periods by practising at home. This will also give you time to make sure your gear is comfortable and in working order.

TREKKING ALONE

Always trek in a group if you can. Ideally, three is the minimum number for trekking in safety. If you plan to travel to Morocco alone, consider taking a guide into the mountains. Apart from showing you the way, which can be very hard to find in parts of the Atlas mountains, you would no longer be trekking solo. Many of the routes are indistinct so other trekkers following the same path can easily miss someone in distress on the same route. Remember the mountain rescue services are very limited so you should tell someone where you're going.

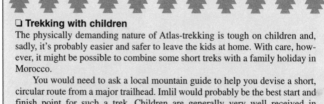

❑ **Trekking with children**
The physically demanding nature of Atlas-trekking is tough on children and, sadly, it's probably easier and safer to leave the kids at home. With care, however, it might be possible to combine some short treks with a family holiday in Morocco.

You would need to ask a local mountain guide to help you devise a short, circular route from a major trailhead. Imlil would probably be the best start and finish point for such a trek. Children are generally very well received in Morocco, where the family is a highly respected institution. There is certainly much to keep them amused and interested.

EXPERIENCE

Trekking in the Atlas mountains is physically demanding and needs to be taken seriously. On the Jbel Toubkal route I've often seen trekkers completely unprepared with totally inadequate clothing and even street shoes. That said, unless you plan to tackle the higher peaks over the winter months, in which case you will need to know how to trek on ice with crampons, you don't need any special experience for the treks in this book. But you will need to be physically fit, well-prepared and, unless you take a guide, you will need to know how to read a map and use a compass.

MOUNTAIN RESCUE SERVICES

Despite the increasing number of visitors who trek in the Atlas every year, there is no official rescue service. CAF huts have a first-aid kit and stretcher but, from most points in the Atlas, it would be faster and safer simply to head for the nearest trailhead by mule to get motor transport to the nearest town. **Evacuation by mule** is quick to organise.

> ❏ **Weather forecasts**
> There are meteorological offices in:
>   Azilal (☎ 3-45.82.36)
>   Casablanca (☎ 2-90.24.24)
>   Marrakesh (☎ 4-43.04.09)
>   Ouarzazate (☎ 4-88.23.20)

If the emergency is too serious for the patient to travel by mule there is a **helicopter** stationed at Marrakesh which can be called to the Atlas. The helicopter is much in demand as it operates over a massive area, so you cannot rely on it reaching you quickly. There will also be a delay while you call the helicopter since you will have to get to a larger village where the mayor should have a short-wave radio with which he can summon it.

Official mountain guides study basic first-aid as part of their training but, in a serious situation, get the patient out of the mountains to proper medical help as soon as you can. For all these reasons, trekkers should consider studying first-aid before visiting the Atlas and should think twice about trekking without local help. Local Berbers are, however, very fast and adept at getting people to medical attention. Your best course of action in any serious situation is to accept their assistance.

Health precautions

Morocco has something of a reputation for felling its visitors with stomach upsets. It is true that, like most developing-world countries, Morocco has generally lower standards of hygiene than one might expect to find in the West. With care and common sense, however, the chances of getting

❏ **Visit your dentist**
Standing in Djemaa al-Fna in Marrakesh watching street dentists yank out teeth with pliers might make you wish you'd sorted out your teeth before leaving home. At least this one appears to have had plenty of practice!

any illness can be considerably lessened. Trekking, of course, carries its own inherent risks. But if you are fit before you start, look after yourself and respond promptly to any problems as they occur, there is no reason why your travels should be marred by medical trouble.

Refer to Appendix B (pp241-6) which tackles **specific health problems** which might confront you in the Atlas mountains.

WHO SHOULD AVOID HIGH-ALTITUDE TREKS?

Since the highest peak in the Atlas mountains, Jbel Toubkal (4167m/13,667ft), is well above the height at which the effects of altitude can begin to take hold, Acute Mountain Sickness (AMS) is a potential danger. AMS can affect anyone regardless of age, gender or fitness level. By following the advice given on p242-3, however, trekkers should be able to avoid this hazard. That said, people with chest, heart or blood pressure problems should seek medical advice before tackling any of the treks described in this book. Children should not be taken above 3000m while teenagers and those in their early twenties should be aware that they may be more susceptible to AMS than older trekkers.

PRE-DEPARTURE PREPARATION

Most trekkers plan to get fit before they go but never quite get round to it. They then spend the first few days of their trek in red-faced, panting agony. The fact is, though, that after a few days it's hard to tell who had arrived unprepared and who had trained for months.

Still, it's sensible to put in some pre-departure training – particularly if you're planning a short trek, in which case you won't want to waste the first half wishing you had found time to follow that elusive fitness regime. If you do decide to train for the trek the best thing you can do is mimic the physical work you will face in the Atlas. This might also help you to try out your gear and break in your boots. Go walking with a full pack or charge up and down a steep flight of stairs everyday. Any exercise will help you to enjoy your trek and, more importantly, will lessen the chance of an early injury or strain.

INOCULATIONS

Morocco officially requires no inoculations but travellers should be up to date with tetanus and polio. Also consider vaccination against hepatitis A and B, diphtheria, typhoid and rabies. Meningitis is no more common in Morocco than Europe. Consult your doctor well in advance of travel to make sure you have received all the immunisations you might need and record them for future reference.

INSURANCE

This is essential. Watch out for the following points: check whether you need to pay extra to be covered for trekking; make sure the cover is adequate for all your gear; read and understand the policy before you go; if you're travelling in a group, don't rely on one person to get to grips with the small-print; know how to claim and follow the procedure to the letter. You should leave a photocopy of your policy with someone at home.

In the UK, the Consumers' Association recommends the following cover as a minimum: £1 million (US$1.6 million) medical expenses; £1 million (US$1.6 million) personal liability; £3000 (US$5000) cancellation and curtailment; £1500 (US$2500) baggage.

Facts about Morocco and the Atlas mountains

GEOGRAPHY

The Atlas mountains form the spine of Morocco, stretching some 1200 miles (1900km) from the Atlantic port of Agadir to the Tunisian capital, Tunis. In Morocco, the several parallel ranges which comprise the Atlas separate Saharan Africa from the Atlantic and Mediterranean basins. The mighty High Atlas range, with Jbel Toubkal (4167m/13,667ft) its highest peak, reaches from near Agadir to northern Algeria in an east-north-easterly direction. From the central High Atlas, another range, the Middle Atlas, stretches north-east. The Anti Atlas range runs parallel to the southern High Atlas to the south. The eastern reach of the Anti Atlas is dominated by Jbel Sahro while the M'goun massif towers over the central High Atlas to the north-east of Jbel Toubkal. Jbel Sirwa forms a bridge between the High and Anti Atlas ranges to the south-east of Jbel Toubkal. The two roads which traverse the High Atlas, the Tizi-n'Tichka and Tizi-n'Test, are said to form the boundaries of the Toubkal region.

GEOLOGY

As suggested by the confusing pattern of the Atlas, the mountains were formed by a complex series of geological events; in fact, the northern and southern sections of the range were created by different processes. The two distinct regions meet in the Middle Atlas.

The northern Atlas, including the Rif mountains, were formed from a sediment-filled basin during a mountain-building period in the Tertiary Period starting some 65 million years ago. Folds were lifted and coated with sheets of flysch (sandstone and clay); as occasional earthquakes testify, the northern Atlas are still forming.

In the south, the Saharan Atlas, a term which includes the High and Anti Atlas, form part of the vast African plateau system and were uplifted with the folding of that substructure and the crumpling of the Earth's crust during the Jurassic and Cretaceous Periods. The Jurassic Period started 208 million years ago.

HISTORICAL OUTLINE

Moroccan history is defined by complex tribal power struggles, religious propagation and often exploitative European influence. Independent since 1956, the nation was only relatively recently coaxed into the modern age through French and Spanish colonialism.

Before European occupation, which took hold from the turn of the century, the lands comprising Morocco were semi-governed by a series of sultans. These successive sultanates tell the story of Moroccan development from the eighth century to the present day. For most of Morocco's history, however, no sultan mustered enough power to control the entire country. Morocco was divided between the *Bled el Makhzen*, or 'governed lands', and the untamed, uncontrollable and essentially Berber-populated regions of the deserts and the Rif and Atlas mountains. Even today, the Atlas mountains, which are technically under government control, are seen by many as a distinct region with questionable regard for the authorities in Rabat. Despite a recent drive by the late King Hassan II to encourage both Berbers and Arabs to consider themselves, above all, Moroccan, the government appears wary of imposing itself too firmly upon the Berbers of the Atlas.

The successive sultanate dynasties which have controlled Morocco since the eighth century started with the Idrissids and continue today with the Alaouites, the seventh dynasty which emerged in the seventeenth century. King Mohammed VI, the current monarch, is an Alaouite.

Earliest inhabitants

The earliest humans to roam North Africa were hunter-gatherers living from 1,000,000 BC. They inhabited the Sahara, then teeming with life, and are thought be among the earliest of our ancestors. Palaeolithic dwellings appeared around 15,000 BC. Later, in the Stone Age, Neolithic Man arrived from Egypt.

Phoenician trading posts developed along the coast from 1100 BC. The Moroccan interior was by then populated by the Barbaroi (Berbers), a collective term applied to Libyan and Ethiopian settlers. A number of ports flourished at this time as pan-African trade routes developed to fuel the increasing prosperity of Carthage (Tunis). One of these ports, Tingis, is now Tangier. Another, Chellah, was near the site of modern-day Rabat, the Moroccan capital.

Roman occupation

Imperial Roman rule was imposed on what had by then become the Berber Kingdom of Mauritania in 24 AD. The kingdom was allied to Numidia, the adjacent Berber state which is today Algeria, and which had enjoyed modest influence in the Maghreb (the Arab term for North Africa). Juba, the most powerful ruler of Numidia, supported the Roman

Empire and married the daughter of Antony and Cleopatra. Despite this, Rome placed Numidia under direct rule, thereby stripping north-west Africa of any real power.

Setting a precedent which lives on, the Moroccan Berbers resisted Roman rule with unexpected vigour. It took years to put down the rebellion. Perhaps shocked by the strength of the Berbers, Rome never attempted to take the Rif or Atlas mountains which, apart from harbouring a fierce population, would have proved almost impossible to penetrate.

After Roman rule disintegrated in 253 AD, northern Morocco fell under the control of the Vandals who had seized power in southern Spain. Perhaps because they saw Morocco only as a staging post en route to Tunisia, the Vandals were reluctant to push further inland from their strongholds in Ceuta and Tangier. Similarly, the Byzantine forces which succeeded the Vandals left the Moroccan interior almost untouched. While the rest of the Maghreb faced a series of changes in the balance of power throughout the region, the Berbers of the High Atlas were able to live above it all – quite literally. It's worth remembering, of course, that at that time there was no precedent for unifying the geographic region which is, today, Morocco. Indeed, it took the power of Islam to draw together the differing cultural strains of the Maghreb Al-Aska, 'The Land of the Farthest West'.

Coming of Islam

By 652 AD, Islam had reached Tunisia. Triggered by the Prophet Mohammed's move from Mecca to Medina, Islam had spread quickly to the north, east and west. This rapid early success was temporarily slowed by strong, unified resistance from Berbers, Christians and Jews in Algeria. Despite Islamic leaders' attempts to carry their religion into Morocco, it took a further half-century before Islam claimed a strong hold over the far west of the Maghreb.

At the turn of the eighth century, a new Arab leader, Moussa Ibn Nasr, succeeded in establishing Islam in the Moroccan plains. His crusade was directed towards Spain and climaxed with the Muslim defeat of the Visigoths is southern Spain in 711 AD. It took just ten more years for Islamic forces to dominate almost all of Spain. This outstanding military success played a large part in converting many more Moroccans to Islam.

Moulay Idriss and the first sultanate dynasty

Elsewhere in the Arab world a split developed within Islam which eventually led to the division between Shia and Sunni Muslims. When the Sunnis took control in Damascus, the Shi'ites retreated to more distant parts of the Muslim world. **Moulay Idriss**, a Shi'ite and great-grandson of the Prophet Mohammed, fled to Morocco where he found refuge in Volubilis.

Here he gathered support through his Muslim pedigree and skilled leadership. In just three years, he set up an Arab kingdom with the support of the Aouraba Berbers and the leadership in Volubilis. His success cost him his life when, in about 790 AD, he was assassinated by the Sunnis. Idriss had achieved enough, however, to ensure his legacy; his son, **Moulay Idriss II**, took control of the first dynasty in Morocco.

Idriss II ruled for 20 years, establishing Arab dominance over much of the north. He also became the Imam, a role his father had created, which made him both political and religious leader. Idriss II welcomed large numbers of Shi'ite refugees to his new court in Fes, so strengthening Arab influence in Morocco, too. The city developed important trade routes and built the Kairaouine University, one of the most distinguished in the Islamic world.

While Fes remained the dominant Arab city, however, the Idrissid state began to deteriorate, forming separate principalities throughout the region. This increasing fragmentation coincided with a similar process in Muslim Spain. Worse was to come when, at the turn of the tenth century, the aggressive Hilali tribe swept west from Egypt in an orgy of destruction which laid waste farms and herds across the Maghreb. The vicious Hilali had been displaced in a clash with the Zirids when the Fatimid dynasty moved into Egypt.

The Almoravids (1062-1145)

As the Maghreb fell into decline, so Idriss II's grip on power began to erode. This weakness created an opportunity for new, stronger movements to come to the fore. The first such movement, the Almoravids (1062-1145), started in the south with the Sanhaja Berbers who had developed a hardline approach to Islam in response to what they saw as widening abuse of Orthodox Muslim practices across the Maghreb and, in particular, in Fes. The Sanhajas were the first of a series of Berber dynasties which ruled Morocco until the end of Saadian rule in 1669.

The Almoravid dynasty grew from a *ribat*, or fortified monastery, from where, in 1054, its people set out on a *jihad* (holy war). They took Marrakesh in 1062, by which time they also had control of Ghana to the south. Their leader, **Youssef bin Tachfine**, extended the Almoravid empire throughout northern Morocco and to Algiers in the east. Youssef bin Tachfine unified Morocco more successfully than at any time before under a simple but harsh form of Sunni orthodoxy.

In 1085, after the fall of Toledo in Spain to the Christians, bin Tachfine was asked to help the Muslims of al-Andalus to repel the crusading Christian armies. This he did and, in 1090, he crossed the Straits again, this time to take Spain for himself. When bin Tachfine died in 1107, he had made Morocco one of the dominant powers in the Maghreb.

While bin Tachfine had established a glorious legacy for his son, Ali, he had also created weaknesses in his empire which would eventually destroy it. He had too few trusted generals or, indeed, soldiers to maintain the empire; his forces were spread too thinly.

The Almohads (1145-1248)

Like the Almoravids, the Almohads (1145-1248) grew from Berber tribes in the south – this time from the High Atlas mountains. The Almohads challenged the Almoravids on religious grounds, claiming the Almoravid leadership had become decadent and arguing that Andalusian influences had weakened their dedication to Sunni orthodoxy.

The Almoravid sultan Ali exiled **Ibn Toumert**, the Almohad leader, from Marrakesh in an act of provocation which led Ibn Toumert to establish a ribat at Tin Mal in the Atlas mountains. Like the Almoravids before them, the Almohads used the ribat as a base to prepare for war. Ibn Toumert attacked surrounding tribes, bringing them into the Almohad fold by declaring himself to be 'the chosen one'.

When Ibn Toumert died, his military chief, **Abd el Moumen**, took control of the movement and expanded its scope. By the end of 1145, Moumen had expelled the Almoravids from Fes and Marrakesh. The Almohads continued to grow in strength and scope, destroying Almoravid resistance and pushing north into Spain. Moumen's successor, **Yacoub el Mansour**, achieved even greater success, extending his eastern boundaries to Tripoli. Morocco now dominated the entire Maghreb. Rabat was founded as the new capital, built with wealth from war.

But the Almohad's 'golden age' began to disintegrate in the face of stronger and more unified resistance in Europe. Mohammed en Nasr, Yacoub el Mansour's successor, suffered punishing defeats in Spain. In the east, too, the Almohad Empire began to crumble, forcing Moroccan rule to retreat into its own neglected interior.

The Merenids (1248-1465)

Fes and Marrakesh fell to the Merenids (1248-1465) amid the collapsing Almohad dynasty. But the end of the Almohads also marked the end of Moroccan dominance in the Maghreb; the Merenids, despite years of struggling, failed to extend their borders into Spain. Even Granada, the last Moorish city in Spain in the early years of Merenid rule, would eventually fall to the Christians.

The Turkish Ottoman Empire was growing apace and the Maghreb began increasingly to gravitate around that great power in the east – thereby isolating Morocco. However, important progress was made within Morocco: a central bureaucracy was established, the *Makhzen*, and the country was divided more clearly than ever between 'the governed lands' and 'the lands of the dissidents'.

This was also something of a golden age for culture, academia and architecture. A new system of taxation, controlled by the Makhzen, allowed the Merenids to build. Grand *medersas* (universities) were established in the imperial cities.

The Wattasids (1465-1554)

A rival but related dynasty, the Wattasids (1465-1554), took control from the Merenids in 1465. But the period of Wattasid rule saw Morocco descend further into chaos. Wattasid power grew increasingly confined to the north, where it was battered by a series of attacks from Portugal, while the south fell into the hands of the emerging Saadian dynasty.

The Saadians (1554-1669)

The Saadians (1554-1669) were the last Berber dynasty to rule Morocco. Their rise to power began through their religious hold; they were descendants of the Prophet. With the Wattasid dynasty struggling even to maintain order in the north, there was little to stop the Saadians growing in power from their capital, Taroudannt, in the south. They took Marrakesh in 1520 and within years were consolidating their power in the north.

Events were made more complex by the arrival of troops from the Ottoman Empire, brought in by the Wattasids, some of whom sided with the Saadians in their bid for dominance of the western Maghreb. The successful Saadian sultan **Mohammed esh Sheikh** was assassinated by a group of Turkish troops in 1557. Moroccan power-politics were plunged ever deeper into almost total chaos. Infighting, violence and assassinations were rife. Ironically, perhaps, the Portuguese, hoping to exploit the power vacuum in Morocco, resolved the situation at the **Battle of the Three Kings**. The Portuguese King Sebastião joined forces with a sidelined Saadian sultan, Mohammed al-Mutawwakil, to attack his Saadian uncle who had seized power with the help of the Turks. The ensuing battle saw all three kings killed and the Portuguese beaten. This allowed **Ahmed al-Mansour**, an underrated Saadian prince, to emerge to take control unchallenged.

Ahmed al-Mansour, the 'Golden One', proved to be a cunning and successful sultan. He demanded such enormous ransoms for the safe return of Portuguese noblemen captured at the Battle of the Three Kings that Portugal was left almost bankrupt. He strengthened his power base within Morocco, partly through extending his boundaries to the south, and turned his attention to European politics. Ahmed al-Mansour's position at home was further enhanced when, having captured great wealth during his southern conquests, he abolished tax.

In 1603 Ahmed al-Mansour died. Since none of his sons could gain enough support to command the empire, the country once again subsided into civil war. Again, a number of separate principalities developed around power bases in Marrakesh, Fes, Souss and Rabat.

The Alaouites (1665-)

This backdrop of disorder allowed a new dynasty, the Alaouites (1665-), to rise to prominence. Following the pattern laid down by previous dynasties, the Alaouites became religious commanders before seizing political power. From their power base in Rissani, they took Taza and Fes before marching into Marrakesh in 1669 under **Moulay Rashid**. Within three years, Rashid was dead. He was assassinated in his own palace. His son, Moulay Ismail, took the helm.

Moulay Ismail governed for 55 years. His is seen as a great era in Moroccan history and his tomb in Meknes still draws thousands of Moroccan pilgrims. European commentators point out that Ismail's cruelty and ruthlessness were almost legendary. There's no denying, however, that he was a charismatic and astute leader. He quickly set about stabilising the country by policing it with an élite guard stationed in kasbahs across the land. This allowed him to monitor his people and, of course, to raise taxes from them. Ismail made Meknes the new imperial capital and used revenue raised through taxes and piracy to build the greatest palace in the Maghreb. Perhaps his finest achievement, however, lay in his ability to deal with the great European powers on an equal footing. Ismail's son, **Sidi Mohammed**, continued his father's work with vigour; he played a prominent role in world politics (he was one of the first rulers to recognise the United States of America) and enjoyed military successes against the Portuguese.

On Sidi Mohammed's death, Morocco again fell into a state of temporary chaos. Once again, the 'Land of the Dissidents' began to encroach on the 'Land of the Governed'. Events elsewhere would also conspire against Morocco as post-Napoleonic Europe turned with hungry eyes to Africa.

When **Moulay Slimane** came to power in 1792 he inherited a difficult situation. He soon made it worse by alienating the Berber population, an error of judgement which led to a serious rebellion in 1818 and a critical weakening of Slimane's grip on power, and by systematically destroying Morocco's relations with the great European powers.

Europe turns to Morocco

When France and Spain began to expand their spheres of influence into the Maghreb in the mid-nineteenth century, there was little the Arab or Berber populations could do to resist. After years of modernisation and war in Europe both France and Spain had well-organised, well-equipped and well-motivated armies.

France led the Europeans into the Maghreb after their defeat over the Ottomans in 1830. They soon controlled Algeria. The Spanish turned their attention to Morocco, taking control of Tetouan.

With these European giants vying for influence in Morocco, successive sultans **Moulay Abn ar-Rahman** and **Mohammed bin Abd ar-Rahman** were almost powerless to prevent the increasing colonisation of Morocco. Great Britain also took an interest, imposing a free trade agreement in 1856. In 1873, Sultan **Moulay al-Hassan** took control of the country. He attempted to resist the growing influence of Britain, France and Spain which had built industrial centres along the coast and took an ever-greater interest in al-Hassan's affairs. But his successor, **Moulay Abd al-Aziz**, invited Europeans to his court and began to adopt European customs. This led to unrest among his subjects, mostly on religious grounds, which allowed a pretender to the sultanate, **Bu Hamara**, to set up a separate court in Melilla. This confusion within Morocco helped the Europeans to extend their influence unchecked.

French control in the region became blatant as its government offered other European powers strong incentives to ignore French colonisation. She allowed Britain a free hand in Egypt and the Sudan, left Italy to colonise Libya and offered Spain a northern sphere of influence in Morocco.

Abd al-Aziz was overthrown by his brother, **Moulay Abd al-Hafid**, in 1907. Abd al-Hafid was disillusioned by his brother's failure to defend the Muslim faith from 'decadent' European influence. Before taking full control of Morocco in 1909, when his leadership was recognised by the Europeans, Abd al-Hafid had launched a half-hearted attack on French troops in Casablanca.

Abd al-Hafid's leadership was hardly more successful than his attempt to deliver Casablanca from French occupation. As he lost control of the country, he had little choice but to accept a French offer of help. In return for propping up his leadership, the French demanded Abd al-Hafid sign the 1912 Treaty of Fes which made Morocco a French Protectorate.

The French Protectorate (1912-56)

After the Treaty of Fes, the French government applied to Morocco the model of colonial domination which it had developed in Tunisia and Algeria. But with a stronger position in Europe, greater strategic importance and a 1000-year history of independence, Morocco would prove more difficult to dominate than its North African neighbours.

Most importantly, perhaps, France was forced to share Morocco with the Spanish who controlled parts of the northern Atlantic and Mediterranean coasts and the region of Tarfaya in the south. While the Moroccan government had little real power during the years of the French protectorate, the French *contrôleurs civils* granted conditional independence to a number of Berber leaders, or *caids*, in the High Atlas and other areas.

Abd al-Hafid, humiliated by his amputated position, found himself unable to support the French régime in Morocco, led by General Lyautey, and retired to Tangier. His brother, Moulay Yusuf, became sultan. He managed to cooperate with the French without losing the respect of his people.

General Lyautey planned to develop Morocco into a modern industrial state without destroying its traditional culture and heritage. He established new cities and centres of industry outside the old Moroccan cities. The administrative capital was moved to Rabat and Casablanca was developed into a grand port city in the French style. World War I hardly slowed this development and regeneration in Morocco. After the war, the

French focused on bringing the Atlas mountains under control. This was achieved by 1934. But by the time Lyautey's reign in Morocco ended in 1926, cracks were developing in the strength of the Paris régime. Arabs were beginning to make demands on their French protectors.

One year after Lyautey's departure, in 1927, Moulay Yusuf died. His successor and youngest son, **Sidi Mohammed**, was chosen by the French. Sidi Mohammed was considered by them to be a diffident personality. But he would later prove himself to be a strong leader and, after independence, would become King Mohammed V. Sidi Mohammed's rise to power coincided with an upsurge in Moroccan nationalism, in part fuelled by a disastrous French attempt to exploit Berber and Arab differences, which climaxed with the expulsion of the nationalist leader, Mohammed Allal al-Fasi, to French Equatorial Africa.

World War II and Moroccan independence

When World War II broke out across Europe in 1939, Sidi Mohammed called on his people to fight alongside the French; Moroccan troops, mainly Berbers, fought bravely against the Axis forces. But when in 1940 German occupation of France began, Sidi Mohammed used the situation to assert his own authority. He met US President Franklin D Roosevelt in 1943 and was impressed to hear him denounce French rule in Morocco.

The Moroccan nationalist movement flourished during the war years, assuming the form of an organised independence party, Istiqlal. In 1944, Istiqlal's formal demand for independence led to a heavy-handed French reaction which in turn caused riots in Fes.

It soon became obvious to the French government that it would have to make some concessions to the nationalists. But the French response, delivered through the new resident general, Alphonse Juin, was to offer elected municipalities in large cities. This was welcomed until it became clear that Juin intended to install French settlers in the municipalities. Sidi Mohammed, whose personal support was growing fast, rejected Juin's offer by refusing to countersign the decree.

While Arabs in Fes, Rabat and Casablanca supported Mohammed's stand against the French, the sultan still lacked support from the Berbers. In 1950, in the hope of using tensions between Arabs and Berbers to put pressure on Sidi Mohammed, Juin began to mobilise support from powerful Berber caids such as **Thami al-Glaoui**. Tension increased still further when Juin surrounded the sultan's palace with Berber tribesman, using his own French troops to prevent them from reaching Mohammed. The sultan was forced to denounce Istiqlal, though he refused to name the party and continued to frustrate Juin by taking a pro-independence stance. In 1952 a series of workers' protests in Casablanca prompted the French to detain scores of nationalists who would not be released until 1954.

During 1953 a number of Berber leaders, including Thami al-Glaoui, conspired with the French to orchestrate Sultan Sidi Mohammed's removal from office. The sultan was eventually deported and a more cooperative leader, **Moulay Ben Arafa**, installed in his place. But Mohammed's forced departure made him a hugely popular figure within Morocco and enraged the Spanish who had not been consulted by the French leadership. The subsequent rift between the two colonial powers made Spanish-controlled Morocco something of a safe haven for Moroccan nationalists.

International opinion and a nationalist rebellion in Algeria began to weaken the French grip on Morocco. In 1954 Paris proposed a crown council, with the support of Sidi Mohammed, to replace the puppet sultan Ben Arafa. Still the pressure mounted against the French as a Moroccan nationalist guerilla army began attacking French units in the north.

Thami al-Glaoui, seeing how the growing independence movement placed Sidi Mohammed at its head, transfered his allegiance to the sultan Sidi Mohammed who returned to Rabat. On 2 March 1956, Moroccan independence was proclaimed and Sidi Mohammed became **King Mohammed V**.

The Spanish Zone

Spain controlled one-tenth of Morocco when, in 1956, France granted independence. The Spanish government followed suit in April 1956 but maintained control of Ceuta on the Strait of Gibraltar and Melilla on the Mediterranean coast

Morocco since independence

On independence Mohammed V inherited an autocratic system. He did, however, introduce a constitution and a cabinet composed of representatives from each group in Moroccan society. Mubarak Bekkai became the first premier. But Mohammed V still chose his ministers and controlled the army and police force. His son, Moulay Hassan, became chief of staff.

As Mohammed V made preparations for a Moroccan parliament, the nationalist movement disintegrated into left- and right-wing factions. Mohammed V used such splits to strengthen his position by claiming to be above 'party politics'. He died unexpectedly in 1961 and his son, Moulay Hassan, succeeded him as **King Hassan II**.

Parliamentary elections took place in 1963. The divided Istiqlal movement formed the opposition to a party supporting Hassan II and his government, the Front for the Defence of Constitutional Institutions. This 'two-horse race' led to a stalemate which was only resolved when, one year later, Hassan II dissolved parliament and made himself premier. He then made two attempts to restore an amended constitution but was blocked both times by the threat of army coups. New elections in 1977 went in favour of Hassan II's supporters. The King had gained great respect when, in 1975, he forced Spain to relinquish control of the phosphate-rich **Western Sahara**.

The Western Sahara was then given over to joint Moroccan-Mauritanian control. Relations between Morocco and Mauritania were strained; Morocco had claimed rights over Mauritania and had argued that the region should be absorbed into the kingdom. An independence movement flared up in the Western Sahara, finding its teeth in Polisario, a group of armed resistance fighters who embarked on a guerilla war against Morocco. Algeria and Libya, sensing an opportunity, supported Polisario. Libya and Morocco reached agreement in 1984, however, thereby denying Polisario Libyan support and arms. Algeria also left Polisario to fight alone after its own internal problems raged out of control.

The United Nations (UN) led Polisario and Hassan II to a cease-fire agreement in 1991 based on the understanding that a referendum in 1992 would decide the region's fate. The cease-fire is in place but the referendum has yet to materialise because of a dispute over who is eligible to vote. This deadlock led UN secretary-general Kofi Annan to appoint James Baker, a former United States secretary of state, special envoy to the area. Baker's aim is to resolve the voting issue to allow the referendum to take place. Commentators have been quick to accuse the Moroccan leadership of stalling; without support from Libya or Algeria, Polisario will find it difficult to resume a guerilla war against Morocco if the UN-brokered agreement collapses, so potentially allowing Western Sahara to fall to Rabat by default.

MOROCCO TODAY

King Hassan II died in 1999 and was succeeded by **King Mohammed VI**. Hassan II was a skilled diplomat. He maintained a useful network of alliances and friendships with both Arab and Western states. During the Gulf War (1990-1991) he supported the Western allies despite the fact that many Moroccans supported Iraq. Unrest has surfaced occasionally in response to difficult economic circumstances. Strikes and clashes shook the country in the early nineties and again in 1994. Both 1996 and 1997 saw demonstrations against unemployment. Islam also caused some difficulties for Hassan II. Fundamentalist views crept across the border from Algeria and the radical Islamist national student union clashed with government forces in 1997.

Moroccans have yet to see in which direction Mohammed VI will steer the nation. His relative youth (he was born in 1963) suggests, perhaps, that he will hope to modernise the leadership. His support for a draft bill improving women's rights appears to prove this. 'How can we hope for progress and prosperity when women, who make up half of our society, see their interests held up to ridicule?' he asked in a public address. He has also appointed a palace spokesman, signalling a softening in the secrecy which traditionally shrouds the monarchy's machinations. The young king can rely on popular support in the first years of his reign.

However, Morocco faces a number of problems which have still to be resolved. The Western Sahara question has yet to be answered. Unemployment is high, over 20 per cent according to some commentators, and an unacceptably high percentage of the population is illiterate. The world will wait with interest to see how the latest scion of the Alaouite dynasty, which has ruled Morocco since 1665, will lead his nation.

Political system

Morocco is a monarchy with a bicameral legislature: the Chamber of Representatives has 325 members elected on a first-past-the-post system; the Chamber of Councillors has 270 members, 60 per cent being elected by local councils, 20 per cent by employers' associations and 20 per cent by trade unions. The constitution was approved in a national referendum on 4 September 1992. The king nominates the prime minister and appoints members of the Council of Ministers based on his premier's advice. The Council of Ministers is responsible to parliament and to the king.

Economy

A four-year development plan from 1988-92 supported by the International Monetary Fund (IMF) and the World Bank saw Morocco take significant steps towards modernisation. But this is still a developing country: around 35 per cent of the population is employed in traditional agriculture. However, the Moroccan economy looks set to benefit from the country's relatively well-developed infrastructure and proximity to Europe as foreign investors turn increasingly to African markets. Today, though, the economy remains held back by foreign debt, unemployment and a high birth rate.

Development

The 1988-92 development plan focused on exports, trade liberalisation, tourism and privatisation. In May 1989 the government established a Ministry of Privatisation to transfer the majority of Moroccan enterprises to the private sector. Morocco was further helped by the cancellation of bilateral debts of some US$3,600 million owed to Gulf States. New injections of cash from the IMF and the World Bank in 1992 supported a second phase of planned development. By 1993 the Moroccan economy was thought to be well on the way to modernisation although growth was slowed by droughts in 1993 and 1995. Privatisation is still seen as the key to attracting much-needed foreign investment; US$2 billion of state companies had been passed into the private sector by 1995. The dirham became convertible in 1994. In April 1994 Morocco joined GATT (General Agreement on Tariffs and Trade) at its annual meeting which was held in Marrakesh. Morocco is a member of the Islamic Development Bank, the African Development Bank and the Union of the Arab Maghreb. Before his death, King Hassan II had expressed a desire to join the European Union; France and Spain are still Morocco's most important trading partners.

Agriculture

Over 55 per cent of Moroccans live in rural areas with 35 per cent of the population employed in traditional agriculture. Agriculture accounted for 20 per cent of Moroccan GDP in 1994. Production is highly vulnerable to poor growing conditions; cereal production fell by 50 per cent in 1981 after a severe drought and in 1995 another drought caused wheat production to drop by over 75 per cent.

Many Moroccan farmers are peasant tenants working land which is owned by a small percentage of the rural population. As a result of these small-scale farms, which are central to the Moroccan economy, the country is usually self-sufficient in vegetable and cereal production. Morocco's principal crops are wheat, barley, maize, citrus fruit, olives, tomatoes and potatoes. Sugar beet and cane is grown on a large scale to help offset sugar imports. Modern agricultural methods are limited to large farms around Marrakesh and the Gharb. Most of these were founded by French settlers but are slowly reverting to Moroccan ownership. Morocco, already the world's largest producer of sardines, is attempting to develop its fishing industry further.

Mining

Mining is still the dominant industry in Morocco and one reason why the government is reluctant to abandon the phosphate-rich Western Sahara. In fact, Morocco is one of the world's largest exporters of phosphates and has two-thirds of the world's known phosphate reserves. Other ores mined include coal, lead, zinc, cobalt, copper and silver. Mining employs around 65,000 people in Morocco.

Energy

There are limited supplies of oil, natural gas and coal but not enough to meet domestic demand; so the government is forced to import fuel. There are a number of plans afoot to develop the country's hydroelectric power potential. A new gas-line from Algeria to Spain via Morocco opened in 1996. The government collects royalties on all gas piped through the country. Morocco's forests are being seriously depleted by the indiscriminate collection of firewood by farmers.

Industry

Agricultural processing is one of the fastest-growing industries in Morocco. The production of construction materials and textiles also forms an increasingly significant part of the Moroccan economy. The traditional craft manufacturing industry, based in Marrakesh and Fes, remains strong.

Tourism

A government drive has seen tourism grow apace during the eighties and nineties. Marrakesh and Agadir have been the main beneficiaries. The total number of visitors to Morocco increased from 1,527,877 in 1995 to

1,832,122 in 1997. Morocco receives mostly French tourists, some 590,034 in 1997, while 108,572 Britons visited Morocco in the same year. Morocco earned 10.5 billion dirhams from tourism in 1997 alone.

Industry in the Atlas

For most Atlas Berbers there are only two industries from which it's possible to make a living: tourism and traditional agriculture. Trekkers will see small villages reliant on farming everywhere in the Atlas. These same trekkers are themselves the only other source of income for many of these villages. This is one reason why it is better to use a local guide and muleteer; that way you give your cash directly to the region in which you are travelling.

To Morocco's larger industries, however, the Atlas mountains are a valuable economic asset. The High Atlas, particularly, is an area rich in minerals. The most important of these deposits are the phosphate reserves found around the Khouribga region. There is also a good deal of hydro-electric potential in the Atlas. Several of the stronger *wadis* (mountain water-courses) have been dammed in an attempt to harness their energy potential.

Defence

With anywhere between 3000 and 6000 troops and a number of captured or donated tanks and armoured vehicles, Polisario (see p52) in Western Sahara is capable of posing a serious threat to Moroccan security. The king is the commander-in-chief of the Moroccan armed forces. His government spends some 4.3 per cent of GDP on the military each year (based on 1995 figures). The army is by far the largest service with 175,000 personnel, 524 battle tanks, 100 light tanks, 900 armoured fighting vehicles and 200 artillery pieces. The Moroccan navy, with 7,800 personnel, boasts one frigate and 26 patrol vessels. The air force, with 13,500 personnel, has 89 fighter aircraft and 23 combat helicopters. Moroccans are conscripted for 18 months.

Education

Education is compulsory in Morocco between the ages of seven and 13; there are government primary, secondary and technical schools. Morocco has 11 universities. But the rate of illiteracy is high, particularly among the elderly, women, and the rural population. Despite the government devoting considerable sums to education, only 25 per cent of the rural population can read and write; that figure is over 60 per cent in the cities. The Moroccan government has been told by its international sponsors, the World Bank and the IMF, that it must continue to improve education if it is to develop its economy in line with the West. Education in the High Atlas, particularly, has some way to go; children, particularly girls, are often kept from school by their parents to work in the fields. However, trekkers will learn to recognise the pink pre-fab buildings which are propped up on the edge of a number of Atlas villages as schools. These *prêt-à-porter* classrooms have been distributed by the government to larger mountain villages in a bid to improve literacy in the Atlas.

Health

For information on potential health hazards in Morocco, see p241. Standards of health care in Morocco are far below those of the West. There is, on average, one doctor per 3000 people. For comparison, there is one doctor per 629 people in Britain and one per 361 in France. There are 26,000 hospital beds, that's one per 1000 people (as opposed to one per 200 in Britain) and the infant mortality rate is 45 per 1000 live births; that rate is 4.9 per 1000 in France.

THE PEOPLE

Generally the Moroccan is clean-shaven or wears a small moustache, while the traditionalist wears a full-grown beard, wraps himself in a fine djellaba and winds a turban round his head. **André Launay** *Morocco*

One of the great joys of trekking in the Atlas mountains is the opportunity it offers to get to know the local population, the **Berbers**. By 1994 Morocco's population had grown to over 26 million people. Around 35 per cent of those are Berbers. Most of the remaining 65 per cent are Arabs. It is a slight simplification but still largely true to state that Moroccan Berbers occupy the mountains while the Arabs dominate the cities. There is some tension between these two ethnographic groups which are different in their origins, outlook, language (see p230) and even appearance. However, most Berbers, like Arabs, are Muslim.

Berbers are famed for their hospitality to strangers. Trekkers will find the locals they meet to be friendly, generous and helpful. It is quite common to be invited to share tea and bread with a local family. Such encounters present a great chance to glimpse the Berber way of life and will enhance any Atlas experience.

Berbers are equally well known for the passion and violence with which they have defended their independence and beliefs. Over the years, Berbers have fought for their freedom against numerous invaders. Traditionally, a slight on the honour of one Berber requires his whole family to avenge the insult. There are also complex codes of conduct which govern courtship and marriage (see box opposite).

Like many mountain peoples, Berbers are often extremely fit. Guides and muleteers will cover vast distances quickly – and without the sort of trekking gear Westerners might consider essential.

The word 'Berber' refers to the indigenous peoples of North Africa who live in widely distributed tribes across Morocco, Algeria, Tunisia, Libya and Egypt. While Moroccan Berbers are, in theory at least, governed from Rabat, there is a strong tradition of independence among the Berbers of the Atlas mountains. Many mountain Berbers live *hors taxe* –

they are exempt from paying tax but, equally, expect no social benefits.

Inevitably, perhaps, Berbers are today beginning to attach more importance to the accumulation of money. As young Berbers aspire to own the sort of products they see city-dwellers possess, so they will gradually be drawn further into a cycle of consumption. That cycle will fuel government interest in collecting taxes from Berbers and, in turn, their independence will begin to erode.

One effect of this is the fact that Berbers are increasingly seeing trekkers as a valuable source of cash. Stories abound of trekkers being invited to share tea with a Berber family and then presented with a bill. This has never happened to me and, in my experience, there is still a world of difference

❏ A Berber wedding

The bride could not have been older than 13. She sat in her mother's house surrounded by women from the village. Shyly, she presented her hands and feet to the women to be decorated with henna. As they worked, the women sang mournful songs. The bride then lifted a line of wool, which had been soaking in henna, and wove it between her fingers. Another girl of a similar age, perhaps her sister, gently tied a small bundle of salt around the bride's neck. Over the following two days the women of the village stayed close to the bride, talking to her in hushed tones, decorating her and singing. The men remained in their own group, preparing the marital home and cooking for the entire village.

On the wedding day itself, the bride dressed in an ornate wedding costume which had been made over months by her mother. The mother, crying and singing a lament to her daughter's leaving, arranged the girl's hair, dyed a colourful stripe through it and painted her face brightly. The mother then retreated into the home as the bride's brother lifted her onto his shoulders and carried her to a waiting horse to cheering and singing from the villagers, all of whom were watching.

Bride and brother rode together to the new marital home. A man then passed a live lamb around her head three times and she was given a copy of the Qur'an which she kissed. She then drank a skin of milk passed to her by the groom's mother. Another woman handed the bride an egg which she threw against the door of the new home.

She was then carried on her brother's shoulders to her new bedroom where she was joined by the groom. The bride's brother, joined by his father, waited outside the room while the couple consummated their marriage. After a nervous wait the groom emerged from the room to show his in-laws his bride's soiled wedding gown, proof that she had been a virgin. The groom then retreated to his room to join his bride while the villagers celebrated at the house of the bride's mother. I was told that Berbers attach great importance to virginity; if the girl had been found to have lost her virginity before the marriage, the wedding would probably have been called off.

between the attitudes of Atlas Berbers and city-dwelling Moroccans.

The most common form of political structure in High Atlas Berber villages is the *jama'ah* (a variant of the word *djeema*, which means square or place), where elders from the village meet to direct village life according to the codes of the *kanun* – a set of laws regarding property and personal behaviour. Nomadic Berber tribes normally choose one chief to command the group's movements.

Contrary to what one might expect, the High Atlas mountains are relatively densely populated. A typical High Atlas village will be home to several hundred people housed in steeply terraced houses (see the section on Berber architecture on p59) grouped around a central threshing floor. The surrounding slopes will be divided between different farming families.

The traditional dress for Berber men, still seen often today, is a brown or dark blue full-length smock. Women wear colourful highly-decorated dresses with distinctive head scarves and bright sandals. Women carry out a good deal of the hard work in the fields and in the home. Men, frankly, appear to do rather little. It's quite common to see an elderly Berber woman struggle past a group of chatting men with a vast sack of crops on her back. The world of business, however, is almost exclusively male. Businessmen and merchants sling a small leather satchel across their chests to signify their position.

Religion

Almost all Moroccans are Muslim and, of these, most follow the Maliki strain of the Sunni faith. There are some Jews and a tiny number of Christians in Morocco; traces of Christianity like the occasional Catholic

❏ Magic and Moroccan women

Moroccan women, bound by the strict Muslim *Sharia* code, live in the shadows of men. Pre-marital sex or infidelity can have appalling consequences for women but Moroccan men can escape imprisonment for rape unless their accuser is able to call two male witnesses.

Magic is one way in which women have attempted to redress this imbalance over the centuries. A surprising number of women claim to practise black magic or to be possessed by *djinns*, intelligent beings from Muslim mythology, often capable of evil, which can gain complete power over individuals. Witches create spells and potions from ingredients bought from *attars* (herbalists) in the souqs.

Many of these ancient potions are poisons. So it's no surprise Moroccan men treat the subject of witches seriously. A cheating husband or a man who beats his girlfriend might have every reason to fear a visit from a djinn or being fixed by the 'evil eye'.

church date from the period of European colonisation. **Islam** was founded by the prophet Mohammed in the seventh century. The word itself, derived from the Qur'an, means to 'surrender to the will of God'. Muslims, those who follow Islam, believe the Qur'an to be the word of God as dictated to Mohammed. As a product of a later age the Qur'an incorporates many earlier 'revealed books' and is thought by Muslims to replace them.

The Muslim creed focuses on six articles of faith: belief in one God; belief in angels; belief in the Qur'an; belief in the prophets; belief in a judgement day; and belief in God's pre-determination of good and evil. Muslims must abide by the five pillars of Islam to lead a devout life. They are: to speak the profession of faith, 'There is no God but God and Mohammed is the prophet of God'; to follow the *muezzin*'s call to prayer five times a day; to pay a *zakat*, or alms, to help the poor; to fast from sunrise to sunset during month of Ramadan; and to perform the *hajj*, a pilgrimage to Mecca, at least once in one's life. For information on travelling in a Muslim country, see p73-4.

Berber architecture

As the Arab and Western worlds infiltrate the Atlas mountains, where some tribes lived in isolation until as recently as the 1930s, the Berber culture will inevitably be influenced. But one has only to explore a typical mountain village to see that the inexorable march of 'progress' has yet to affect traditional Berber architecture – one of the most distinctive features of the High Atlas mountains.

Sun-scorched, red-brown terraced villages hug mountainsides and valleys in defensive huddles. Berber history is a story of violence and traditional architecture reflects the need to repel attackers. Villages blend into their surroundings because transport problems led Berbers to build from the closest materials to hand: mud, stone, wood and *pisé* (mud wedged between wooden boards). The dominant types of building in Berber architecture are the kasbah, the *ksar* (self-contained village), and the *agadir* (fortified granary).

Kasbahs are generally square, fortified pisé structures with turrets at each corner. They were either large, communal houses or small fortresses. Some kasbahs are enormous, like the one at Aït Benhaddou near Ouarzazate, while some are large enough for just a few families. The familiar tapering towers found on many kasbahs have led experts to conclude that these structures borrowed some of their style from Arab-Moroccan architecture.

The ksar (plural *ksours*) is a larger structure, a self-contained village surrounded by a high even wall. One entrance through the wall leads to a central alley from which a labyrinth of houses, mosques and wells fill the space between the main thoroughfare and the walls. Like the kasbah, there are corner towers for defence and few openings. The designs of both kasbahs and ksours, which are similar, grew from the fact that Berber tribes were little more than extended families. The entire tribe and its animals would shelter within their fortified villages.

Agadirs are large, fortified communal granaries. Tribes would build one strong granary in which each family would have a separate store area. The agadir would protect stored food from marauders and provide a place of refuge for women and children during times of war; almost a wartime bunker complete with a well and often an animal enclosure, mosque and blacksmith's workshop. Because of their social and economic importance, agadirs were frequently destroyed during inter-tribal conflicts. But one of the most complete still surviving is near Tabant in the M'goun area.

Fauna and flora

FAUNA

Mammals

There are many more species of wild mammal in the Atlas mountains than one might expect. Small mammals include the **North African elephant shrew** and the **Algerian hedgehog**. Elephant shrews, also called Jumping shrews, are so named for their long snouts and large ears. The only primate to live in the Atlas is the **Barbary ape**, actually a terrestrial macaque monkey. These animals, which are also found in Algeria and on the Rock of Gibraltar, are about 60 centimetres long with pale fur and pink faces. Legend has it that British control over Gibraltar will end when there are no Barbary apes left there.

Rabbits, **brown hares** and **Barbary ground squirrels** are common throughout the Atlas up to 4000m (13,120ft). One might also come across the **otter**, **ratel**, **ferret** or **weasel**. A ratel is a honey-loving weasel which looks rather like a badger.

The chance of meeting a large carnivore in the Atlas is slim but there are small populations of **lynx**, **African wildcat**, **common red fox**, **jackal** and **striped hyaena**. African wildcats (also called Caffre cats) are like large, muscular tabby cats. They hunt alone at night for small mammals. **Leopard** might still inhabit the Atlas but none have been seen for some time. Less threatening are the **Edmi gazelle** and **Barbary sheep** (*mouflon*) which are present in the Atlas but rarely seen.

Reptiles

The Atlas range, like all Morocco, is the habitat of a number of different species of **lizard**, **gecko** and **chameleon**. Many of these prefer to live in the walls of houses or on stony ground. Geckoes are essentially nocturnal lizards. Chameleons, of course, are known for their long tongues with which they snap up insects and also by their ability to change colour to disguise themselves against different backgrounds. **Snakes** are prevalent in Morocco but become less common at altitude. Few species present any danger to humans except perhaps those from the viper family, particularly the horned viper. They can be recognised by their triangular-shaped heads and the diamond pattern on their backs.

BIRDS OF THE ATLAS MOUNTAINS

Alpine chough

Male and female Alpine choughs have a similar all-black plumage with a blue-green tinge. Pale yellow bills provide the easiest way to distinguish an Alpine chough from a common chough. Alpine choughs also have longer tails. Choughs are noisy, sociable airborne acrobats. **Length**: 38cm; **Wingspan**: 75-85cm.

Barbary falcon

A Barbary falcon is similar to the peregrine but with a longer tail and brown colouring around the nape. The underside is spotted. Females are larger and bolder than males. The flight of a falcon is fast and powerful with dramatic dives for prey. Barbary falcons often hunt in pairs. **Length**: 45-50cm; **Wingspan**: 95-115cm.

BARBARY FALCON

Black kite

Both sexes of black kite, despite their name, have dark brown-red plumage with paler heads. Tails, in common with most kites, are forked. A kite's flight is graceful with slow wing-beats. Kites can sometimes be seen scavenging for food at souqs. **Length**: 55cm; **Wingspan**: 150-165cm.

BLACK KITE

Black redstart

The black redstart, from the chat-thrush genus, is a small insect-eating bird. The male has dark wings and back and a chestnut tail with a dark-brown central stripe. Females are similar with lighter, more grey colouring. Both have black bills and legs.

BLACK REDSTART

Length: 14cm; **Wingspan**: 25cm.

Blue rock thrush

Male blue rock thrushes are all-blue songbirds with darker wings. The female is dark grey with buff spots across her breast and underparts.

BONELLI'S EAGLE

Young blue rock thrushes resemble the female. These are timid birds with a loud call. **Length**: 20cm; **Wingspan**: 35cm.

Bonelli's eagle

Adult Bonelli's eagles have pale bodies and are dark underwing. On closer inspection, the wings have contrasting dark and grey sections. There is also a strong, dark grey stripe across the end of the tail. These eagles hunt daily in the same territory and in pairs. **Length**: 70cm; **Wingspan**: 150-170cm.

Booted eagle

The booted eagle in flight has a clear aquiline form but is the smallest eagle found in Europe or North Africa. There are two forms, pale and dark, varying from a pale, yellowish underside with dark flight feathers to an all-dark bird with a slightly paler head. **Length**: 45cm; **Wingspan**: 110-130cm.

Common buzzard

Buzzards, both male and female, are varying shades of brown with darker underparts. Paler buzzards usually have dark flight feathers. Tails are curved. Buzzards often perch in the open. **Length**: 50cm; **Wingspan**: 120-130cm.

Dipper

Both sexes of dipper are similar with dark-brown heads and very dark wings and upper bodies. The breast and throat, in contrast, are striking white. Bills are dark. Dippers reveal white eye‑

DIPPER

lids when they blink. They tend to live near mountain streams. **Length**: 17cm; **Wing span**: 25-30cm.

EGYPTIAN VULTURE

Egyptian vulture

Also called the Pharaoh's Chicken, Egyptian vultures are relatively small and white with black flight feathers and bald heads. Both sexes are similar. Like all vultures, the Egyptian vulture eats carrion but might occasionally prey on small, vulnerable live animals. **Length**: 65-70cm; **Wingspan**: 160-180cm.

Golden eagle

Golden eagles take over five years to grow their adult plumage which, when mature, is a mix of grey and dark-brown which looks dark from below when the birds are in flight. Powerful wings create a seemingly effortless, fast flight and sudden swoops to catch prey. The golden eagle is a much admired bird which, like other eagles, has often been used as a symbol to represent power and aggression. **Length**: 75-90cm; **Wingspan**: 190-230cm.

GOLDEN EAGLE

Housemartin

Housemartins are common across Europe and North Africa but are most likely to be seen near habitation. They feed on small insects at high altitude and often nest in buildings. Adults have dark blue underparts with white legs and rump. Bills are black. **Length**: 12cm; **Wingspan**: 25-30cm.

Lammergeier

The Lammergeier, also known as the bearded vulture, is a giant eagle-like vulture which feeds on carrion. Lammergeiers drop bones from heights of up to 80 metres onto rock in order to break them open to reach the marrow inside. Wings and tail are black, the head orange. **Length**: 105-120cm; **Wingspan**: 270-280cm.

LAMMERGEIER

Little swift

Little swifts are rare birds which spend almost all their time on the wing. They are dark brown in colour with white rumps and throats with a loud, piercing call. **Length**: 13cm; **Wingspan**: 35cm.

MERLIN

Merlin

Merlins, sometimes described as dashing merlins after their fast flying style, are attractive birds which fly low to hunt smaller birds which they often catch on the wing. The merlin is the smallest bird in the falcon family and capable of impressive aerobatics. Females are larger with brown upper bodies while the males are grey-blue with red-brown underparts. **Length**: 25-30cm; **Wingspan**: 60-65cm.

Moussier's redstart

The smallest redstart endemic to north-west Africa, it has a reddish-brown throat, a black and white head, a black back with conspicuous white wing patches. Its song is a warbling sound; its main call 'weet' followed by a rattle rasping. Seen in forests, scrubland and on rocky hillsides. **Length**: 12cm

Red-billed chough (aka chough)

A black bird with red bill and legs. Its call is more like a gull's than a crow's viz 'kyow' or 'k'chuf', hence its name; no song but rarely a subdued chattering like starlings. It both walks and hops and its flight is acrobatic. Found in mountainous areas and round steep cliffs. **Length**: 39-40cm.

Red-rumped swallow

It has a reddish-brown nape and rump, almost black plumage with slightly shorter in-curved tail streamers and slower flight than the swallow. Its song is less musical but its calls are similar. It breeds chiefly near cliffs or bridges, and often in towns. **Length**: 16-17cm. **Wingspan**: 14cm

Rock thrush

Chunkier than most swallows, the red-rumped swallow has a blue-back upperwing, a black tail and a chestnut stripe across the nape. Underparts are tan with black markings. The bill is black and legs dark. **Length**: 16cm; **Wingspan**: 25-32cm.

Roller

This large bird resembles the crow in shape but displays a bright blue plumage with chestnut back and dark flight feathers. Legs, feet and bill are black. **Length**: 30-32cm; **Wingspan**: 67-72cm.

Tristram's warbler

Male has reddish-brown wings, whiteish rings round the eyes and a whiteish streak under its bill turning to brown underparts; the female's colouring is more muted. Its song is musical; its call a clear 'chit' or chit-it'. It breeds and winters in north-west Africa.

FLORA

In summer, the Atlas mountains appear far from lush; barren, perhaps. A close inspection, however, will reveal that there is a lot more plant life in the range than one might suppose. Many of the plants which do flourish in Morocco are similar to those which one would find at altitude in southern Europe. Look out for cedar, prickly pear and juniper trees. Incense Juniper, Cupid's Dart and Woad are plant species of particular interest.

Cladanthus arabicus
Tofs

Erinacea anthyllis
Hedgehog Broom

Papaper rhoeas
Common poppy

Scrophularia canina
Dog's Figwort

Nerium oleander
Oleander

Asphodelus ayardi
Ayard's Asphodel

Catananche caerulea
Cupid's Dart

Verbascum
Mullin

Euphorbia
Spurge

Astragalus ibrahimianus
Ibrahim's Shrubby Milk-vetch

Cirsium chrysanthum
Golden-spined Thistle

Daphne laureola
Spurge-laurel

Xanthium spinosum
Cocklebur

Juniperus thurifera
Incense Juniper

Muscari comosum
Tassel Hyacinth

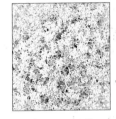

Isatis tinctoria
Woad

Onopordon
Cotton Thistle

Bupleurum spinosum
Spiny Hare's Ear

Alyssum saxatilis
Spiny Alison

Helianthemum
Rockrose

Arundo donax
Reed-plant

Phoenix dactylifera
Date Palm

Buxus balearica
Balearic Box

Practical information for the visitor

LOCAL TRANSPORT

By air

Trekkers using this guide will find little use for the internal flight network offered by Royal Air Maroc (RAM). But if you need to dash to Casablanca from Marrakesh for a flight out of Morocco, or if you decide to explore further afield, you might choose to fly. RAM serves most major cities in Morocco and flights are relatively cheap. Marrakesh to Casablanca, for example, costs about £35/US$50 for a one-way fare. The flight takes a little over half an hour. Students, young travellers and children can all benefit from hefty discounts on all routes.

By bus

Travelling on a Moroccan bus can be interesting. At their best they are moving carnivals of colour, music and friendly locals. At their worst they are steaming, fly-infested wrecks driven by madmen. The bus network itself is extensive and there are few places you can't get to by bus if you're prepared to wait long enough for one to turn up.

There are dozens of bus companies on the road but the best, and worth using wherever possible, is Compagnie de Transports Marocains (CTM). CTM is basically the national bus operator serving most routes. These buses are generally faster, safer and cleaner than the alternatives. They are also more expensive but still cheaper than trains and very inexpensive by European standards – you'll pay about 65dh from Marrakesh to Casablanca. Details of relevant bus services are given at the appropriate points in this book.

By rail

The ONCF rail network provides the best way to cover long distances. Trains are normally clean and air-conditioned, tickets are cheap (around 80dh to get from Marrakesh to Casablanca, for example) and the stations safe. There are, however, few opportunities for trekkers to take advantage of rail travel because the network is rather limited. Trains from Marrakesh go to Casablanca, Rabat, Tangier, Meknes and Fes. For details of getting to and from Marrakesh by train, see p88.

Opposite: Prickly pear (*Opuntia maxima*) in flower. The fruit is surprisingly refreshing. (Photos opposite and on C1 and C3 © Patrick Maguire).

By car

There can be few more enjoyable adrenalin sports than driving in Morocco. Roads outside the major cities are often deserted and the freedom a car provides allows you to travel at your own pace. But be careful. Many Moroccan roads are in poor condition and local drivers regularly attempt suicidal driving manoeuvres. The rules are the same as those in France: drive on the right; give way to the right; and the speed limit is 100kph on the open road and 40kph in urban areas. The police enjoy nothing more than a good roadblock and you will almost certainly encounter one if you drive for more than a few days. Just show your passport and a friendly smile.

You will find fewer petrol stations than you would expect to come across driving in Europe. Fill up whenever possible if your route is remote and consider taking a jerry-can for an emergency supply; your car-hire company should be able to lend you one. If you're setting off for a really long road trip, pack some bottled water and spare clothes in the car as well. Remember that roads in the Atlas can be made dangerous by ice, wind and snow in winter.

Car-hire firms are scattered across every major town and city in Morocco (see p89 for information on car hire in Marrakesh). You will normally need to be over 21 and have held your driving licence for over a year in order to hire a car. It's quite common to be asked to give a credit card imprint as a deposit, too. If you plan to head out to the more remote areas of the south, south-east and the mountains, consider paying extra for a 4WD vehicle (*quatre quatre*). One final tip: when parking in towns and cities it's a good idea to appoint a *gardien* (parking attendant) to look after your car. One will probably approach you as soon as you park. For two or three dirhams they will make sure no one breaks into your car.

By taxi

Morocco is brimming with taxis. There are two sorts: *grands taxis* are giant old Mercedes into which six passengers are expected to squeeze; they've generally been pounded to a heap by their lifetime of service on Moroccan roads but they are inexpensive (when full) and useful for longer journeys. There is no meter so you will need to agree the price in advance. You should find a sticker on the window in the back which explains standard prices for set routes.

Petits taxis are equally battered Fiat Unos which are restricted to short runs around town. See the appropriate sections for information on specific grand taxi journeys and prices. For information on taxis and prices in Marrakesh, see p88. Generally, however, a short hop in a petit taxi should cost 5-10dh. Always take extra care when you first arrive at a Moroccan airport; like taxi drivers the world over, airport drivers will attempt to overcharge you outrageously.

❑ **Weekly souqs**
A number of strategically-placed villages and towns hold weekly souqs (markets) where locals from the surrounding area do all their buying and selling. These colourful, day-long events are useful for **transport** as well as supplies. Taxis and camions arrive for the souq the day before and leave the day after. So your best chance of finding onward transport is always the day after a souq.

Aït Tamlil	Tuesday
Asni	Saturday
Azilal	Thursday
Ouarzazate	Sunday
Tabant	Sunday

By truck (camion)

Hitching a lift on the back of camion is a well-established practice in the High Atlas – albeit a frightening one. You'll soon find yourself muttering '*Inshallah*' like the nervous Berbers in the back with you. But there are sometimes few alternatives and this is, at least, a cheap mode of transport. Expect to pay 10dh for a ride regardless of the distance. For safety reasons, however, you should avoid camions if you possibly can.

LANGUAGE

Most Moroccans speak Arabic or one of three Berber dialects. Many also speak French. English is not widely spoken but Moroccans are generally very adept at languages; you will find someone who speaks at least a little English in all but the most isolated parts of the country.

It's fairly easy to get by with French alone. But in the mountains some knowledge of Berber is useful if only to be polite. Arabic and Berber are difficult languages to English-speaking minds. At the very least, however, one should learn some basic pleasantries. The effort will always be appreciated and, on a more practical note, you will find people are much better disposed towards you if you inject some of the local tongue into your small talk. The section on p230-7, while far from comprehensive, introduces basic Arabic, French and Berber words and their pronunciation. There is also a glossary of relevant Moroccan-Arabic and Berber terms on p238-40.

EMBASSIES AND CONSULATES

Most foreign embassies (see p68) are in Rabat but there are British and French consulates in Marrakesh. For Moroccan embassies see p19.

❑ When to bother your embassy...

If you lose your passport, your embassy should be able to help but travellers must understand that there are very few other circumstances under which embassy staff can act. It is very rare for an embassy to assist someone who is arrested by the local police; you are, of course, bound by the laws of the country in which you are travelling. In Morocco, this advice is particularly pertinent with regard to drugs (see p75). It is also very unusual for an embassy to help with travel expenses if you find yourself penniless or unable to get home in an emergency.

British Embassy
BP 45, 17 boulevard de la Tour
Hassan, Rabat
☎ 07-72.09.05

British Consulate
55 boulevard Zerktouni
Marrakesh
(☎ 04-43.40.95)

Canadian Embassy
CP 709, 13 bis, rue Jafaar As-Sadik
Rabat-Agdal
☎ 07-67.21.34

Embassy of the French Republic
3 rue Sahnoun
Rabat
☎ 07-77.78.22

French Consulate
rue Ibn-Khaldoun
(next to Koutoubia)
Marrakesh

Spanish Embassy
3 rue Madnine
Rabat
☎ 07-76.89.89

Embassy of the USA
BP 003, 2 avenue de Marrakesh
Rabat
☎ 07-76.22.65

ELECTRICITY

The Moroccan standard electrical supply, like that of Europe, is 220 volts AC, 50Hz. Depending on the age and situation of the building, however, the old 110 volt supply is occasionally still used. Plugs follow the European two-pin format. American- and Canadian-bought appliances require current adaptors. Few villages have electricity in the Atlas interior. Some have communal generators which are used for a few set hours each evening.

TIME AND DATE

Morocco keeps Greenwich Mean Time (GMT). Muslims use a lunar calendar, which starts about 11 days earlier each year, with the following months: Muharran, Saphar, Rabia I, Rabia II, Gamada I, Gamada II,

Rajab, Shaaban, Ramadan, Shawwal, Dhulkaada, Dhulheggia. The ninth month, Ramadan, is the Muslim equivalent of Lent and commemorates Allah's dictation of the Qur'an to Mohammed. Muslims are required to fast between sunrise and sunset for the entire month (see p22).

Each 30-year period in the Muslim calendar is divided between 19 years which have 354 days ('common' years) and 11 which have 355 days ('intercalary'). Muslim years equate to the Gregorian as follows: 1422 (2001), 1423 (2002), 1424 (2003).

The Muslim New Year falls on the following approximate Gregorian dates: New Year 2001 (1422): 27 March
              New Year 2002 (1423): 17 March

Thus the Muslim calendar falls behind the Gregorian calendar by about 10 days each year. Almost all Moroccans, particularly those working in business or tourism, understand and use the Gregorian calendar as well as the Muslim.

OPENING HOURS

Bank hours vary but expect to find them open between 8.30 and 11.30am and 3 and 4.30pm Monday to Thursday with early closing, perhaps 3pm, on Fridays. Shops and souqs stay open longer; expect them to stay open for business between 8am and 6pm – perhaps longer in summer in tourist destinations like Marrakesh. Post offices (PTT or La Poste) are open between 8am and 3pm in winter or from 8am to 12.30pm and 3 to 6pm in summer. Museums and tourist sights will usually stay open between 10am and 5pm. However, this can vary from one place to the next; aim for mid-morning or mid-afternoon to avoid disappointment. Banks, post offices and a number of shops and museums will close for the weekend. Banks, post offices, museums and souqs close during public holidays (see below). Many cafés and food shops close for the month of Ramadan.

HOLIDAYS AND FESTIVALS

Seven **secular public holidays** (*fêtes nationales*) are celebrated on the same Gregorian dates each year:

1 January – New Year's Day
3 March – Feast of the Throne
1 May – Labour Day
23 May – National Feast
14 August – Allegiance Day
21 August – King's birthday
6 November – Anniversary of the Green March

There are also a number of **Muslim festivals** each year; the dates of these, based on the Muslim calendar (lunar-based) and set by Islamic authorities, are difficult to predict with any certainty.

Ramadan

The most important festival in the Muslim calendar is **Ramadan.** The festival begins with the first sighting from Mecca of the new moon; approximate dates are as follows:

  1-27 December 2000
  21 November to 16 December 2001
  11 November to 6 December 2002.

Ramadan is the ninth month in the Muslim calendar. The five pillars of Islam (see p59) state that devout Muslims must fast between sunrise and sunset for the entire month. In that respect, at least, it mirrors Lent for Christians. In practice, however, Ramadan is taken far more seriously. Ramadan commemorates the time when the Qur'an was revealed to Mohammed.

The fast applies to drinking, eating, smoking and sex during daylight hours. This makes it a testing time for travellers but, frankly, a far more testing time for locals. Trekkers should avoid the month of Ramadan completely; guides and muleteers will not work or, if you do persuade one, they will charge far more than usual. Ramadan is also a celebration. If you do decide to visit Morocco during this time you will find the streets alive with activity, celebration and good humour. Tourists are not obliged to join in the fast but don't be surprised to receive a lot of dirty looks if you decide to sit in the centre of Marrakesh tucking into a chocolate bar and a cigarette while all around you are craving both.

Other religious holidays and festivals

Next comes the feast of **Aïd es Seghir** which marks the appearance of the new moon that signals the end of Ramadan. Still traditionally a family-orientated festival, Aïd es Seghir is celebrated as much in the home as on the streets. In Marrakesh, however, this festival sees Djeema al-Fna as lively, colourful and dazzling as it ever gets. Following Aïd es Seghir by around two months, **Aïd el Kebir** honours Abraham and is, again, a family affair. Families all over the country slaughter a sheep to mark Abraham's sacrifice of a ram in the place of his son, a bad day for sheep but a much-loved festival in Morocco. **Achoura** (sometimes **Moharran**), about three weeks later, is the festival of the Muslim New Year. It's followed about a month later by **Mouloud** which celebrates the prophet Mohammed's birthday. This is, perhaps, the second-most important festival in the Muslim calendar and it is celebrated with enthusiasm. Moussems (see below) take place all over the country.

A **moussem** is a religious festival originally staged around a pilgrimage to the tomb of a saint (*marabout*). They happen all over the country throughout the year and are often very small, rural affairs. Berbers, particularly, stage a number of moussems in the 'true' sense of the word; local celebrations at a saint's tomb. But the word has grown to encompass almost any religious celebration. Moussems are not always very spectacular from a tourist's point of view. One that is, however, takes place at **Imilchil** sometime in September. This is the marriage moussem, high in the Atlas mountains, where a mass Berber wedding is held.

Not a religious festival but well worth seeing, the **Marrakesh Folk Festival** is growing in stature every year. Berber and folk musicians from all over Morocco, and increasingly the Arab world, inundate the city every summer. The festival takes place around June but check with the tourist office in spring to find out for sure.

MONEY

The Moroccan currency is the **dirham** (dh) which is divided into 100 centimes. You cannot get dirhams outside Morocco. It's best to change money at banks; there is almost no black-market in currency exchange and, even if you do find a shark willing to make a deal, it's very unlikely you'll get a better rate than the banks offer.

One legacy of French colonialism is the fact that French francs are sometimes accepted in hotels. Dollars, too, can occasionally be used in the same way.

As always, **travellers' cheques** are a safe way to carry money but you will need cash for day-to-day expenses. In the Atlas mountains in particular, you cannot rely on finding somewhere to change your travellers' cheques; stock up with dirhams in Marrakesh before you set off.

❏ Rates of exchange	
	Dirham
Aus$1	6.19
Can$1	7.00
Euro1	9.93
FF1	1.51
DM1	5.07
NLG1	4.50
NZ$1	4.90
Ptas1	0.06
UK£1	15.70
US$1	10.30

Credit cards are not accepted outside the largest and most up-market hotels, restaurants and shops. There are **ATMs** in the larger towns and cities, most of which accept cards from international networks such as Cirrus, Visa and MasterCard.

International money transfer agents are fairly easy to find. Crédit du Maroc is the agent for Moneygram and WAFA Bank is affiliated to Western Union. Don't get money wired to you unless you really must; it's a slow and expensive operation. Much better to take a credit card with a PIN for emergencies.

Tipping

A waiter in a restaurant will expect a tip of around 5dh while café staff are used to a little less; taxi drivers are not normally tipped at all. If you take a photograph of someone, or someone's camel, you should offer around 5dh. Car gardiens are paid 2dh. If you listen to live music or story-telling, particularly in Marrakesh, you should offer some coins, perhaps 5dh or more depending on the length of time you were entertained. Mountain guides and muleteers will expect a tip of one day's pay. Some guides, however, might prefer gifts, perhaps some trekking gadget which you can't easily buy in Morocco.

Haggling

Bartering is an essential prop in the theatre of Moroccan life. Restaurant, hotel and most transport costs are fixed. But beyond that, prices must be established through a long-winded ritual which some travellers hate and others love. Remember to keep a cool head. Stay friendly and cheerful and never bargain for something you don't actually intend to buy. It helps to know how much an item is really worth but, more importantly, decide how much it's worth to you. Keep a fixed upper limit in your mind and don't exceed it.

Praise the shopkeeper for his fine goods and then show casual, unenthusiastic interest in whatever it is you hope to buy. It's best to get the shopkeeper to name his price first. Open your bidding at one-third of that.

Ignore the shopkeeper's sob stories and bargain hard. He will expect nothing less. Whatever the outcome, shake the salesman's hand and keep the whole transaction friendly. It is after all as much about entertainment as it is about buying and selling.

KEEPING IN TOUCH

Post offices

Moroccan post offices (look for PTT or La Poste signs) are usually swamped by irritated customers. You can avoid the hassle by buying stamps at some news-stands and *tabacs* (tobacconists). Stamps cost 5.5dh for Europe or 11dh for the United States. You can send parcels from post offices and most have a rather expensive Express Mail Service (look for the EMS logo) which should see letters or parcels arrive in Europe within a few days.

Poste restante This international postal system allows letters or parcels to be sent to a general post office (see addresses below) and held there for one month for the recipient to pick up. There is a nominal fee for picking up post this way. When sending post use a bright envelope and remember to use a simple form of the recipient's name and underline their surname, also write your name and address on the reverse. When picking up post, take your passport for identification. Most American Express offices offer a similar and perhaps more reliable service free of charge for clients with AmEx travellers' cheques.

Poste Restante
La Poste
place 16 du Novembre
Marrakesh
Morocco

Poste Restante
La Poste
rue de la Poste
Ouarzazate
Morocco

Telephones and fax

Most post offices have a telephone room attached (look for the Itissalat al-Maghrib sign) where you can make reverse-charge calls (ask to make a PCV) or pay after you've finished. You will also find card-phones outside most post offices. Cards are available in post offices or from news-stands and tabacs. Probably the easiest way to call home, however, is to look for a *téléboutique*. These privately-run phone rooms are always easy to find, carry lots of change and are usually slightly more peaceful than post offices (with the exception of the phone room in the Marrakesh-Medina PTT which is an oasis of calm). Many téléboutiques have fax machines as do the better hotels. However, sending faxes from hotels, like making telephone calls, can be very expensive.

> ❏ **Dialling codes**
> International codes must be preceded by 00 and the first 0 of the area code should be omitted.
>
> **Calling from Morocco:**
> Australia   +61
> Belgium   +32
> Britain   +44
> France   +33
> Germany   +49
> Netherlands   +31
> New Zealand   +64
> Spain   +34
> USA and Canada   +1
>
> **Calling to Morocco**
> Country code   +212
> Marrakesh and Ouarzazate
> area code   +4

E-mail

The Internet provides a cheap and easy way to keep in touch overseas through free web-based e-mail services like hotmail.com and fireball.co.uk. In Morocco, however, Internet access is hard to find. Your chances of finding somewhere to log-on in the High Atlas are slim. In Marrakesh, though, you can check your e-mail at Hôtel Ali and an Internet café is said to be on its way.

MEDIA

French- and Arabic-language newspapers are published daily. The main French-language newspapers are *L'Opinion* and *Le Matin du Sahara*. Foreign publications are readily available in the major cities, including Marrakesh, and are usually just one day late.

Any trekker in the High Atlas equipped with a short-wave radio will find it easier to pick up the **BBC World Service** (MHz 17.71, 12.10, 11.78, 9.410) or **Voice of America** (MHz 9.760, 6.040, 1.197, 0.792) than an international newspaper.

TRAVELLING IN A MUSLIM COUNTRY

Morocco is a Muslim country and as such there are a number of social conventions which visitors should understand. Although travellers are not expected to follow all Muslim manners, failure to make sufficient effort will be considered a little lazy or even insulting. Don't eat or offer gifts with your left hand, which is ritually 'unclean'. (If knives and forks are available, you can use both hands.) Don't point bare feet at anyone. Don't ask for alcohol, which is forbidden under Islamic law, unless your host is drinking or alcohol is clearly available. Don't ask for pork.

As a non-Muslim, do not try to enter a mosque or religious building unless you are sure you are allowed inside. Dress should be modest; slacks rather than shorts for men (even in the Atlas, trekkers should cover their legs in villages) and women should be particularly discreet. If you do get chance to see inside a mosque, take off your shoes and cover up your legs, arms, shoulders and, for women, hair. Scarves and *jallabah* (large hooded full-length garments) are normally available inside mosques for visitors who are exposing too much flesh.

WOMEN IN ISLAM, WOMEN TRAVELLERS & SEXUAL MORES

The position of women in Islam underpins Moroccan sexual politics. Adultery committed by men seems almost accepted while a wife or mother has little power or independence at all. The Qur'an allows polygamy as long as the man is in a position to provide for all his wives.

The degree of freedom given to Muslim women varies from one Islamic country to the next. This often provides a useful guide to the level of fundamentalism in a particular country. A growing number of non-Muslim visitors have helped relax attitudes in some parts of Morocco. In the cities particularly, women enjoy freer lives than they might in more

fundamentalist Muslim societies. That said, Quranic principles are widely adhered to and for most women opportunities are very limited. Moroccan women are expected to wear the veil in public and to preserve their virginity until their wedding night. Arranged marriages are the norm. Women who ignore these codes are often treated harshly by society.

Western women are generally seen as promiscuous and female travellers will need to take great care to avoid unwelcome attention. Lone women travellers will be pestered while those accompanied by men will fare better. Women travellers, married or not, should consider

Berber woman (photo © Rupert Evers)

wearing a wedding ring to indicate that they are not available. Since most Moroccans are polite and courteous, women should not be afraid to shout out if a man's pestering becomes intimidating. Almost all Moroccans fear public reproach and will seek to avoid the humiliation that a yelling Western woman might cause.

Although homosexuality is thought to be fairly common, lesbianism is rare. Despite a drive by the late King Hassan II to raise awareness, the dangers of AIDS remain relatively little-understood.

DRUGS

The Rif mountains in northern Morocco are a major centre of marijuana (*kif*) production. (The word 'kif' is derived from the Arabic '*kayf*' which means 'pleasure'.) The industry is even semi-tolerated by the authorities. The drug trade makes the Rif a dangerous area in which to travel; whatever your views on kif, most marijuana farmers are suspicious of trespassers.

Elsewhere in Morocco, kif is widely available. If you look like someone who might want to indulge, you are sure to be offered some with shouts of 'chocolate!' or 'kif!'. Contrary to a popular misconception, however, the purchase, possession or transportation of kif is illegal in Morocco and could lead to very heavy penalties. An alarmingly high number of Western visitors end up in some dank Moroccan prison each year; a fairly unpleasant place in which to reside for five years.

If you do decide to smoke a little kif, the chances are you will not be caught. But be careful; some dealers work with the police to frame tourists who are then forced to pay hefty bribes to avoid jail. Apart from looking out for that danger, there are three golden rules for kif smokers: don't transport drugs anywhere; don't offer drugs to anyone; and only buy very small amounts for immediate use. You would be wise to avoid drugs altogether; it is really the only way to be sure of avoiding running into problems with the law and, indeed, the low-life who peddle kif in Moroccan cities. Remember, too, that your embassy will not help you if the local constabulary 'feel your collar' for a drug-related offence.

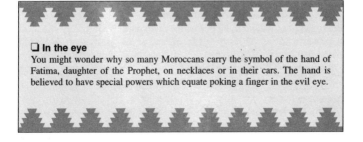

❑ In the eye
You might wonder why so many Moroccans carry the symbol of the hand of Fatima, daughter of the Prophet, on necklaces or in their cars. The hand is believed to have special powers which equate poking a finger in the evil eye.

FOOD

Moroccan cuisine reflects the country's history; it's a blend of Berber dishes, Arab spices, Spanish ingredients, desert staples and, more recently, French interference. The Berber influence is best tasted in *couscous* and *tagines*. Soups, particularly *harira*, are common starters. Apart from couscous and tagines, *pastilla* and *brochettes* (kebabs) are popular main dishes. *Harissa* is a commonly-used sauce for flavouring almost any Moroccan recipe. Outside the main cities, restaurants tend to offer a very limited choice. Moroccans eat fairly early so that choice will grow increasingly limited throughout the evening. Meals are a social event in Moroccan families; if you get chance to eat with a local family, take it.

● **Harira** This thick soup is eaten as an entire meal or a starter. It's a rich and filling concoction made from chick peas, lamb, tomatoes and spices.
● **Tagine** It's impossible to visit Morocco without becoming acquainted with this ubiquitous dish. The word 'tagine' actually refers to the earthenware pot with a chimney in which the meal is cooked. The meal itself is a delicious meat or vegetable stew cooked slowly in spices. If you're eating with others, the tagine will be placed in the middle of the table and shared.
● **Couscous** This classic Moroccan dish, like the tagine, is found all over the country. Semolina is steamed in the top part of a *couscoussier* (a two-tier cooking pot) while a meat or vegetable stew cooks slowly underneath. After several hours, the two are combined and coated in harissa sauce. Like tagines, the couscous dish will be placed in the centre of table and shared. You can't beat home-cooked couscous but if you do order it in a restaurant you will often need to give notice.
● **Pastilla** Moroccans consider this to be a luxurious speciality – and at its best it is excellent. It is a very sweet, rich pigeon pie made with light, crispy pastry and covered in sugar. This must be the most filling dish in the world.
● **Harissa** Almost always used on couscous but a popular addition to any Moroccan dish, harissa is a spicy sauce made from chillies and garlic. Test its strength before you pour it on.
● **M'choui** A m'choui is a whole lamb roasted slowly in a sealed clay oven. This Berber speciality is usually reserved for weddings or feats so, if you are offered one, you should consider it a great kindness. The lamb's heart and liver will be eaten before the main dish. Traditionally, the most succulent parts of the lamb will be offered to the guests first; this could mean the eyes or even the testicles. Refusal *will* offend. More worldly-wise Berbers will have encountered Western reluctance to eat steaming lamb's gonads before but if not there's no way out.

Western food
The French left Moroccans with a taste for milky coffee and croissants. Most major cities have several French-style restaurants and some offer

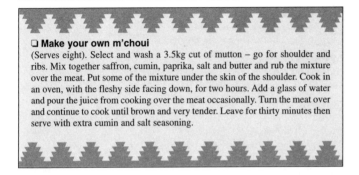

❏ **Make your own m'choui**
(Serves eight). Select and wash a 3.5kg cut of mutton – go for shoulder and ribs. Mix together saffron, cumin, paprika, salt and butter and rub the mixture over the meat. Put some of the mixture under the skin of the shoulder. Cook in an oven, with the fleshy side facing down, for two hours. Add a glass of water and pour the juice from cooking over the meat occasionally. Turn the meat over and continue to cook until brown and very tender. Leave for thirty minutes then serve with extra cumin and salt seasoning.

what can best be described as Franco-Moroccan cuisine. Poor imitations of American-style fast-food dishes are available in cities like Marrakesh and Casablanca when one can also find the occasional pizza. Outside the cities, however, non-Moroccan or Berber food is hard to find.

Eating in the Atlas
Larger trekking groups might consider employing a cook who will often double as the muleteer to join them. With just a gas stove and a couple of pans, these highly-skilled mountain people are capable of rustling up tasty three-course meals (usually soup followed by a tagine and fruit). Otherwise it's possible to find a meal in most gîtes d'étape but often you will need to give several hours' notice. It would be dangerous to rely on finding well-stocked gîtes for the duration of your trek; take a cook or, at least, generous emergency supplies of your own. One Berber speciality which should not be missed is *m'choui* (see above). Staples such as dried fruit and nuts are easy to buy in the souqs and make useful, light energy food to carry with you on long treks.

DRINK
Faithful to tradition, our host rises to prepare the green mint tea...oh, that odour that touches the throat with an iced finger, which plumbs the depths of the lungs, tells of snow and subtle pepper, wakens the spirits and deludes thirst!
Colette *A Moroccan Luncheon*, from *A Book of Travellers' Tales*

Tea and coffee
Moroccans drink sweet mint tea almost constantly. It appears at first to be a glass of sugar with a hint of mint tea but one acquires a taste for it surprisingly quickly. The proper way to pour tea is to fill one glass from a great height, taste it then pour it back into the teapot. Then fill each glass. Pouring from a height makes the tea frothy. Coffee is usually French-style, strong and milky.

Soft drinks

All the usual brands are available everywhere – even in the most unexpected places in the High Atlas mountains.

Water

Don't drink tap water and, when trekking, purify stream water with iodine (see p242). Otherwise drink Sidi Harazem bottled water. Check the seal.

Alcohol

Booze is forbidden under Islamic law but non-Muslims are allowed to make, sell and drink it. The better international hotels have decent bars but, apart from these, the average Moroccan bar is a seedy den. Heineken is the most commonly available international beer but Morocco does have two brands of its own. The better of these is Flag, which claims to have won an international prize in Amsterdam in 1981. Some wine is produced in Morocco but, generally, it's not great.

HAMMAMS

These communal steam baths are an essential part of Moroccan life. Groups of men and women meet to wash in a setting which places as much emphasis on the social opportunity to chat to friends as it does on washing. Men and women are strictly divided. Outsiders are normally welcome and, if you don't know what you're doing, someone will probably show you. There's nothing better for those post-trek aches than a *hammam*, which can include a vigorous massage, but the actual baths can be hard to find. Ask someone to show you. A hammam should cost no more than 30dh and will often be much less. Many of the larger international hotels offer versions of the hammam for over 100dh. These are seldom as interesting as the real thing.

TOILETS

Up-market hotels and restaurants have Western-style flush lavatories but, in most homes and cafés, a hole in the ground is more common. The big issue for outsiders is whether to adopt the local 'left hand and tap' method of hygiene or to carry acres of loo roll around. You won't often find a toilet roll provided. Trekkers should burn used toilet paper.

THINGS TO BUY

Moroccan Arabs, Berbers and, in the past, Jews conspired to create an art and craft tradition in Morocco which has been strong and exciting for hundreds of years. This tradition still flourishes in souqs across the country. Larger towns also have an *ensemble artisanal*, a government-run craft market, where prices are fixed but higher than those in the souqs. Often, however, the better craftsmen supply the ensemble artisanal while there's no doubt that the souqs peddle a lot of cheap made-for-tourists tat alongside genuine high-quality articles.

Carpets

Moroccan carpet-dealers could teach any double-glazing salesman a thing or two about high-pressure sales techniques. But if you are prepared to take the time to find a good dealer with some genuinely interesting wares, the experience can be rewarding; you will find yourself sitting cross-legged on the floor, plied with mint tea, while an enthusiastic salesman rolls carpets out for your inspection. Carpets differ depending on the region in which they were made. Cheap, machine-made fakes are normally easy to spot: look out for unsubtle colours and fewer knots per square inch than the on the genuine article. High Atlas carpets (often *hanbels* – designed for general domestic use rather than purely ornamental purposes) are called *glaoua* and are quite plain and black and white. The area around Jbel Sirwa produces more colourful, complex patterns. Carpets can be enormously expensive so be careful; you should also consider how you propose to get the carpet home. Don't make the mistake of thinking that a carpet will be an investment or the start of a thriving import-export business; once you've bought your carpet, you'll never see that money again.

Ceramics and pottery

Carpets which look fantastic in the large Moroccan carpet shop can look daft back home, unless you have a good eye. Pottery, however, normally looks as good at home as it did in Morocco. Look out for beautiful plates and bowls decorated in classic Moroccan geometric designs. A tagine pot also makes an amusing memento.

Clothes

When you find yourself poised to buy some Moroccan garb, ask yourself whether you're really likely to wear it back home. The answer is normally 'no'. If you plan to buy Moroccan clothes to wear in Morocco, however, you're on to a good thing. Jallabah, *kaftans* and *burnous* (all variations of hooded full-length smocks) are useful for trekking, to keep the sun off and for travelling unpestered through the streets of Marrakesh.

Jewellery

The sort of jewellery one finds in souqs is attractive but not very valuable. So haggle accordingly. It is possible however to pick up some real bargains, particularly if you search for simple, hand-crafted silver necklaces, rings and pendants which can be beautiful and symbolic. It is also possible to find genuinely valuable emerald-studded pieces among the more up-market dealers but unless you really know what you're doing you should try not to part with too much cash.

Leather

You will find high-quality leather wallets, slippers, belts and other acces-sories all over the souqs. Morocco-bound book-covers are world-famous for their quality and, if you plan ahead, it's a good idea to take a treasured book to Morocco with you to be bound.

Metal

Again, the souqs are full of decorative metalwork such as candlesticks, bowls and stands. Much of it is beautiful but the more complicated items are not always very durable. A Moroccan tea-pot makes a great souvenir; there can be no more appropriate symbol of the Moroccan experience.

Semi-precious stones

Wherever you drive in the Atlas mountains, small boys will leap out from the roadside with coloured stones for sale every few hundred yards; they are selling amethyst or Sahara Rose which, again, make beautiful reminders of Morocco.

Spices

A small bag of saffron or cumin makes an interesting gift; explore the spice souqs in Marrakesh where each stall is laden with colourful sacks of spices. The trader will invariably be happy to let you taste different spices.

Wood

Of all Morocco's craftsmen, wood-workers are probably the least depen-dent on tourism. Gorgeously ornate panels are still created to furnish the homes of the rich and woodworkers are often employed in maintaining religious buildings and in building high-quality furniture. Tourists can take a sample of these magnificent skills home in the form of luxurious, inlaid draughts and chess boards or jewellery boxes made from the wood of evergreen *thuja* trees.

SECURITY, CRIME AND THE POLICE

Morocco is often perceived to be a difficult country in which to travel but, in fact, the crime rate is low. Muslims are asked by the Qur'an to show kindness to strangers and, more often than not, travellers remember Moroccan hospitality as one of the best things about their trip. Like any country, however, wherever tourists swarm in numbers, conmen and thieves operate. This applies to Marrakesh, and travellers will need to employ common sense and exercise caution. In the Atlas mountains, how-ever, crime is almost non-existent. If you do run into trouble, contact the police by dialling ☎ 19. Remember that the Moroccan police are a quasi-military and, if rumours are to be believed, highly-corruptible bunch and you will need tact and patience in dealing with them.

PART 3: MINIMUM IMPACT

The need for minimum impact trekking

As increasing numbers of people explore the mountains which Pliny described as the most wonderful in Africa, so the Atlas itself might change. The damaging effects of tourists' presence can be limited only if trekkers try to minimise their impact by considering how their actions and decisions might affect the people, environment and economy.

Unlike some other popular trekking regions, the Atlas has no organised environmental group striving to protect it, so no guidelines have previously been written with the Atlas trekker in mind. These below have been developed to help readers think about how they might minimise the impact of their visit. They have been devised with the help of the British Mountaineering Council's *Mountain Tourism Codes* and the *Himalayan Tourist Code* published by the charity Tourism Concern.

For more information on responsible tourism, contact Tourism Concern, based in London, on ☎ 020-7753 3330.

ENVIRONMENTAL IMPACT

Waste management
Don't pollute the Atlas with waste. All waste has some consequence. Each individual trekker should play his or her part in disposing of waste or removing it from the mountains.
- **Minimise group size** The bigger the group, the more serious its impact.
- **Minimise supplies** Don't carry more supplies than you really need.
- **Educate others** With diplomacy and tact, encourage others in your group, including locals, to help manage waste properly.
- **Burnable waste** Food, paper, card and wood waste can be burnt.
- **Toxic and non-burnable waste** Metals, plastics, foams, batteries, petrol, paraffin, methylated spirits, oil and medical waste should be carried out of the mountains.
- **Human waste** This should be buried in pits dug downhill of camps and water sources. Don't relieve yourself within 20m (70ft) of a water source. Burn toilet paper.
- **Remove packaging** Get rid of excess packaging before setting off for the mountains. This will also help you to reduce the weight of your pack.
- **Don't ignore others' waste** Make the effort to clean up any other waste which you find on your trek.

Limit deforestation

Local Berbers are guilty of contributing to deforestation but that's no reason why visitors should add to the problem. Locals tend to use firewood efficiently while visitors might provoke inefficient use of wood without realising it simply by demanding food or hot water at irregular times.

● **Avoid open fires** Only make a fire when you really need the warmth. Berbers will almost certainly build fires, since it is a part of local life, but you should at least make sure they use dead wood.

● **Don't ask for boiled water for drinking** There are better, more efficient methods for purifying water (see p242).

● **Order food at the same time and keep it simple** Complicated orders cause problems for remote Atlas cafés which might use wood-burning stoves inefficiently in order to meet your demands.

Keep water clean

This is crucial. Simple 'green' routines will prevent water contamination which might lead to serious problems further downstream.

● **Human waste** Find a place away from the nearest water source and bury your waste. Burn toilet paper.

● **Washing** Fill a bucket or bowl to use soap or shampoo and dispose of the dirty water at least 20m away from the water source. Use biodegradable products and use them sparingly.

Protect plants

The effect of your removing one mountain flower might appear to be minimal; but the Atlas is a fragile environment which will not tolerate large-scale tampering with its plant and flower populations. Don't pick flowers.

● **Don't take cuttings** Never remove cuttings, seeds or roots from plants.

● **Avoid trampling plants** Watch where you walk.

Avoid erosion

Take care not to add to erosion any further than you can possibly help.

● **Stay on the main trail** Where possible, follow the trail to avoid creating new paths or shortcuts which might erode the landscape.

● **Respect fields and crops** Pay particular attention when walking near fields and crops to make sure you don't damage the produce or any irrigation system which, while not always immediately obvious, might have been built around the field.

ECONOMIC IMPACT

Use local services

Think about where the money you spend will go. Where possible, inject what you've set aside for your holiday directly into the local economy.

● **Use guides and muleteers** Consider employing a local guide and muleteer rather than joining a trek organised by an international tour operator.

There are a number of other very good reasons for doing this (see p10).
● **Lodges and refuges** Staying in lodges or refuges rather than camping is one way to invest some money in the Atlas economy.
● **Provisions** Buy locally rather than bringing supplies from home.

Observe standard fees

Remember to keep costs in perspective. Most Atlas Berbers are poor people who live hard lives working an unforgiving land. Pay a fair price for the goods and services they offer. Haggle for gifts and trinkets, it's the Berber way, but accept standard prices for food, guides, muleteers and accommodation (see p10-11).
● **Don't pay too little** Paying less than the standard price is exploitative.
● **Don't pay too much** Paying too much creates dependency, promotes an inflationary cycle and sets a precedent for future visitors. It might also create resentment in the local community; the beneficiaries of your generosity will be envied by others.
● **Tips** Tipping is normally expected (see p71) but avoid overtipping for the same reasons as you should avoid overpaying. Give your tip separately from the payment.

Maintain good relations

Never let business negotiations lead to ill feeling. Be friendly and respectful.
● **Don't lose your temper** Keep calm when negotiating. Berbers often become very animated when conducting business but are rarely rude.

CULTURAL IMPACT

Photograph with sensitivity

It's all too easy to snap away without realising that your interest might appear voyeuristic, rude or even dangerous. Remember that, to most Berbers, to pose for your photograph is to give you something.
● **Ask first** Never take a photograph of a person or their property without first asking permission.
● **Send photographs** Many Berbers in the more remote Atlas villages will never have seen a photograph of themselves. If you photograph someone, ask whether they would like to be sent a copy of the photograph and be sure that you send it; this is a good way to reward their kindness.

Respect holy places

Regardless of your own views, extreme sensitivity should be shown to holy people and places. See p74 for more information.

Don't give to beggars

You will be pestered with demands for sweets, medicine and money but you should not give in. Encouraging begging fosters a dependent attitude which, in the long-run, can be very damaging to the culture and economy. There are genuinely needy people in the Atlas but if you want to help you might do better to contact village leaders than to hand out money to strangers; village leaders will apply your gift to where it's most useful.

Respect local customs

See p73-4 for more information about local etiquette and customs. Pay particular attention to this when in a public place, visiting a home, eating and drinking or negotiating with local people.

Don't play doctor

Don't hand out medicine. This is potentially harmful and sets a negative precedent. If you treat someone but make things worse, you could be blamed. It would be better to donate any spare medical supplies to some-one in a position of authority than to offer treatment to strangers.

Don't flaunt wealth

No matter how poor you might be by Western standards, to an Atlas Berber you are wealthy. Flaunting wealth is insulting and chips away at local pride.

Ask questions but never patronise

You will learn more and foster better relationships with the people if you are genuinely interested in their way of life. Don't behave condescendingly.

Don't expect special privileges

You are one of many thousands who visit the Atlas mountains. Never expect special treatment because you are from the West or because you are relatively rich.

Paint a realistic picture of the West and encourage local pride

Tell them what you enjoy about the Atlas mountains and what you respect about their way of life. Answer questions about the West in a balanced way. If you are asked what you earn, explain that the very high cost of living in the West makes your income rather less impressive than it might at first appear to be; make comparisons to which they can relate.

Don't make a 'home from home'

Engage in the local way of life and enjoy it. If you attempt to create a 'home from home' in your trekking party, you might just as well have stayed at home in the first place.

Don't make promises you can't or won't keep

If you offer to do something for someone, do it. This is particularly perti-nent with regard to photographs which you might offer to send (see above). It's easy to forget promises when you get home, but failing to fol-low through breeds resentment and ill-feeling.

Keep your sense of humour

Trekking can be hard and uncomfortable and cultural gaps might prove frustrating. Humour will help everyone. You will notice that Berbers are an exuberant people who enjoy music, jokes and stories. Join in.

PART 4: MARRAKESH

Marrakesh

Dark, fierce and fanatical are these narrow souqs of Marrakesh. They are mere mud lanes roofed with rushes, as in South Tunisia and Timbuctoo, and the crowds swarming in them are so dense that it is hardly possible, at certain hours, to approach the tiny raised kennels where the merchants sit like idols among their wares. One feels at once that something more than the thought of bargaining – dear as this is to the African heart – animates these incessantly moving throngs. The souqs of Marrakesh seem, more than any others, the central organ of a native life that extends far beyond the city walls...
Edith Wharton, *In Morocco*

Arriving in the imperial city of Marrakesh is an almost overwhelming experience: the combined assault of sounds, smells and sights will set your senses reeling. Djemaa al-Fna, the city's central square and its cultural pulse, is where the assault is at its most intense. Snake-charmers, story-tellers, street dentists and Berber drummers compete for attention with frenzied enthusiasm. This almost non-stop display is not aimed at tourists; look at the crowds around the musicians and fortune-tellers and you will see mostly Moroccans. Djemaa al-Fna is the single most important feature of the city. There is no other sight quite like it in the Arab world.

Marrakesh, the Red City, has another great draw: its low-rise sprawl of red-pink buildings which appear to have grown out of the ground in a moment of blossoming, then baked solid in the scorching African sun. It's difficult to see where one house stops and another starts. Indeed, the souqs and narrow streets of the old Medina form a beguiling labyrinth. All this is framed by the peaks of the High Atlas which appear to curl around the city. In turn, the mountains are set against a consistently perfect deep blue sky. The effect is quite staggering.

The city is a mix of ancient and modern; in the east the walled Medina suggests time has made only limited progress. The streets, architecture and souqs appear to have changed little over hundreds of years. Only television aerials and the constant roar of taxis and scooters piloted by crazed locals hint that the third millennium AD has arrived. The west of Marrakesh is the *Ville Nouvelle*, or new city, in which modern blocks of apartments and businesses were built during the years of the French Protectorate. But a combination of questionable construction and a faithful dedication to Marrakesh's universal colour scheme has left even the Ville Nouvelle looking strangely worn by the Saharan sands of time.

Marrakesh is defined by a fascinating blend of Arab and Berber cultures; this is one reason why the city has become such an important centre for arts and crafts. As a fast-growing tourist destination Marrakesh has seen an influx of Western visitors who have to some extent diluted the city's attitudes. So one might see a Muslim woman veiled in the traditional manner walking alongside a younger Moroccan girl dressed in jeans or even a short skirt. But this is still a deeply religious city. Calls to prayer boom from the tops of mosques and Koutoubia, the 220ft-high minaret which dominates the city's skyline, is closed to non-Muslims.

For trekkers Marrakesh is above all a sort of base camp. This is where you will most likely start and finish your Moroccan Atlas trip. And here you will find supplies, advice, telephones and fax machines. More importantly, perhaps, Marrakesh will be ready to welcome you back from the mountains with a warm shower, an extravagant dinner and a smooth, cold drink. That almost overwhelming assault on the senses with which the Marrakesh Medina greets new visitors might cause some to run for cover. But travellers have little or nothing to fear from the colourful theatre of life in Marrakesh. You would be well advised to allow several days to explore this extraordinary city.

HISTORY

Marrakesh was founded in 1062 by Yusuf Ibn Tashufin from the Almoravid dynasty, although there was probably a settlement here from Neolithic times. The city became the capital of Berber culture, a role which it still enjoys today. Almoravid rule, an era of wealth in Morocco, bequeathed Marrakesh its city walls, irrigation system and many of its mosques and gardens. The city served as an important Almoravid centre for 85 years until the Almoravids were defeated by the Almohads in 1147. The Almohads destroyed much of the city but later rebuilt it using mainly Andalusian craftsmen to make it capital of Almohad Morocco. Marrakesh's famous Koutoubia mosque, whose minaret towers above the city, was built under the Almohad sultan Abd el-Moumen.

In 1269 the Merenids seized power and made Fes their capital. By that time, however, Marrakesh had already established itself as one of Morocco's great cities. Still, Merenid neglect did much to damage Marrakesh which was attacked by the Portuguese in 1515 and later suffered a series of famines. Marrakesh had another spell as capital under the Saadians in the sixteenth century.

The Saadians presided over a period of great success in Morocco and revived the city to establish it as a major trading and cultural centre. Under Saadian rule Marrakesh gained the El Badi Palace and the Saadian tombs. The subsequent dynasty, the Alaouites, took Marrakesh in 1668 but preferred to rule from Meknes, Fes and later, of course, Rabat.

Marrakesh regained a hint of its former glory when Moulay al-Hassan I was crowned sultan there in 1873. But in 1912 al-Hiba, a Saharan rebel, invaded and briefly took control of the city before French forces expelled him and his fellow insurgents.

During the years of the French protectorate (1912-1956), it was administered by the influential Glaoua family. The last Glaoua pasha, Haj Thami al-Glaoui, played a large part in the deposition of Sultan Mohammed V in 1953. Sultan Mohammed would become king of an independent Morocco in 1956. Haj Thami al-Glaoui's power helped restore Marrakesh's influence; the city attracted wealthy traders who built extravagant homes and palaces amid the city's olive groves and palms.

After taking control of Marrakesh in 1912, in collaboration with the Glaoua family, the French built the new areas of Gueliz and Hivernage to form a Ville Nouvelle to the west of the old Medina. Despite French interest, Marrakesh failed to keep pace with the development of Rabat and Casablanca which became the leading industrial and power centres of the country. More recently, however, tourism has grown to become the city's key industry. Moroccans have worked hard to develop the country's tourism potential; Marrakesh has benefited from that drive more than any other city in the country – with the possible exception of Agadir – but, unlike Agadir, has maintained enough of its original charm to keep visitors coming back.

As travellers become increasingly aware of the potential of the High Atlas mountains, Marrakesh looks set to continue to enjoy wealth from tourism. In 1994 the important position of Marrakesh in modern Morocco seemed sealed when it was chosen to host the signing of the GATT world trade agreement. Today, Marrakesh is a city of over 500,000 people.

ARRIVAL AND DEPARTURE

By air
The small international Aéroport Marrakesh-Menara (☎ 44.78.63) is seven km south-west of the city-centre. A petit taxi to or from Djemaa al-Fna should cost 50dh but it's difficult to get one at that price. Grands taxis will cost at least 80-100dh. Bus No 11 goes from Djemaa al-Fna to the airport and back every 30 minutes. At least it does in theory. In practice, the No 11 bus is a pretty elusive beast.

There is a bureau de change which closes at 6pm in the airport building. Airport taxis will normally accept foreign currency but you will need to think fast to avoid paying over the odds. The airport is also home to a legion of brown-coated porters who will expect to be tipped heavily for wheeling your baggage from the carousel to the kerb – a distance of no more than 20 metres.

By train

The train station, or *gare ferroviaire*, on avenue Hassan II in Gueliz (☎ 44.77.68) is a 10-15dh petit taxi ride from the Medina. Hotels in the Ville Nouvelle should cost no more than 7dh to reach. Bus Nos 3 and 8 are alleged to run from the station to the Medina but, again, the service is not always reliable. There are normally plenty of taxis waiting to meet arrivals. The station itself is well lit to provide a non-threatening environment with plenty of uniformed staff on hand. There is a small snack bar and a kiosk selling newspapers, drinks and chocolate bars. If you don't feel comfortable waiting for a train in the station you could wait with a drink in Hôtel Moussafir which is next door. There are four trains a day to Fes, eight to Casablanca and six to Rabat. Second class single fares cost around 70dh to Casablanca or 95dh to Rabat depending on the type of train. If you're travelling overnight – and you're not counting your pennies too closely – it's worth buying a first-class ticket for comfort; first-class fares are not much more expensive than second-class.

By bus

All long-distance buses use the **main bus station**, or *gare routière*, next to the city walls by Bab Doukkala. Expect to pay 10dh or so for a petit taxi from here to Djemaa al-Fna. Otherwise it's a 30-minute walk. The main building is lined with booths representing different bus companies which serve different destinations. Go to window No 10 for the CTM bus company which serves Ouarzazate. After buying your ticket you will need to find out which bay your bus will leave from and queue there. At peak times the bus station is packed and noisy; keep your wits about you: pickpockets operate here. There is never any shortage of bus company touts inside the station nor shortage of taxis outside.

There is a **local bus station** by the Bab Robb gate by the Medina. It's actually just a patch of ground but it's the place to go for buses to Asni which is en route to Imlil and Jbel Toubkal.

LOCAL TRANSPORT

Taxi

Marrakesh is a fairly compact city so it's easy to get around on foot or by taxi. Yellow **petits taxis** operate in town while beige grands taxis cover longer set routes and out-of-town journeys. Petits taxis are easy to find almost anywhere in the city. They have meters which you should insist on using. You should pay 7-10dh for a ride from Djemaa al-Fna to Gueliz.

Grands taxis are usually giant old Mercs. You will need to negotiate the price in advance but there should be a sticker in the car which lists standard prices for common routes. These taxis are normally shared and on longer journeys you shouldn't be surprised when the driver crams four people onto the back seat and two on the front passenger seat. This is con-

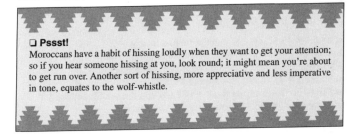

❑ **Pssst!**
Moroccans have a habit of hissing loudly when they want to get your attention;
so if you hear someone hissing at you, look round; it might mean you're about
to get run over. Another sort of hissing, more appreciative and less imperative
in tone, equates to the wolf-whistle.

sidered normal and safe. It's very uncomfortable but at least it makes the
journey cheaper. The best place to pick up a grand taxi is Djemaa al-Fna
or Bab Robb.

Calèche

Calèches, or horse-drawn carriages, are quite a good way to get around
although some of the horses don't look too well cared for. The price, (10-
15dh), depends on whether you're going outside the city walls or staying
in the Medina; a sticker inside the windscreen displays set fares. In practice, however, most calèche drivers charge what they feel like. Agree the
price in advance. You can charter a calèche for sightseeing for about 70-
80dh per hour. Pick them up at Djemaa al-Fna or at place de la Liberté.

Bus

Since Marrakesh is very easy to negotiate there is little need to grapple
with the local bus service. If you do feel inclined to wedge yourself onto
a bus, however, you might find No 1 useful; it runs along avenue
Mohammed V between Djemaa al-Fna and Gueliz. Bus No 11 goes to the
airport and Nos 3 and 8 go to the train station from the Medina.

Car hire

Piloting your own vehicle through Marrakesh's frenzied streets is an even
more alarming experience than travelling on a Moroccan bus. Cars aren't
particularly useful in the city itself but obviously allow visitors to explore
further afield. If you do decide to a hire a car you should make certain
you're well insured. Give the vehicle a quick check before you take it
away. Be prepared to encounter regular acts of lunatic driving and keep
one hand firmly on the horn at all times.

Local car-hire firms – and there are nearly 30 of them – offer cheaper prices than the major chains and are open to haggling. In fact you
should be able to reduce the price significantly by claiming to have found
a better deal elsewhere. Most firms will attempt to match their competitors' prices. You are likely to pay around 415dh per day plus 2.5dh per
kilometre for a basic Fiat Uno from one of the major chains. A similar car
could cost as much as 50 per cent less if you go to a small company and

negotiate well. The following car-hire companies are not necessarily recommended; this is simply a list to get you started.

- **Avis** (☎ 43.37.27) 137 avenue Mohammed V
- **Budget** (☎ 43.11.80) 68 boulevard Zerktouni
- **Europcar** (☎ 43.12.28) 63 boulevard Zerktouni
- **Hertz** (☎ 43.46.80) 154 avenue Mohammed V
- **First-Car International** (☎ 43.87.64) 234 avenue Mohammed V
- **Lune-Car** (☎ 43.43.69) 111 rue de Yugoslavie

Scooter and bicycle hire

Locals love their scooters; you'll see whole families buzzing around town on one machine. To join the fray visit **rue Bani Marine** near Djemaa al-Fna where there are a number of companies with bikes and scooters for hire. Otherwise go to **Peugeot** at 225 avenue Mohammed V or **Marrakesh Motos** on the road to Casablanca. Both **Hôtel Ali** and **Hôtel de Foucauld** rent bikes. Bicycles go for around 35dh per half day, scooters for 250-300dh per day.

ORIENTATION

Marrakesh sits at an altitude of 470 metres above sea level in the heart of the fertile Haouz plain within reach of the High Atlas mountains and the sub-Saharan south. The city, like many in Morocco, is divided between the old town, or Medina, and the new town, or Ville Nouvelle, which is itself split between the areas of Gueliz and Hivernage.

Hivernage is of little interest to most travellers, although well-heeled visitors will find some of the better hotels here. **Gueliz** is the modern, commercial hub of the city where most banks, offices, shops and a number of mid-priced modern hotels are situated.

The **Medina** holds more interest; the souqs, cafés and cheap but charming hotels here are more in keeping with the popular image of Marrakesh. Place Djemaa al-Fna, the main square in the Medina, is the city's cultural heart. The old and new towns are connected by avenue Mohammed V; most visitors find themselves darting regularly between Gueliz and the Medina along this central street. It takes about 20 minutes to walk from the Medina to Gueliz. A petit taxi will cost 7-10dh. The mighty Koutoubia mosque marks the point where avenue Mohammed V turns into the Medina proper.

Head south from Djemaa al-Fna to find the **city's palaces** (see p112) or north for the more important mosques (see p110). The southern Medina walls are bordered by olive groves while the principal **palmeries** surround the city to the north. Marrakesh is well-known for its ancient gardens which have been maintained since the city's foundation by an ingenious underground irrigation system. The **main gardens** (see p114) are Jardin Menara to the west, Jardin Agdal south of the Medina and Jardin Majorelle north-east of Gueliz.

WHERE TO STAY

Hotel areas

Most cheaper hotels are in the old Medina area, clustered around the narrow streets to the south of Djemaa al-Fna. This is a more exciting and atmospheric part of town and wherever you stay you are bound to spend a lot of your time here. More modern hotels including many of the more expensive places are found in the Ville Nouvelle areas of Gueliz and Hivernage. The Ville Nouvelle holds less interest for travellers but is a calmer, cleaner place to stay. Both areas are connected by a short, cheap taxi ride and both have banks, shops and places to eat.

Prices

Cheap hotels start at around 30dh for a single room without bathroom. Prices range from there to vast sums for a suite at the exclusive La Mamounia hotel. Prices given here are for the high season (May to September) and should be treated as an approximate guide only; some hoteliers will adjust their charges according to supply and demand. If a hotel appears under-subscribed you might be able to negotiate a discount of 10 or 20 per cent. Room prices rarely include breakfast.

Budget hotels

Almost all low-priced hotels in Marrakesh are clustered in the streets south of Djemaa al-Fna. They are all located in typical old merchants' houses, two or three storeys built around an open courtyard. The majority of these charge similar rates for a very similar level of accommodation. A few are markedly better than others. The best of these hotels can be at least as pleasant – and certainly more interesting – than their modern, classified counterparts in the Ville Nouvelle. Common (com) or attached (att) bathrooms are indicated after the price. Most 'cheapies' **charge for showers in common bathrooms; the price is indicated thus: eg (com, 5dh)**. Prices for a single room are given first, with the price for doubles shown second.

Medina *Hôtel Hilal* (☎ 44.51.87), at 15 rue de la Recette, is one of the cheapest hotels in the city. Rooms cost 30dh (com, 5dh for shower) per person. Since the Hilal appears in few guidebooks, it's often worth investigating when accommodation is in short supply. *Hôtel Sahra*, at 87 Riad Zitoune Kedim, has a range of rooms for 35dh (com); that price includes showers. Again, the Sahra fills up more slowly than many other hotels in this price bracket so could be worth trying when the better-known hotels are full.

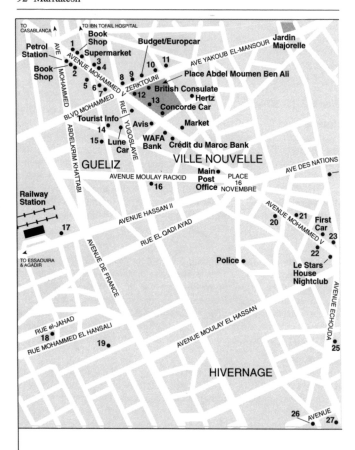

TO
CASABLANCA

TO IBN TOFAIL HOSPITAL

Book
Shop

Petrol
Station

Budget/Europcar

Jardin
Majorelle

AVE YAKOUB EL-MANSOUR

1

AVENUE MOHAMMED V

Supermarket

3

11

Book
Shop

4

10

2

9

Place Abdel Moumen Ben Ali

8

RUE ZERKTOUNI

5

6

7

British Consulate

12

Hertz

13

BLVD MOHAMMED V

Concorde Car

Tourist Info

14

RUE YUGOSLAVIE

Avis

Market

15

Lune
Car

WAFA
Bank

Crédit du Maroc Bank

AVE MOHAMMED V

ABDELKRIM KHATTABI

GUELIZ

VILLE NOUVELLE

AVE DES NATIONS

AVENUE MOULAY RACKID

Main
Post
Office

PLACE
16
NOVEMBRE

16

AVENUE MOHAMMED V

21

First
Car

20

Railway
Station

AVENUE HASSAN II

23

17

RUE EL QADI AYAD

22

TO ESSAOUIRA
& AGADIR

AVENUE DE FRANCE

Police

Le Stars
House
Nightclub

AVENUE ECHOUDA

RUE el-JAHAD

18

AVENUE MOULAY EL HASSAN

RUE MOHAMMED EL HANSALI

19

25

HIVERNAGE

26

AVENUE

27

Places to Stay

1 Hôtel Oasis
2 Hôtel Amalay
5 Hôtel Tachfine
8 Hôtel des Voyageurs
9 Hôtel Franco-Belge
10 Hôtel Al Bustan
17 Hôtel Moussafir
18 Youth Hostel

19 Camping
20 Hôtel Hasna
23 Hôtel Le Marrakesh
24 Hôtel de la Ménara
25 Hôtel le Grand Imilchil
26 Hôtel Es Saadi
27 Hôtel Imperial Borj
28 Hôtel La Mamounia

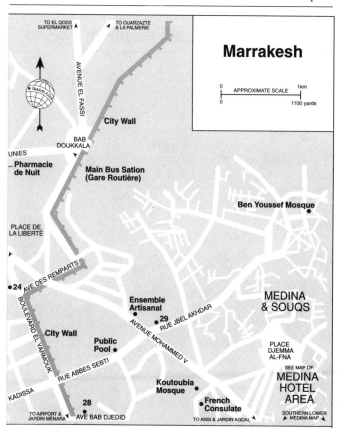

Marrakesh

TO EL QODS
SUPERMARKET

TO OUARZAZTE
& LA PALMERIE

AVENUE EL FASSI

City Wall

BAB
DOUKKALA

UNIES

Pharmacie
de Nuit

Main Bus Sation
(Gare Routière)

Ben Youssef Mosque

PLACE DE
LA LIBERTÉ

AVE DES REMPARTS

24

BOULEVARD EL YARMOUK

City Wall

Public
Pool

RUE ABBES SEBTI

KADISSA

Ensemble
Artisanal

29

AVENUE MOHAMMED V

RUE JBEL AKHDAR

MEDINA
& SOUQS

PLACE
DJEMMA
AL-FNA

SEE MAP OF
MEDINA
HOTEL
AREA

Koutoubia
Mosque

French
Consulate

28

TO AIRPORT &
JARDIN MÉNARA

AVE BAB DJEDID

TO ANSI & JARDIN AGDAL

SOUTHERN LOWER
MEDINA MAP

APPROXIMATE SCALE

0 — 1km
0 — 1100 yards

TRAILBLAZER

Places to Eat

3 Café Agdal
4 Le Petit Poucet
6 Le Petit Auberge
7 Restaurant Chez Jack'Line
11 Le Dragon d'Or
12 Starfood

13 Brasserie du Régent
14 Restaurant la Taverne
15 La Trattoria du Gian Carlo
16 Rôtisserie du Café de la Paix
21 Restaurant Al-Fassia
22 Pizza Hut
29 Restaurant Diaffa

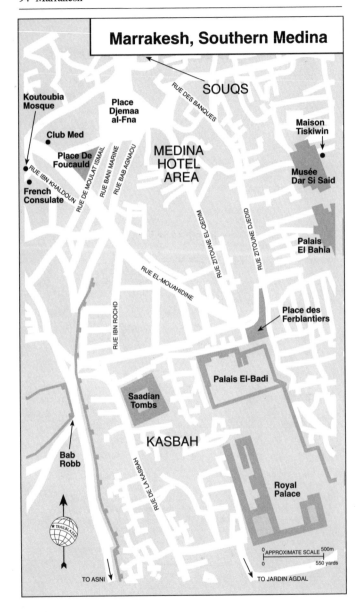

Marrakesh, Southern Medina

Koutoubia Mosque

Club Med

Place De Foucauld

French Consulate

RUE IBN KHALDOUN

Place Djemaa al-Fna

RUE DES BANQUES

SOUQS

RUE DE MOULAT ISMAIL

RUE BANI MARINE

RUE BAB AGNAOU

MEDINA HOTEL AREA

Maison Tiskiwin

Musée Dar Si Said

RUE ZITOUNE EL-QEDIM

RUE ZITOUNE DJEDID

Palais El Bahia

RUE EL-MOUAHIDINE

RUE IBN ROCHD

Place des Ferblantiers

Palais El-Badi

Saadian Tombs

KASBAH

Bab Robb

RUE DE LA KASBAH

Royal Palace

TRAILBLAZER

0 APPROXIMATE SCALE 500m
0   550 yards

TO ASNI

TO JARDIN AGDAL

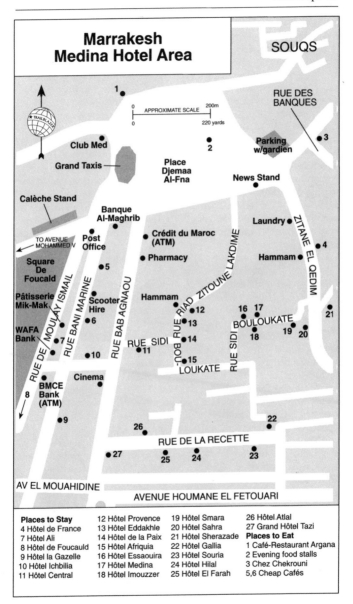

Marrakesh
Medina Hotel Area

SOUQS

RUE DES BANQUES

APPROXIMATE SCALE

0 — 200m

0 — 220 yards

TRAILBLAZER

• 1

Club Med

Grand Taxis

• 2

Parking w/gardien

• 3

Place Djemaa Al-Fna

News Stand

Calèche Stand

Banque Al-Maghrib

Laundry •

ZITANE EL QEDIM

Post Office

Crédit du Maroc (ATM)

• 4

TO AVENUE MOHAMMED V

Hammam •

Square De Foucald

• 5

Pharmacy

RIAD ZITOUNE LAKDIME

Pâtisserie Mik-Mak

Scooter Hire

Hammam •

WAFA Bank

• 6

• 12

16 • • 17

• 21

BOULOUKATE

• 7

• 13

• 18

• 19

• 20

RUE DE / MOULAY ISMAIL

RUE BANI MARINE

RUE BAB AGNAOU

• 10

RUE SIDI

• 11

• 14

BOU

RUE SIDI

• 15

LOUKATE

• 8

BMCE Bank (ATM)

Cinema

• 9

• 26

• 22

RUE DE LA RECETTE

• 27

• 25

• 24

• 23

AV EL MOUAHIDINE

AVENUE HOUMANE EL FETOUARI

Places to Stay
4 Hôtel de France
7 Hôtel Ali
8 Hôtel de Foucauld
9 Hôtel la Gazelle
10 Hôtel Ichbilia
11 Hôtel Central

12 Hôtel Provence
13 Hôtel Eddakhle
14 Hôtel de la Paix
15 Hôtel Afriquia
16 Hôtel Essaouira
17 Hôtel Medina
18 Hôtel Imouzzer

19 Hôtel Smara
20 Hôtel Sahra
21 Hôtel Sherazade
22 Hôtel Gallia
23 Hôtel Souria
24 Hôtel Hilal
25 Hôtel El Farah

26 Hôtel Atlal
27 Grand Hôtel Tazi
Places to Eat
1 Café-Restaurant Argana
2 Evening food stalls
3 Chez Chekrouni
5,6 Cheap Cafés

Budget hotels: Medina (cont) *Hôtel El Farah* (☎ 44.15.46), at 30 rue de la Recette, is a fairly shabby affair but should prove adequate for those on a tight budget. Rooms are just 30dh (com, 5dh for shower) per person.

For a slight step up-market, head for *Hôtel Atlal* (☎ 42.78.89), at 48 rue de la Recette, which offers above average rooms for 40/80dh (com, 10dh). The Atlal is clean and well maintained but the showers are a touch pricey. Better value still, perhaps, is the ornate and attractive *Hôtel Essaouira* (☎/▤ 44.38.05) at 3 Sidi Bouloukate. Rooms are good value at 40-50/80-90dh (com, 5dh) but most are quite small. The nearby *Hôtel Medina* (☎ 44.29.27), at 1 Riad Zitoune Lakdime, is another good bet. The friendly owner speaks good English (he spent four years touring Britain in a circus) and the hotel is kept to a good standard. Rooms cost the usual 40/80dh (com, 5dh). On the same street, the reliable *Hôtel Eddakhle* (☎ 44.23.59; ▤ 44.23.57), at 43 Riad Zitoune Lakdime, is slightly cheaper at 40/70dh (com, 5dh). The Eddakhle has been decorated with enthusiasm – it seems quite shambolic – but travellers will enjoy the easy-going atmosphere.

Few hotels in Marrakesh can legitimately claim to be quiet; traffic, the clamour of businessmen, calls to prayer and the general hubbub of Moroccan life infiltrate the atriums of most. Some visitors have reported, however, that *Hôtel Provence* (☎ 44.35.39) on rue Riad Zitoune Lakdime is more peaceful than the average Medina accommodation. The Provence has a clean, bright atrium and small rooms for 35/80dh (com, 5dh).

The tiny *Hôtel de France* (☎ 44.30.67), at 197 Riad Zitoune el-Qedim, is not one of the best but at 40/80dh (com, 5dh) is at least well within the budget bracket. Much better is *Hôtel Afriquia* (☎ 44.24.03) at 45 Sidi Bouloukate. This is one of the best value hotels in the old city with small rooms from 40/70dh (com, 5dh). The helpful, English-speaking owner will be only too pleased to show you to the wonderful rooftop terrace which boasts remarkable tiled walls and views to the High Atlas; the open, tree-filled courtyard is also very attractive.

The basic *Hôtel Imouzzer* (☎ 44.53.36), at 74 Sidi Bouloukate, offers tiny, cell-like rooms but is at least staffed by friendly and helpful people. Rooms are, predictably, 40/80dh (com, 5dh). Another hotel at that price is *Hôtel Smara* (☎ 44.55.68) at 77 Sidi Bouloukate; it is small, shady and clean. On the same street – and at the same price – *Hôtel de la Paix* (☎ 44.54.31), at 46 Sidi Bouloukate, is another simple but acceptable option.

Moving up in price again, *Hôtel Souria* (☎ 42.67.57), on rue de la Recette, costs 60/120dh (com, 10dh). The owner speaks English, Spanish

---

(Opposite) Acrobats performing in Djemaa al-Fna (see p107), Marrakesh's central square. (Photo © Patrick Maguire).

and Italian which might be one reason why the price is a little higher than usual – or perhaps guests pay for the outlandish decor. *Hôtel Central* (☎ 44.02.35), at 59 Sidi Bouloukate, has always been a fairly safe budget choice at 50/120dh (doubles att). But the owners are at present adding a third level to the house while keeping the hotel open at the same time. The mixture of builders and guests is not a good one; wait till the work's finished before staying here. *Hôtel la Gazelle* (☎ 44.11.12; 🖹 44.55.37) and *Hôtel Ichbilia* (☎ 39.04.86) are at Nos 12 and 1 rue Bani Marine respectively. Both offer rooms for 60/100dh (com, 5dh). Both are clean, reliable choices. The Ichbilia is probably the better of the two because it's slightly more peaceful – admittedly serenity in the Medina is relative.

Hôtel Ali (☎ 44.49.79; 🖹 44.05.22), on rue de Moulay Ismail, has long been a favourite for backpackers. It is good value with en suite rooms for 70/90dh, an excellent rooftop dinner buffet and even Internet access. More importantly, this is where mountain guides and muleteers look for clients in Marrakesh. So if you plan to engage a guide before leaving the city, start by asking the staff at Hôtel Ali. The staff here can also advise on routes and how to get hold of maps.

Ville Nouvelle The Ville Nouvelle is not good hunting ground for those in search of a cheap night's sleep, although there is a *youth hostel* on rue el-Jahad south of the train station. Since a bed in a shared room here costs 30dh, and the hostel is not conveniently located, the cheaper Medina hotels are better value.

There are just three budget hotels worth investigating in the Ville Nouvelle: *Hôtel Franco-Belge* (☎ 44.84.72), on boulevard Zerktouni, is a one-storey collection of rooms huddled around a courtyard. It's modern but fraying at the edges. Rooms cost 60/100dh (com) or 100/130dh (att); slightly better, perhaps, is *Hôtel des Voyageurs* (☎ 44.72.18) at 40 boulevard Zerktouni. Rooms go for 80/120dh (com) or 120/150dh (att); Hôtel des Voyageurs is rather more atmospheric than the Franco-Belge, but both have seen better days – at least one would hope so.

A third choice in the Ville Nouvelle is *Hôtel Oasis* (☎ 44.71.79) at 50 avenue Mohammed V. It, too, is perfectly acceptable but less than inspiring. Rooms cost 110/130dh (com) or 130/155dh (att). The Oasis is more popular with Moroccans than travellers which some might see as a bonus. If you find the manic pace of the old town detrimental to sleep, it might suit you better to stay in the Ville Nouvelle; while life here is hardly restful, the Ville Nouvelle is noticeably less frenzied than the Medina.

(Opposite) Henna'ed hands, Djemaa al-Fna, Marrakesh. (Photo © Patrick Maguire).

Mid-priced hotels

The modern Ville Nouvelle has traditionally been the best area to look for moderately-priced hotels. These days, however, there are almost as many good choices in this price range in the Medina as there are in the Ville Nouvelle. Ville Nouvelle hotels tend to be modern with more facilities while the better Medina hotels win on charm and attention to detail.

Medina By far the best hotel in this category and one of the best value in Marrakesh is *Hôtel Sherazade* (☎/🖹 42.93.05) at 3 Derb Djama off Riad Zitoune el-Qedim. The Sherazade, a beautifully restored and traditionally decorated merchant's house, is run by exceptionally helpful and efficient staff. The atrium, complete with a fountain, cushions and carpets, is a delight – as is the rooftop terrace from where one can see as far as the High Atlas mountains. Prices start from 150/180dh (com) and climb

❏ Hammam and massage

There's nothing better after a long trek than a **hammam**; the Moroccan equivalent of a Turkish bath. If you pay for the full works you will normally be shown into a series of increasingly hot and steamy rooms. You'll then be expected to wash from a tap in the hottest room before some wrinkled but often surprisingly strong old character steps out to give you the traditional massage. This is normally pretty vigorous but despite what you might think while it's happening you will feel better for it afterwards.

Hammams are either men-only, women-only or shared with set times for women (usually earlier) and men. A recent story tells of a 20-year-old boy who, fascinated by the opposite sex but frustrated by his inability to meet girls, disguised himself as a woman and sneaked into a women-only hammam to take a peek. Sadly for him he was caught and, apparently, sentenced to a very long prison term. Hammams are social places where groups of men and of women gather to discuss the day's events while washing in the steamy water. Since relatively few Western travellers find their way into hammams you can expect to be welcomed by the locals who will happily show you the proper routine.

One of the better hammams for men is on rue Zitoune el-Qedim on the right a little way before the left turn to Hôtel Sherazade (if you're walking from Djemaa al-Fna). It's hard to find since there's no sign; look for a traditionally-decorated arched doorway with bicycles and scooters propped up just inside. The fee appears to be negotiable but expect to pay 30-50dh for the full hammam including massage. There are two hammams side by side off rue de Bab Agnaou – one for women and one for men. Turn left at Hôtel de la Paix to find them. Expect to pay 30dh here for the full treatment. Don't forget to take a towel.

If you would prefer to relax with a Western-style massage go to Hôtel Nassim on avenue Mohammed V and make an appointment with their in-house masseuse. A 30-minute massage will cost 100dh.

steadily as rooms increase in size and facilities. Most rooms are en suite. The only problem with the Sherazade, and it's a problem shared by many hotels in the Medina, is its proximity to a mosque; the early morning call to prayer booms around the atrium. You get used to it. The Sherazade also offers dinner for residents only; set menus start at 85dh.

Another good choice is *Hôtel de Foucauld* (☎ 44.54.99; 🖹 44.13.44) on avenue El-Mouahidine. The Foucauld is impressively decorated in traditional Moroccan style although it's clearly past its glory days. It offers comfortable and clean rooms for 150/190dh (att). There is a good restaurant and a small pool. Creeping up the price scale, *Hôtel Gallia* (☎ 44.59.13; 🖹 44.48.53), at 30 rue de la Recette, is another attractive hotel set in an old house. Rooms cost 201/270dh (att). Breakfast is also included in that price. The hotel's best feature is its arboretum-like courtyard.

If none of these suit, you could try *Grand Hôtel Tazi* (☎ 44.21.52) on rue de Bab Agnaou. Like Hôtel de Foucauld, the Tazi is a gargantuan place extravagantly kitted out in traditional Moroccan fixtures and fittings. There's a restaurant which offers a good dinner buffet, a bar (although it's not up to much) and a very pleasant swimming pool. Rooms are en suite, cosy and cost 240/275dh. The Tazi is at least as good as several of the more expensive mid-priced hotels in the Ville Nouvelle. *Hôtel Islane* (☎ 44.00.81/83; 🖹 44.00.85), opposite Koutoubia mosque on avenue Mohammed V, offers air-conditioned rooms with satellite television, telephones and en suite facilities for a very reasonable 214/275dh.

Ville Nouvelle One of the better mid-priced hotels is the three-star *Hôtel Hasna* (☎ 44.99.72/73/73; 🖹 44.99.94) at 247 avenue Mohammed V. The hotel is well equipped with both European and Moroccan restaurants, a pool, hammam and sauna. Although the pool is rather small, the rooms, which go for 321/392dh, are very good; they're all en suite and come with satellite television.

Another good one is the slightly cheaper but still three-star *Hôtel Amalay* (44.86.85/44.90.23; 🖹 43.15.54) at 87 avenue Mohammed V. The Amalay offers tidy en suite rooms for 292/358dh. *Hôtel de la Ménara* (☎ 43.64.78/43.23.55; 🖹 4-44.73.86) on avenue des Remparts, near place de la Liberté, has a good pool and en suite rooms for 316/440dh including breakfast. The pool is open to non-residents for 50dh.

Nearby and similar in standards, *Hôtel Le Grand Imilchil* (☎ 44.76.53; 🖹 44.61.65), on avenue Echouhada, offers rooms for 274/350dh and a pool, solarium and European restaurant. Admittedly, it's hard to imagine why anyone would want to use a solarium in Marrakesh. A very reliable hotel in this price range is *Hôtel Moussafir* (☎ 43.59.29/33; 🖹 43.59.36) which is part of the international Ibis chain. It's right next door to the railway station on avenue Hassan II which means it's just a little off the beaten track. The Moussafir has a good pool and is a safe bet for anyone looking for European standards without breaking the bank. En suite rooms go for 318/426dh including breakfast.

The three-star *Hôtel Al Bustan* (☎ 44.68.10; 🖹 44.68.13), at 66 boulevard Zerktouni, is acceptable but not great value at 306/372dh for functional en suite rooms with TV, telephone and breakfast. Another hotel worth considering is *Hôtel Tachfine* (☎ 44.71.88; 🖹 43.78.62) which is also on boulevard Zerktouni. The Tachfine has rooms for 292/358dh; it's adequate but not the best in this price range.

Expensive hotels

It is quite possible to stay in a first-rate hotel in Marrakesh without spending vast sums. For travellers with deep pockets, however, the best Moroccan opulence can rival any of the world's most sumptuous hotels.

The least expensive hotel in this category, *Hôtel Le Marrakesh* (☎ 43.43.51; telex 72067), on place de la Liberté, has well-furnished en suite rooms for 500/600dh. Breakfast is 55dh and dinner 160dh. Le Marrakesh represents a clear step up from any of the mid-priced hotels and is reasonably good value. The pool is open to non-residents for 100dh. Prices then jump at the enormous *Hôtel Imperial Borj* (☎ 44.73.22; 🖹 44.62.06) on avenue Echouhada; this impressive place boasts all the facilities you would expect from a hotel which charges 900/1100dh for excellent en suite rooms.

Moving up in price again, the five-star *Hôtel Es Saadi* (☎ 44.88.11; 🖹 44.76.44; 🖥 essaadi@royal.net), on avenue Kadissia, has a very good reputation and, again, all the facilities expected of a major international hotel. Rooms cost 1200/1400dh. The Es Saadi, an elegant fifties building, has a great swimming pool and patio which form a tranquil haven from the bustle of the city.

A more recent addition to Marrakesh's collection of élite hotels is the sprawling *Palmerie Golf Palace* complex (☎ 30.10.10; 🖹 30.50.50) just out of town in the Jardins de la Palmerie. The Golf Palace is impressively well equipped with over 300 rooms (these cost well over 2000dh), a magnificent set of swimming pools, nine restaurants, squash courts, horse-riding and an 18-hole golf course. Not bad. The pool is open to non-residents for 100dh but a taxi from Djemaa al-Fna to the Golf Palace will cost at least 50dh each way.

There's no doubt, however, that the best hotel in Marrakesh (and many claim it to be one of the best in the world) is *La Mamounia* (☎ 44.89.81; 🖹 44.46.60; 🖥 reserv@mamounia.com) on avenue Bab Djedid. La Mamounia, built between 1925 and 1929 and redecorated by French designer André Paccard in 1986, is itself a Marrakesh landmark well worth visiting if only for a cup of coffee. The wonderful pool and gardens are a delight and the fine Moroccan decor – juxtaposed with flashes of Art Deco – is among the best you will see anywhere in the city.

No wonder, then, that Winston Churchill declared La Mamounia to be one of his favourite places in the world – or so the management will tell you. Churchill's suite has been preserved for visitors to admire. Look out for pictures of the former prime minister painting in La Mamounia's gardens in the forties and fifties. The downside to all this extravagant luxury, of course, is that room prices start at over 2000dh.

There is a casino attached which is open to non-residents who, to the bouncer, look to be the 'right sort'. A small collection of slot machines in the casino foyer caters to the crowd who fail to make it into the casino proper; walk with a certain swagger and wear respectable clothes and shoes if you want to bypass the one-armed bandits and hit the card tables. Indeed, you will need to avoid jeans, shorts and sandals even if you plan to visit the gardens of La Mamounia.

WHERE TO EAT

At its finest, Moroccan cuisine (see p76) is among the best in the world and, as in most cities in Morocco, it's quite possible to eat well in Marrakesh for very few of your hard-won dirhams. The city also offers a number of palatial and expensive restaurants for those who feel they deserve a royal blow-out after a hard High Atlas trek.

But the average *tagine* (meat or vegetable stew) or bowl of couscous will often be at best unmemorable or, at worst, all too memorable for the wrong reasons. Clearly, it's particularly important to avoid picking up a stomach bug before you set off for the mountains. To minimise your chances of becoming ill, eat hot, freshly-cooked food and avoid salads, rice or ice-cream; these might have been prepared using water of dubious quality. Stick to hot or bottled drinks. The restaurants given below are listed from the least expensive upwards.

In the Medina

Each evening, before the storytellers and drummers have taken over completely, rows of food stalls are set out across **Djemaa al-Fna** under the setting sun. White-coated chefs man the stalls which offer fish, salads, couscous, kebabs, chicken or simple egg sandwiches. Noisy conversation hangs over the square along with smoke from the barbecues.

Given Morocco's reputation it is, perhaps, no surprise to see that many Western travellers view this open-air food court with a certain amount of suspicion. In fact, this is the place to come for some of the best and cheapest eating in the city. The food is almost always delicious and, since it's cooked right in front of you, pretty reliable. Just 20-25dh will buy you a fine feast of lamb kebabs, olives, bread and tea. This is also a good time and place to sit back to watch the continuous fiesta in the square.

If you would prefer to head inside, try ***Chez Chekrouni*** on the east side of Djemaa al-Fna near rue des Banques. Chez Chekrouni offers cheap but tasty tagines and soups in a simple but pleasant environment. There are quite a number of cheap and cheerful café-restaurants along **rue Bani Marine**. Few are very inspiring but most are quite adequate if you're looking for a proper but reasonably-priced meal.

A better bet but a step up in price is the evening buffet on the rooftop terrace of the ***Hôtel Ali***. The buffet is served from around 7pm; it's excellent value with a wide choice of salads, tagines, fish, couscous and vegetables for just 60dh. Musicians sometimes serenade diners in summer. Another good value buffet is served up in the restaurant of the ***Grand Hôtel Tazi*** for 80dh. This buffet starts at 8pm and has the advantage of a licensed bar. The Grand Hôtel Tazi's sister property, ***Hôtel de Foucauld***, serves a similar but slightly more expensive buffet on its rooftop terrace. Again, the buffet has a wide choice of traditional Moroccan dishes prepared to a high standard. Each of these hotels also offers à la carte and fixed-price menus. Hôtel de Foucauld serves a particularly good pastilla – a traditional, sweet pigeon pie.

Back in Djemaa al-Fna, a very good bet is ***Café-Restaurant Argana*** which is easy to find thanks to its bright flashing sign. The Argana is a favourite among a number of mountain guides who meet here for celebratory ice-creams after trekking; come here to enjoy the view from the terrace across the square and to sample excellent fixed-price menus from 75dh and good service. A typical menu will include a salad for starter, a tagine to follow and ice-cream for dessert. If you're in need of a break from traditional Moroccan fare you could try the reasonably-priced ***Pizzeria Venezia*** in Hôtel Islane. The service can be painfully slow but the pizzas are fine and the terrace overlooks Koutoubia. It's also licensed.

More expensive restaurants in the Medina include ***Restaurant Yacout*** at 79 Sidi Ahmed Soussi, which serves exquisite French-Moroccan cuisine in palatial surroundings. Expect to pay at least 400dh for your meal. You need to be guided to the restaurant which is at the heart of the Medina amid particularly labyrinthine streets. Another excellent restaurant in this price range is ***Diaffa*** at 1 rue Jbel Akhdar. The décor and cuisine are both wonderful but don't expect too much change from 500dh per person. Belly-dancers and Berber musicians entertain diners most nights.

The well-known ***Restaurant Maison Arabe***, at 5 Derb Ferrane, has long been regarded as one of the finest restaurants in Morocco. With fantastic food and a beautiful setting you will no doubt agree. Again, the price per person will come to around 500dh.

Hôtel La Mamounia has a number of restaurants, the best of which is ***Restaurant Marocain du Mamounia***. As you would expect for over 700dh, the food here is hard to fault. Diners will also enjoy the incredibly ornate decor and impressive if slightly hackneyed folklore acts which are staged most evenings. You will need to make a reservation and dress well to visit any of the restaurants in this upper bracket.

In the Ville Nouvelle

For cheap, fast-food fare head for **Starfood** on the corner of boulevard Mohammed Zerktouni and avenue Mohammed V. Starfood serves reliable burgers, fries and chicken for 15-20dh. Another budget choice for snack food is **Café Agdal** on avenue Mohammed V opposite Hôtel Amalay. **Le Petit Auberge** opposite Hôtel Tachfine is a slight step up. The menu includes pizza and simple French-style dishes.

If none of those appeal **Le Petit Poucet**, at 56 avenue Mohammed V, a pleasantly shabby hangover from the days of the French Protectorate, serves simple French food at reasonable prices. Travellers desperate to find a familiar taste from the West could try **Pizza Hut** at 6 avenue Mohammed V. It's a pretty poor example of the genre but it is, at least, a bona fide Pizza Hut. Meals will cost from around 50dh. At the top end of the budget restaurants, **Brasserie du Régent**, at 34 avenue Mohammed V, can supply a good set menu meal from around 70dh.

Nudging up the price scale, **Restaurant Bagatelle**, at 101 rue Yugoslavie, serves good French food in a pleasant setting; the vine-shaded courtyard is the restaurant's best feature. For a more international menu try **Restaurant Chez Jack'Line** at 63 avenue Mohammed V. It doesn't look much from the outside but the European and Moroccan food is good and excellent value (expect to pay 80-100dh for your meal). Another restaurant which offers French-Moroccan cuisine is **Restaurant La Taverne** at 23 boulevard Mohammed Zerktouni. Set menus start at around 80dh. There's an attractive garden and bar.

Heading up-market again, **Rôtisserie du Café de la Paix**, at 68 rue Yugoslavie, is a very well-established place which dates back to the days of the French Protectorate. It serves good grilled food in a pleasant garden in summer or inside by a fire in winter. Expect to pay around 150dh.

The best Italian food in Marrakesh is served at **La Trattoria du Gian Carlo**, at 179 rue Mohammed El-Beqal, amid extravagant but slightly odd surroundings. For a Vietnamese meal head for **Le Dragon d'Or** at 10 boulevard Mohammed Zerktouni.

Perhaps the best Moroccan cuisine in the Ville Nouvelle is found at **Restaurant Al-Fassia** at 232 avenue Mohammed V; the food is very good but quite expensive. Al-Fassia is not as impressive as the better restaurants in this category in the Medina.

Pâtisseries

Moroccans go to such lengths to satisfy their collective sweet-tooth that the country's economy is actually held back by the enormous amounts of sugar Morocco is forced to import. So it's hardly surprising that Marrakesh is a good city for cake lovers. There are a number of excellent

French-Moroccan pâtisseries in the city. One of the best, *Pâtisserie Mik-Mak*, is next to Hôtel Ali on rue de Moulay Islane. There's another good one a little way along rue de Bab Agnaou opposite Hôtel Ichbilia.

NIGHTLIFE

Drinkers will find a pretty limited selection of **bars** in Marrakesh. Outside the better international hotels, bars are generally fairly dubious places frequented almost exclusively by dodgy men or prostitutes. There are cheap rooftop bars in the *Foucald* and *Grand Tazi* hotels but both are quite poor. The bars in *Le Petit Poucet* restaurant and *La Renaissance* hotel on avenue Mohammed V are a step up. A more stylish drinking environment is on offer at the **Piano Bar** in *La Mamounia* hotel – where there is also a **casino** (see p101).

There are all-night **discos** in most of the large, top-price hotels. One of the best of these is *Diamant Noir* in *Hôtel Le Marrakesh*. Admission, which includes the first drink, is usually around 80dh. Subsequent drinks are quite expensive. Of the independent discos, *Le Stars House* on avenue Mohammed V is just about bearable.

Some of the more expensive Moroccan restaurants put on impressive **folklore** displays. Djeema al-Fna, of course, provides plenty of after-dark folklore entertainment in itself.

SERVICES

Banks and currency exchange

The best place to change money is probably at **Crédit du Maroc** on rue Bab Agnaou near Djemaa al-Fna. There is also an ATM machine which claims to accept cards from most major networks; for some reason, however, it seldom does. The **BMCE Bank** on rue de Moulay Islane, just a few metres from Hôtel Ali, has a more reliable ATM machine which accepts most international cards. The machine is behind a red wooden door with no sign.

Most Moroccan banks have large branch offices in the Ville Nouvelle. **Crédit du Maroc** is on avenue Mohammed V, **WAFA Bank** is nearby at 213 avenue Mohammed V and **Banque Populaire** is at 69 avenue Mohammed V. If you need money wired to you, Crédit du Maroc is the agent for Moneygram and WAFA Bank is the agent for Western Union. Patience is often required when dealing with Moroccan banks.

Bookshops and newspapers

There are two bookshops on avenue Mohammed V: Librairie Chatr at No 19 and, almost opposite, Librairie Papeterie. Both have a good selection of

French-language books and a limited collection of titles in English. Librairie Chatr has a slightly better range of English books including a number of classics and, strangely, an almost complete collection of Ernest Hemmingway's novels. Librairie Papeterie has a handful of paperbacks by the likes of John Grisham and Tom Clancy. There is another bookshop at the top of rue Bab Agnaou near Djemaa al-Fna which offers a good number of French-language books and a tiny handful of English ones. The larger hotels can supply newspapers from the international press. Otherwise the best place to try is the news-stand next to Café Glacier on the south side of Djemaa al-Fna. International newspapers normally arrive one day late.

Communications

● **Telephone and fax** There are téléboutiques scattered all over the city. They all give change for the phone and all require 1dh pieces for local calls or 5dh pieces for international connections. Otherwise you can make reverse-charge (collect) calls from the quiet telephone office under the post office on Djemaa al-Fna. The main post office on place 16 Novembre no longer offers this service. Most of the bigger hotels have fax machines which visitors can use for varying fees. Some of the better téléboutiques also offer a fax service.

● **E-mail** Marrakesh has been slow to get wired. Hôtel Ali offers Internet access but there is as yet no Internet café. One is said to be planned.

● **Post** The almost impossibly busy main post office (PTT) is on place 16 Novembre in the Ville Nouvelle. Head here for post restante and other normal postal services. There are several pay-phones outside. The branch office on Djemaa al-Fna is quieter and offers a better telephone service.

Embassies and consulates

Britain and France have consulates in Marrakesh. Nationals from other countries will need to travel to Casablanca or Rabat (see p68). The **British consulate** (☎ 43.40.95) is at 55 boulevard Zerktouni. The **French consulate**, next to Koutoubia on rue Ibn-Khaldoun, is easier to find – just head for the French flag.

Laundry

Perhaps the best place to get your clothes washed is the small laundry next to the téléboutique on rue Zitoune el-Qedim. Prices need to be negotiated but 50dh should get a fair-sized bundle of clothes cleaned and pressed.

Medical emergencies

● **Ambulance** (☎ 44.37.24)

● **Hospitals** Hôpital Avenzoar (☎ 04.42.27.93), rue Sidi Mimoun; Hôpital Ibn Tofail (☎ 04.44.80.11), rue Abdel Ouahab Derraq

● **Doctors** Dr Mansouri (☎ 43.07.54); Dr Perez (☎ 43.10.30); Dr Benzakour (☎ 43.10.50)

● **Dentists** Dr Mekouar (☎ 44.66.81); Dr Bennani (☎ 43.11.45); Dr Hicham (☎ 44.86.04)

● **Pharmacies** There are a number of small pharmacies near Djemaa al-Fna and along avenue Mohammed V. The Pharmacie de Nuit on rue Khalid ben Oualid is open all night and has a doctor. Also recommended is Pharmacie Centrale at 166 avenue Mohammed V.

Supermarkets
There are several small food shops in the streets around Djemaa al-Fna. For a better selection there's the supermarket on avenue Mohammed V near Librarie Papeterie and Hôtel Oasis. If you're planning a major spree it might be worth taking a petit taxi to El Qods supermarket on boulevard Allal El-Fassi. El Qods is the biggest supermarket in Marrakesh with a good selection of European imports.

Swimming pools
Most of the up-market hotels in Marrakesh have wonderful pools and some welcome non-residents for a daily fee of 50-100dh. Others don't. It's tempting to try slipping into La Mamounia for a swim. Bad idea; the management don't take kindly to finding non-residents in their pool. The same goes for Hôtel Es Saadi.

The **Palmerie Golf Palace**, however, is a different matter. Non-residents can use the Palmerie's fantastic pool for a hefty 100dh – and the staff there are pleasingly inefficient when it comes to collecting that fee. **Hôtel le Marrakesh**, on place de la Liberté, also invites non-residents into its pool for 100dh. It's a good pool but not in the same league as the Palmerie. For a carefully-collected 50dh you could swim at **Hôtel Moussafir** on avenue Hassan II or **Hôtel de la Ménara** on avenue des Remparts. The Moussafir's pool is the better of the two; it's set in an attractive garden and is always immaculate.

In the Medina, **Grand Hôtel Tazi** has a small pool which is also open to non-residents for a charge. There's a **public pool**, open in summer only, on rue Abbes Sebti. It's adequate and cheap but usually overcrowded. Women visitors should be aware that the pool is almost exclusively used by young men.

Trekking agencies
Agencies are not always good value for money since it is relatively easy to organise a mountain guide and muleteer independently; nevertheless solo trekkers might prefer to travel with a group – not least for safety. See p9-12 for more information about whether to trek independently or with a group.

● **Adrar Aventures**, 111 rue Saada (☎ 43.56.63/43.93.86; 🖹 43.56.82)
● **Atlas Sahara Trek**, 72 rue de la Liberté (☎ 44.93.50; 🖹 44.96.99)
● **Sport Travel**, 154 avenue Mohammed V (☎ 43.99.68/43.05.59; 🖹 43.99.69)

- **Ribat Tours**, 6 rue des Vieux Marrakchis (☎ 43.86.93; 🗎 43.86.94)
- **Tourisport**, 213 avenue Mohammed V (☎ 44.81.39; 🗎 44.81.65)
- **Trekking Tours Maroc**, 107 rue Saad Ben Errabia (☎ 30.80.55; 🗎 30.80.55)

Tourist office
The main tourist office is in the Ville Nouvelle on place Abdel Moumen Ben Ali. It isn't a very useful place but if you ask politely you might come away with an armful of photocopied literature about the city.

WHAT TO SEE

Djemaa al-Fna
The largest crowds are drawn by the storytellers. It is around them that people throng most densely and stay longest. Their performances are lengthy; an inner ring of listeners squat on the ground and it is some time before they get up again. Others, standing, form an outer ring; they, too, hardly move, spellbound by the storyteller's words and gestures. Sometimes two of them recite in turn. Their words come from farther off and hang longer in the air than those of ordinary people.
Elias Canetti, *The Voices of Marrakesh*

Djemaa al-Fna means 'assembly of the dead', referring to a time when the heads of executed criminals were displayed on poles around the square. The French administration in the fifties tried to close it by turning it into a car-park, fortunately failing to do so.

This vast open square at the heart of the Medina continues to be one of the most extraordinary sights in Morocco because of the people working there: story-tellers, snake-charmers, healers, clairvoyants, musicians, cooks, dentists and water-carriers; together they form a constantly shift-

---

❏ **Safety in Djemaa al-Fna**
Tourists are conspicuous in Djemaa al-Fna and you will find yourself attracting a lot of attention. Most hustlers are simply salesmen trying to make some money, or Djemaa al-Fna regulars offering to pose for photographs in return for some coins. Remember that if you listen, watch or take photographs you will be expected to pay. It's useful to be ready with a pocketful of small change.

Not everyone in the square is honest; watch for thieves, pickpockets, drug dealers and threatening beggars. Be particularly careful at night. Keep your valuables close or, better still, travel light through the square. Don't be fooled by bogus 'guides' who offer to show you around (see p109), 'students' who claim to want to practise English with you or hustlers who hand you 'presents'; if you accept the 'present' you will most likely be accused of stealing it just minutes later.

ing scene of vivid colour. During the day the square is relatively quiet. A few snake-charmers sit under parasols while traders set out their wares on faded carpets; water carriers in their outlandish costumes stroll about attracting attention by shaking bells; 50 or so identical orange-juice stalls are set up around the perimeter. But when night falls the square hits a more urgent note, intoxicating, intimidating, insistent, timeless; crowds gather as drummers and Berber musicians compete, the players shrouded in smoke from the many food stalls.

If you tire of fighting your way across the busy square, or would prefer to watch in relative peace, head for one of the cafés or restaurants overlooking all the activity; the terraces of Café Glacier and Restaurant Argana form fine vantage points; you must buy a drink at Café Glacier as the waiter will explain quite emphatically.

Koutoubia mosque

At 220ft Koutoubia towers over the Marrakesh Medina. It's the most visible landmark in the city; at night when the minaret is lit you can see Koutoubia for miles. The mosque was built on the site of a kasbah in the twelfth century by the Almohads. The design follows traditional Almohad patterns which later formed the basis for many themes in classic Moroccan architecture. Koutoubia is closed to non-Muslims but it is possible to walk around its landscaped surroundings. One interesting story attached to Koutoubia claims that only a blind muezzin was permitted to call the faithful to prayer from the tower because it overlooked the *harem,* where women of the court lived. Another claims the three copper balls atop the tower were once gold. They were apparently presented by Sultan El-Mansour's wife as a penance for breaking her fast during Ramadan.

The souqs

It is spicy in the souqs, and cool and colourful. The smell, always pleasant, changes gradually with the nature of the merchandise. There are no names or signs; there is no glass. Everything for sale is on display. You never know what things will cost; they are neither impaled with their prices, nor are the prices themselves fixed...You find everything – but you always find it many times over.
Elias Canetti, *The Voices of Marrakesh*

Marrakesh is an important centre for arts and crafts which is why the city's sprawling souqs are among the most fascinating in North Africa. Trawling the souqs for bargains is, however, a stressful experience. Be prepared to be harangued at every turn by eager salesmen. See the box opposite for some tips on how to deal with over-enthusiastic merchants. See p79 for information about Moroccan crafts.

Although there are now a number of all-purpose craft shops in the souqs, it is still true that for the most part different souqs specialise in particular products; thus you will find all the silver dealers clustered in one place or all the textiles merchants grouped around another. The souqs have operated like this for many hundreds of years.

Souq Semmarin forms the main route through the souqs from the northern side of Djemaa al-Fna. Semmarin is traditionally the textiles souq. Since it sees the bulk of tourist traffic, however, it has become something of an all-purpose crafts market with larger 'shops' selling everything from carpets to jewel-encrusted travelling chests. There are still a number of textiles merchants here. After passing the clothes **kissaria** on the left, you will come to **Rahba Kedima**.

This square, once the corn souq, is fascinating for its wool market on the south side and animal skin souq on the east. You must get to the wool market early in the morning to see any trading taking place. The ancient skins market is open for business all day. There are also a number of stalls selling traditional remedies and potions in Rahba Kedima. Many of the goods on offer seem extraordinary to Western visitors – and the merchants'

❏ SURVIVING THE SOUQS

Orientation

On first impressions the souqs seem to have developed to no particular plan at all; indeed, it's quite easy to get lost in this seemingly random web of streets and markets. In fact, the souqs have been shaped by religion and economics: only goods deemed 'clean' in the Islamic sense can be sold close to mosques. Thus in the Marrakesh souqs the coppersmiths' trade, for example, is 'clean'; valuable products like silver are generally made and sold close to main streets while less impressive or cheaper products, dyed wool perhaps, will normally be found deeper in the side streets.

Guides or touts?

Do not go into the souqs with a *faux guide* (false guide). These rogues act as agents for merchants, simply guiding tourists to particular carpet dealers where they then take a commission. There are qualified guides in Marrakesh but there is, in fact, little need to take a guide into the souqs at all. Just pay close attention to where you are and take care not to get lost. It might even be worth taking a compass.

What to pay

Haggling will go more smoothly if you are polite, well-dressed and conduct negotiations in a spirit of fun. Don't haggle for anything you are not genuinely interested in. It's a good idea to allow the merchant to name his price first. Then retort with your price; start at one third of his. You have probably done well if the end price is between half and two thirds of the merchant's first price. Don't worry when the merchant launches into the inevitable sob story about how at that price you are practically robbing him. No merchant will agree to any price with which he doesn't feel entirely happy. Unless you're an expert it is very hard to know whether the price you reach is fair. The best advice is this: if it's worth that price to you, buy it.

claims are often even more staggering; you will find here 'cures' for all manner of illnesses, aphrodisiacs and bizarre ingredients for working black magic.

After Souq Semmarin the street splits. The right-hand fork, **Souq el-Kebir**, leads next to **La Criée Berbère**. This was a slave market until the French occupation in 1912 and kidnapped black Africans were sold like mules at auctions here. These days the small square is dominated by carpet-sellers. Anyone with any experience of Morocco will know that carpet-sellers are nothing if not persistent, so it takes steely determination to keep a cool head and find a genuine bargain here where there are more carpet-sellers per square foot than anywhere else in the country! There are bargains to be had, though, and you will no doubt be shown beautiful carpets from various regions in Morocco. Different patterns show regional variations and most of the designs have some hidden meaning. There will often be a carpet auction during mid-afternoon. Only participate if you're confident you know what you're doing.

The next souq after La Criée Berbère is the **Souq aux Bijoutiers** – for jewellers – after which you will find yourself in the tight streets of the **Souq Cherratin**. Before reaching the Souq Cherratin, however, you will pass the **kissarias** to the left; these rather tacky stalls sell mainly Western goods, or copies of Western goods, at inflated prices. The Souq Cherratin is the place to come for leather goods. Haggle here for handmade shoes, bags and jackets.

To loop back to Djemaa al-Fna, head left after the leather workers' souq before reaching the **Ben Youssef Mosque**. This will take you to the **Souq Haddadine** where blacksmiths ply their trade with noisy enthusiasm. From here walk south along **Souq el-Attarin**, which is itself the souq for perfumes and spices, to the **Souq aux Chourai** (for carpenters) and, just a little further on, the **Souq des Huivres** where oils are bought and sold. Beyond here the colourful **Souq des Teinturiers**, or dyers' souq, is for many visitors the most attractive feature in this labyrinthine market. Dyed wool is hung out above the sun-dappled streets to form a beautiful, bright and colourful canopy.

Continue south on the Souq el-Attarin to reach the Souq Semmarin and Djemaa al-Fna. Alternatively you could go right before reaching the dyers' souq. This street takes you to the **Mouassin Mosque** and its intricate sixteenth-century Saadian fountain. Turn left at the mosque onto rue Mouassin to head back to Djemaa al-Fna. There is another interesting souq, the **Souq des Forgerons** (coppersmiths) along a narrow street behind the mosque.

Ben Youssef mosque and medersa

Go north through the souqs past the Almoravid Koubba to find the Ben Youssef mosque, the largest in the Medina, which was first built by the

Almoravids in the twelfth century but was rebuilt in the Merenid style in the nineteenth century. It's closed to non-Muslims.

A medersa, one of the most impressive in Morocco, stands alongside the mosque. Medersas were used to house religious students while they committed the Qur'an to memory. This one was founded by the Saadians in 1565; today it remains one of the most attractive buildings in Marrakesh and follows many of the principles common to most Moroccan medersas. But it's larger than any other and, contrary to custom, some of the students' cells look out over the street. Another unusual feature is the number of small courtyards which complement the main central courtyard, arcade and pool. Look out for the intricate carvings and Kufic lettering in the prayer hall and *mirhab* (prayer alcove). The medersa is open to non-Muslims but is closed on Fridays.

Almoravid Koubba

South of the Ben Youssef Mosque, just beyond the leather workers' souq, stands an early twelfth century Almoravid *koubba* (dome-shaped tomb of a Holy Man). Its significance far outweighs its immediate aesthetic appeal. As one of the very few Almoravid buildings still intact, it is one of Morocco's oldest examples of an architectural form which would underpin almost all subsequent classic Moroccan architecture. You will notice a number of patterns and shapes which subsequently became standards in Moroccan design – most notably, perhaps, the interior dome support and the squared battlements (*merlons*).

This koubba was discovered in 1952 amid excavations around the Ben Youssef mosque and is one of very few Almoravid buildings in Marrakesh to survive the Almohad rampage which destroyed much of the city. It is open to non-Muslims for a 10dh entrance fee.

The Jewish Quarter

A separate Jewish Quarter, or *Mellah*, was created in the mid-sixteenth century. At that time the Jews were successful in commerce and finance but were unable to own land or property and were exploited by the city as a useful tax resource trapped within the Mellah. The streets and houses look very different from those in other areas of the city; in the sixteenth and seventeenth centuries these narrow streets formed an almost separate city within Marrakesh. These days there are very few Jews left; most have emigrated or moved to the northern cities. The Mellah is run-down but there is still one functioning synagogue. It's difficult to find; you will need to ask a local to show you. The main entrance to this walled quarter is on place des Ferblantiers.

Tanneries

Head out to the north-east of the city to Bab Debbagh to find Marrakesh's tanneries. Here workers treat and dye skins using techniques which have changed little over hundreds of years. The main change is the replacement of traditional vegetable dyes with chemical equivalents, exposing the workers to serious health risks in the process. But the sight of the great vats of churning dye and hundreds of animal skins stretched across the rooftops under the sun is a compelling one. The smell is equally striking – and very unpleasant.

Saadian tombs

Discovered in 1917 between Bab Robb and the Palais el-Badi, the Saadian tombs are today considered the most prized attraction in Marrakesh. The mausoleum was built in the late sixteenth century for the Saadian sultans and their families. Moulay Ismail, the dynamic Alaouite sultan, sealed the tombs in the late seventeenth century, which is why they remained hidden for so many years.

The high-walled enclosure is a surprise: attractive gardens shelter two separate mausoleums and a number of graves of princes and other notables. The **first mausoleum** is on the left as you enter. This is the more impressive of the two, perhaps because it houses the tomb of Sultan el-Mansour during whose reign the tombs were built. The delicate, spectacular designs inside the three chambers of the mausoleum are breathtaking. The **second mausoleum** also has three rooms in one of which lies the body but not the head of Mohammed Esh Sheikh. He was killed by Turks who took his head back to Istanbul to prove his demise.

Entrance to the tombs is signposted from the Kasbah mosque. There is a 10dh charge to get in. Staff will often suggest you take a guide but this is no longer compulsory.

Palais el-Badi

Like the Saadian tombs, the Palais el-Badi dates back to the reign of Sultan el-Mansour, the 'Golden One', in the late sixteenth century. El-Mansour used his considerable power and wealth to build a palace which would rival any other in Morocco or, indeed, the world. The Palais el-Badi was the fruit of that ambition; known as 'the Incomparable Palace' it incorporated the finest display of Moroccan wealth and craftsmanship.

Sadly, the palace was largely destroyed in 1696 by Moulay Ismail who sacked much of Marrakesh and sealed the Saadian tombs (which he left intact out of fear of divine retribution). El-Badi's extravagant materials, which el-Mansour imported from all over the Maghreb and southern Europe, were carried away by Ismail's troops to adorn his new palace in Meknes. Still, the fact that it took over 10 years for Ismail's men to complete that task suggests that the great palace was indeed incomparable.

These days it takes some imagination to get a sense of how impressive it once was, although the height of the walls hints at the vast scale of the rooms and courts. All that is left now is the external walls, on the tops of which birds have built untidy, straggling nests, a series of internal pools and a koubba, once a great hall for state occasions. This was famed for its 50 giant columns which were shipped to Morocco from Italy. There's also a series of underground rooms and corridors under the southern edge of the ruins; exploring these is fascinating but take a torch.

The best way to find the palace is to follow rue Zitoune el-Qedim south from Djemaa al-Fna to place des Ferblantiers. Go through the large gate off the place and head to the right. Entrance costs 10dh. Guides are not compulsory. Palais el-Badi is attached to the Royal Palace which is still used sometimes by the Moroccan royal family.

Palais el Bahia

Perhaps the next most visited palace in Marrakesh is el Bahia (*Bahia* means 'brilliant') which was built towards the end of the nineteenth century by Bou Ahmed, a former slave who became a powerful *grand vizier* (Muslim leader) and is said to have been the most influential man in Morocco until he died in 1900.

He was a tough and cruel man. Immediately after his death, his slaves and harem ransacked the palace stealing everything of value. Bou Ahmed's family was driven out and the state took possession of the great palace. The palace itself remains intact. Its craftsmanship, while undeniably impressive and certainly extravagant, cannot compare to the genius which must once have adorned the Palais el-Badi and can still be seen in the Saadian tombs.

Built for the most part to traditional Moroccan-Muslim patterns, the palace is secluded and cool. Each member of Bou Ahmed's court had a place within the complex. His wives had a separate courtyard each while his harem lived in a different part of the palace with another cool courtyard in which to wait for the grand vizier to call. The palace is more an example of a rich man's whims than a classic model of Moroccan architecture; it is, however, mainly undamaged thus offering a clear picture of the way in which these great homes were organised.

Find the palace from place des Ferblantiers by heading north. There is normally an unhappy policeman on place des Ferblantiers directing traffic. Ask him for directions if you are unsure. Entry to the palace is free but you are required to take a guide with you for about 10dh.

Musée Dar Si Said (Museum of Moroccan Arts)

Dar Si Said is another palace, far less grand than el-Bahia, which was built at the end of the nineteenth century by Bou Ahmed's brother; it now houses an excellent Museum of Moroccan Arts.

The collection, beautifully displayed in a series of rooms around the building, focuses on jewellery, carpets and curiosities from Berber tribes in the High, Anti and Western Atlas. You will also come across the most prized exhibit: a 1000-year-old marble basin brought to Marrakesh from

Spain by Ben Youssef to be placed in the Ben Youssef medersa. It was transferred to the museum some years ago. The museum is organised on several floors, so allowing visitors to explore not just the art but much of the mansion as well. Remember to look up: the carved ceilings which adorn many of the rooms are among the most exciting in the city.

Explanatory cards are written in Arabic and French but English-speaking guides can be hired. It's rather difficult to find the museum. Head south on rue Zitoune Djedid from rue des Banques and turn left about halfway down. Then turn left again at a cluster of craft shops. You might need to ask a local to help you. Once there the entrance fee is the standard 10dh.

Maison Tiskiwin

Just around the corner from Dar Si Said at 8, rue de la Bahia is the Maison Tiskiwin. This attractive house, built in Andalusian-Moroccan style at the turn of the century, has been turned into a museum of Moroccan culture by Dutchman Bert Flint. Flint made Marrakesh his home in the fifties. There's also a small shop and café attached to the museum. The collection is housed in a number of rooms each of which focuses on a particular Moroccan region. You will find carpets, textiles and jewellery from Tangier, Fes, and the Rif and Atlas mountains. The notes again are in French. The museum is open only in the mornings.

Musée Dar Al Funun Ashaabia

This is another museum which is well worth visiting for an explanation of Moroccan culture – this time the oral and musical heritage which is so important a part of life in Marrakesh. The museum, at 154 Derb Sahrige, shows short explanatory films.

Old walls and gates

Old Marrakesh is enclosed behind a predominantly Almoravid defensive wall which boasts 200 towers and 20 gates (*babs*). The orange-pink walls make a splendid sight, particularly under a setting sun. It's worth walking out to the olive groves south-west of the Medina during sunset when the view of the walls against the High Atlas mountains is wonderful.

The gates themselves are masterpieces of defensive design. They are also useful for orientation. **Bab Robb**, to the south-west, is the best place to pick up a grand taxi to Asni. Head for **Bab Doukkala**, to the north-west, to find the bus station. **Bab Debbagh**, on the east side, is the 'tan-ners' gate'. Climb to the top of the gate for a fine view of the tanneries.

Gardens

Marrakesh, like most Moroccan cities, hides a number of secret and not-so-secret gardens. Sounds of gently running water escape from behind high walls to hint at oases just out of reach. Moroccan-Muslim architec-ture places great emphasis on privacy. So many of the city's most impressive homes and gardens are discreetly kept out of sight. But Marrakesh is also famous for its public gardens which were first created by the Almoravids in the twelfth century; they developed a revolutionary irrigation system which allowed them to build the finest gardens in Morocco. If you feel the need to escape the heat and hubbub of Marrakesh, go to one of the following gardens to relax.

● **Jardin Agdal**, which stretches for some three kilometres south of the Medina, was established in the twelfth century under Sultan el-Moumen and later improved under the Saadians. The size and scale of the garden makes it difficult to navigate but you will come across olive groves and orange tree orchards and a number of ornamental pools and pavilions. The gardens close when the King is in town.

● **Jardin Menara**, reached from Bab el-Djedid (next to Hôtel La Mamounia) along avenue de la Menara, is an enormous olive grove. A rectangular pool at the centre, with a *menzeh* (summer pavilion) alongside, is the biggest draw. You'll recognise the pool, pavilion and High Atlas backdrop from postcards and posters all over the city. The garden gets quite busy because it is so easy to reach from the Medina.

● **Jardin Majorelle** is a particularly attractive and secluded paradise north of Gueliz off avenue Yacoub el-Mansour. The small garden, designed in the twenties by French artist Louis Majorelle, is now owned by Yves Saint-Laurent. The wonderful bright blue art deco house at the centre of the garden now houses an interesting collection of Islamic art. Entrance is 15dh plus an extra 15dh to get inside the house to see the art collection. Children aged under 12 are not allowed in.

● **Hôtel La Mamounia,** on avenue Bab Djedid, is set in magnificent gardens which, in Saadian times, were enjoyed solely by royalty. The gardens are meticulously well looked after and completely hidden from the world outside. Unless you're staying at the hotel you will need to buy a drink to justify exploring them. You should also dress up; the hotel staff will ask you to leave if you're wearing shorts, sandals or the like.

PART 5: OUARZAZATE

Ouarzazate

Modern Ouarzazate was built by the French in the twenties to act as a garrison and administrative centre. In that respect, at least, the town is a success. It is a fairly dull and functional place which has little to offer tourists except transport, supplies and comfortable hotels. The fact is, however, that you can hardly avoid Ouarzazate if you plan to trek in the Sirwa or Sahro regions.

Ouarzazate is a boom-town with a prosperous film industry and a growing number of visitors. Impressive new hotels have sprung up to welcome arrivals at the international airport and tourism looks set to be a big earner for the town.

On the surface, Ouarzazate seems calm after the frenetic buzz of Marrakesh. Dig a little deeper, however, and you will discover that Ouarzazate's film industry has attracted a huge number of wanna-bes, general desperadoes and other amusing characters to the town. Poverty is common, though not immediately apparent, and the police are subtly keen to harass locals, unless they are official guides, if they talk to tourists; the town tries hard to present a good image to its visitors but, if you look hard enough, there are a few such cracks in the veneer.

HISTORY

Ouarzazate sits at the junction of the Drâa, Dadès and Ouarzazate valleys which makes it a site of strategic importance. As a result, subsequent dynasties made a habit of posting troops here which in turn made Ouarzazate a focal point for inter-tribal battles. Little survives of those early skirmishes which were often violent enough to wipe out any trace of the previous settlement.

At the turn of the century, however, the powerful Glaoui family seized Ouarzazate and built a kasbah to dominate the area. Fortunately for Ouarzazate, the kasbah is still standing; it's the only site of historic interest in the town.

The Glaoui clan later became allies of the French occupiers who, in 1928, built a garrison for their Foreign Legion near the kasbah. Unimaginative French planners then proceeded to develop Ouar-zazate as a regional centre.

ARRIVAL AND DEPARTURE

By air

Taourirt Airport is about two kilometres north of the town-centre. A petit taxi between the two should cost around 25dh. Royal Air Maroc (RAM) offers flights from Ouarzazate to Marrakesh, Casablanca and Paris.

By bus

There are two bus stations in Ouarzazate; the new gare routière north-west of the town-centre and the old CTM bus-stand on avenue Mohammed V. The **CTM station** has several departures to Marrakesh every day. The first is at 8.30am, the last 9.45pm. There are three departures a day to Casablanca and one at 12.30pm to Zagora and M'Hamid. There is also a service to Boumalne and Q'laat M'gouna at 10.30am and a daily departure to Agadir. The **left-luggage** desk charges 5dh per item per 24 hours with a 48-hour limit.

The **gare routière** is where all non-CTM buses pull in so there are more services from here. There are seven services a day to Marrakesh, three to Casablanca and five to Boumalne and Q'laat M'gouna. There are also services to Zagora and M'Hamid, Rabat and Agadir. The **left-luggage** desk here, open 24 hours a day, charges 5dh for large items or 3dh for small items per 24-hour period.

LOCAL TRANSPORT

Taxis

A journey in a petit taxi costs 3.5dh from and to anywhere in town during the day or 5dh after 9pm. They are easy to hail. There's a grand taxi stand opposite the CTM bus station.

Buses

See above for information about long-distance bus routes.

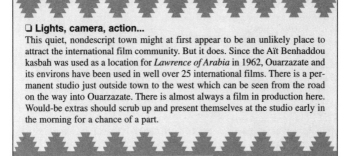

❑ **Lights, camera, action...**
This quiet, nondescript town might at first appear to be an unlikely place to attract the international film community. But it does. Since the Aït Benhaddou kasbah was used as a location for *Lawrence of Arabia* in 1962, Ouarzazate and its environs have been used in well over 25 international films. There is a permanent studio just outside town to the west which can be seen from the road on the way into Ouarzazate. There is almost always a film in production here. Would-be extras should scrub up and present themselves at the studio early in the morning for a chance of a part.

Car hire
These are the main players in Ouarzazate. Don't assume that every company listed here is reliable.

- **Avis** (☎ 88.48.70; 🖹 88.43.10), avenue Mohammed V.
- **Azir Sud** (☎/🖹 88.58.51), place Al Mouahidine.
- **Budget** (☎/🖹 88.42.02), avenue Mohammed V.
- **Europcar** (☎ 88.20.35; 🖹 88.40.27), place 3 Mars.
- **Hertz** (☎ 88.20.84; 🖹 88.34.85), avenue Mohammed V.
- **Mars Car** (☎/🖹 88.69.82), avenue Mohammed V.
- **Rosa Cars** (☎/🖹 88.69.32), 100 rue de Marché

ORIENTATION

Ouarzazate is a strip of development bounded to the east by the kasbah and to the west by a cluster of petrol stations. Anything in between is fair game. Since one can easily walk from one end to the other in 25 minutes, it is a very easy town to navigate.

WHERE TO STAY

There are some excellent hotels in Ouarzazate but the budget traveller will need to be wily to find a bargain; there are only a few places which are really cheap and these fill up fast in summer. On the other hand, the town's top-class hotels rarely fill up outside peak season so it might be worth attempting to haggle. Dress well to improve your chances.

Common (com) or attached (att) bathrooms are indicated after the price. Some cheapies charge for showers in common bathrooms; the price is given where appropriate. Prices for a single room are given first, with the price for doubles printed second.

Budget accommodation
The *municipal camp-site* is signposted off the main road east about a kilometre past the kasbah. It's a decent place with a café, a murky pool, show-

---

Ouarzazate (centre)

Where to stay	Where to Eat
1 Hôtel Bab Sahara	2 Firstnet Internet Café
4 Hôtel/Café Royale	3 Café with no name
5 Hôtel Es-Salaam	6 Restaurant Chez Dimitri
11 Hôtel Atlas	7 Hilal Café
12 Hôtel Zahir	8 Café Snack El Hassania
14 Hôtel Amlal	9 Café de la Renaissance
	10 Café Aloifa
	13 Restaurant es-Salam

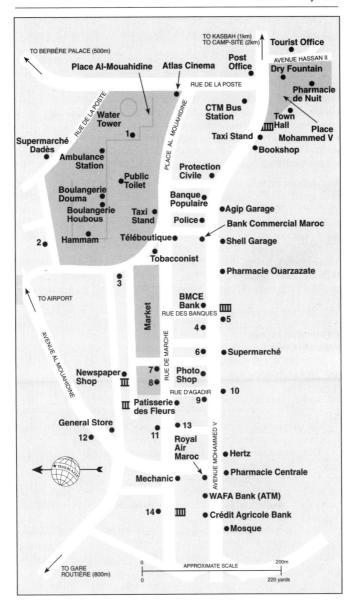

TO KASBAH (1km)
TO CAMP-SITE (2km)

Tourist Office

TO BERBÉRE PALACE (500m)

Place Al-Mouahidine   **Atlas Cinema**

Post Office

AVENUE HASSAN II

Dry Fountain

Pharmacie de Nuit

RUE DE LA POSTE

RUE DE LA POSTE

Water Tower

CTM Bus Station

Town Hall

Place Mohammed V

1

Taxi Stand

Bookshop

Supermarché Dadès

Ambulance Station

PLACE AL MOUAHIDINE

Public Toilet

Protection Civile

Boulangerie Douma

Banque Populaire

Boulangerie Houbous

Taxi Stand

Police

Agip Garage

Bank Commercial Maroc

2

Hammam

Téléboutique

Shell Garage

Tobacconist

Pharmacie Ouarzazate

3

TO AIRPORT

BMCE Bank

AVENUE AL MOUAHIDINE

Market

RUE DES BANQUES

4

5

6

Supermarché

RUE DE MARCHE

Newspaper Shop

7

Photo Shop

8

RUE D'AGADIR

10

9

Patisserie des Fleurs

General Store

13

12

11

Royal Air Maroc

AVENUE MOHAMMED V

Hertz

Pharmacie Centrale

★ TRAIN IN A ZU

Mechanic

WAFA Bank (ATM)

14

Crédit Agricole Bank

Mosque

TO GARE ROUTIÈRE (800m)

0   200m

APPROXIMATE SCALE

0

220 yards

ers and electricity hook-ups for camper vans. The price is relatively expensive, however, with a charge of 5dh to pitch a tent plus a per person charge of 10dh.

The three best of the cheap, unclassified hotels are **Hôtel Atlas** (☎ 88.23.07), on rue de Marché, with rooms from 35/45dh (com), **Hôtel Royale** (☎ 88.22.58), on the corner of avenue Mohammed V and rue des Banques, with similar prices, and **Hôtel Es-Salaam** (☎ 88.25.12), opposite, which has rooms from 40/80dh (com, 5dh) or 50/100dh (att) and a helpful owner who always seems pleased to see you.

Moving up in price a touch, there's **Hôtel Amlal** (☎ 88.40.30), on rue de Marché, west of the centre behind avenue Mohammed V (see map), where you'll find decent en suite rooms from 110/170dh.

Mid-priced hotels

Ouarzazate is sadly limited in this area but you could try **Hôtel Zahir** (☎ 88.57.40; 🖹 88.67.79) on avenue Mouahidine. The Zahir has en suite rooms for 140/190dh. It's a large, modern place with spacious rooms which are just a little worse for wear. The pool table is quite a plus. There's also **Hôtel La Gazelle** (☎ 88.21.51; 🖹 88.47.27) on avenue Mohammed V. Rooms here go for 130/160dh (att). La Gazelle is a step up from the Zahir although it has seen better days. The management makes much of the fact that Timothy Dalton stayed here during his stint as James Bond; it's a shame that Dalton looks so miserable in all their photographs. There's a bar attached.

Expensive hotels

Booming Ouarzazate has several options for the well-heeled visitor. At the lower end of this category, there are two hotels in the Salam chain which are worth investigating. The three-star **Hôtel Oscar Salam** (☎ 88.22.12/88.21.66; 🖹 88.21.80), on the main road out of town to the west, has well-appointed en suite rooms for 280/350dh. Its sister hotel, **Hôtel Riad Salam** (☎ 88.33.35; 🖹 88.27.66), is at the other end of town towards the kasbah off avenue Mohammed. Rooms go for over 500dh but the hotel is undeniably impressive with tennis courts and a good pool.

Three of the best four-star hotels are **Hôtel Hanan Club** (☎ 88.25.55; 🖹 88.57.37) on avenue Erraha, **Hôtel Belere** (☎ 88.28.03; 🖹 88.31.45) on avenue My Rachid and **Hôtel Karam Palace** (☎ 88.22.25/88.25.22; 🖹 88.26.42) nearby. There's little to choose between these three plush hotels each of which offers all the luxuries one would expect for the 650-750dh price bracket.

The best hotel in town, however, is the magnificent **Hôtel Berbére Palace** (☎ 88.31.05; 🖹 88.33.77) on rue Sharia ar-Raha. The Berbére Palace offers fantastic rooms, first-class service and a really good pool. All this for just 800dh a night.

WHERE TO EAT

Don't expect to find in Ouarzazate the sort of top-class gourmet treats which Marrakesh offers in its better restaurants. That said, there are plenty of good places around. All the **four- and five-star hotels** (see above) have restaurants attached and most offer Moroccan and international cuisine.

Starting at the other end of the price scale, however, head for the market area where cheap **food stalls** are set out during the evenings. You can eat well here for just 15dh. One street north, No 3 on the map, is a *café* with no name where a lovely Berber woman dishes up great food. You can eat till you're full for 15dh. Just west of the market, look for *Café-Snack El Hassania* where greasy staff serve cheap but reliable fast food. Next door, *Café Hilal* is equally good value.

Café Aloifa, opposite the photo shop on avenue Mohammed V, can set you up with a quarter of a chicken and a tomato salad for 20dh. Heading up in price, try *Restaurant Es-Salam* between avenue Mohammed V and rue de Marché. If you can find a table, there's a whole range of good set menus on offer. Expect to pay no more than 60dh for your meal. Nearby, *Café de la Renaissance* serves cheaper snacks.

The licensed *Restaurant Chez Dmitri*, next to Hôtel Royal, is one of the most popular places in town and something of a local institution. The cuisine is a blend of Moroccan and French and prices range from about 150dh for a three-course meal.

NIGHTLIFE

After-dark entertainment in Ouarzazate is truly abysmal. There is a bar in *Hôtel La Gazelle* but it's the sort of place where everyone stares at you when you walk in. The better hotels, of course, most notably the *Berbére Palace*, have pleasant but expensive bars. For nightclubs, try *Hôtel Hanan Club*, *Karam Palace* and *Belere*. Don't expect too much from these places, however. Hôtel Belere, for example, charges 50dh entry and 50dh for a beer. Its denizens are almost all male with a smattering of prostitutes, and the music is a medley of the very worst Europop ever recorded.

SERVICES

Banks and money exchange

There are several banks in the centre of town along avenue Mohammed V, including the BMCE and Banque Populaire. The WAFA Bank, on the north side of avenue Mohammed V towards the mosque to the west of town, has reasonable rates of exchange and an ATM machine.

Marrakesh/Ouarzazate area code: ☎ 04. From outside Morocco dial ☎ +212-4

Bookshops and newspapers

The one bookshop in town is opposite the CTM bus station on avenue Mohammed V. It sells very few English-language titles and even the French-language range is limited. It's difficult to find the international papers at news-stands in Ouarzazate but your best chance is at the news agent behind the market. Also try the better hotels.

Communications

● **Telephone and fax** For reverse-charge calls, head for the main post office. There are téléboutiques all over town and several offer a fax service as well.

● **E-mail** Walk north up rue de la Poste and take the first left to find the Firstnet Internet Café; you can log-on for 25dh per hour (20dh after 8pm).

● **Post** The main post office is at the southern end of rue de la Poste.

Hammams

There are a few hammams in town but the best is the one to the north-west of place Al Mouahidine where you can get the full treatment for about 30dh. The price seems fairly fluid so might depend on your approach.

Medical emergencies

● **Hospitals** Ouarzazate hospital is near the kasbah at the east end of avenue Mohammed V. There is an ambulance station in place Al Mouahidine.

● **Pharmacists** Try the Pharmacie Centrale next to Hertz rent-a-car on avenue Mohammed V, the Pharmacie Ouarzazate about 500 metres east, also on the south side of the road, or the Pharmacie du Nuit by the fountain (dry – at the time of research).

Supermarkets and shopping

Ouarzazate is a good town for shopping; there are a number of craft shops geared to passing tourists and two well-stocked supermarkets. The Supermarché Dadès on rue de la Poste is better than the one right in the centre of town on avenue Mohammed V. There's also a general store on the corner of avenue Al Mouahidine and the airport road and two good bakers on place Al Mouahidine. The Ouarzazate souq is held on Sundays.

Swimming pools

By far the best pool in town is hidden behind the high walls of Hôtel Berbére Palace. All the top hotels in town have good pools which, like that of the Berbére Palace, can be enjoyed for a fee of 50dh.

Trekking agencies

Désert et Montagne (☎ 88.51.46; 🖹 88.63.52; 🖵 desert@iam.net.ma) BP 93, 45 000 Ouarzazate (offices within the walls of the kasbah), is an excellent agency with treks to several parts of the Atlas and helpful, knowledgeable staff.

Tourist office

The tourist information office (☎ 88.24.85) is by the dry fountain off avenue Mohammed V. The staff here are more helpful than most and they should be able to make suggestions if you have problems finding a place to stay in your price range.

WHAT TO SEE

Taourirt Kasbah

Ouarzazate has just one historical showpiece and this is it: the 100-year-old kasbah was built by the Glaoui clan to control their southern trading routes. Although the clan chiefs never made it their residence, close relatives were placed in charge and for a time the kasbah was one of the most significant in Morocco.

Today the kasbah is in a state of decline although recent efforts to restore it have helped. Parts of the kasbah are structurally unsafe but what tourists can see is worth exploring. Enter through the northern gate, where you will be set upon by guides, to a courtyard. Here you will see the old cannon given to the Glaoui at the turn of the century. It might not look much now, but it caused havoc across the south in the hands of the merciless Glaoui. Once inside the kasbah, you can explore some of the main rooms where the traditional Moroccan artistry is well worth a close look.

A labyrinth of streets and houses crowd the kasbah which no longer stands alone as it must once have done; still, there are a number of craftsmen working in this part of town so, if you've yet to buy a carpet or a Berber necklace, this is the place to look for it. There is an ensemble artisanal opposite the kasbah.

The kasbah itself is open from 8.30am to 12pm and 3 to 6pm Monday to Friday and mornings only on Sundays. Entrance costs 10dh.

Zagora, about 160km south-east of Ouarzazate, stands beside the Sahara and is just 52 days' camel trek from Timbuktu. This signboard has become something of a tourist attraction but don't attempt to test its claims unless the border has reopened.

Using this guide

ROUTE MAPS

Scale and walking times

These treks have been organised into convenient stages. Since everyone walks at a different speed, however, all timings should be treated as approximate guides. Don't feel compelled to divide your trek into the same stages; walk at your own pace. You will soon get the measure of how this relates to the timings on the maps. Until you do work out how your speed relates to mine, allow extra time. Timings are given along the side of the map with arrows showing the direction to which the time refers. Black triangles depict the points between which the timings were taken. Since these timings are for walking only; you will need to add on time for rests or stops along the way. If you are planning a long trek, allow a rest day every five days or so. Finally, don't try to cover too much ground too quickly; the appeal of trekking is, after all, the slow pace that gives you the chance really to see the country.

Up or down?

The trail is shown on our maps as a dotted line. An arrow across the trail depicts a slope; two arrows show the slope is steep. The arrows point to the higher part of the trail. If, for example, you were walking from A (at 900m) to B (at 1100m) and the trail between the two were short and steep, it would be shown thus: A--->>---B.

Staying overnight

The High Atlas is more populated than you might think, although this is less true of the Toubkal region, so you will often find a village to stay in overnight. Many villages have basic gîtes d'étape which are seldom full. The nature of Berber hospitality is such that if you do find yourself in a village with no gîte d'étape or a full one, there's a good chance you will be offered alternative accommodation by a local. Don't expect five-star luxury in the Atlas; even the better gîtes can be quite uncomfortable by European standards. (A good tip is to take a universal basin plug; there seems to be a shortage of these in Morocco.)

You will enjoy greater freedom if you take a tent with you. In fact, camping is often the only alternative. Since the ground is normally sharp and hard you should take elastic loops to allow you to pitch your tent using rocks to weigh down the fly-sheet. Remember to ask permission to camp if you can and carry all your litter away with you.

WHEN TO GO

See p21 for information on when to trek in the Atlas. Should you go at times other than that recommended, avoid parts of treks where you might encounter rivers in spate and the possibility of flash floods.

The Toubkal region

Most High Atlas trekkers make Jbel Toubkal (4167m/13,670ft), the highest peak in North Africa, their first goal. Toubkal is easy to reach from Marrakesh and can be tackled in just a couple of days. This is also an exceptionally striking region with a sharp, imposing splendour which never fails to impress its visitors. There is nothing gentle about Toubkal; this is Snowdon on steroids. At the summit of Jbel Toubkal one gets a clear sense of the way in which the Atlas mountains form Morocco's spine, dividing a gleaming Atlantic coast from the scorching vastness of Saharan Africa. Most Toubkal trekking takes place in the Mizane valley. The region itself is bound by Tizi-n'-Tichka in the west and Tizi-n'-Test to the east. Imlil is the main trailhead in the area.

GETTING TO IMLIL

Take a bus or grand taxi south along the Taroudannt road from Marrakesh to Asni. Eight buses a day go to Asni from the local bus station (there is no actual bus 'station' as such, just a dusty plot of ground) next to the Bab Robb gate in Marrakesh. The price is 11dh. Otherwise go to Bab Robb to pick up a grand taxi. Expect to pay 15dh for a shared taxi or 90dh to travel alone. The journey to Asni takes just under an hour.

At Asni there are three ways to get to Imlil, a further 17km into the mountains. Your grand taxi driver might take you but since the road is poor he will charge extra. Otherwise you will need to wait for the Asni–Imlil mini-bus or a lorry (camion) to take you. Lorries regularly pass through Asni on their way to Imlil and it is common practice to ride on the back for a 10dh fee. The petrifying mini-bus costs about the same but you might wait a long time for it. There is always plenty of Asni–Imlil traffic on Saturdays when the former holds its main souq.

Asni

You will probably have to wait around in Asni for a while before getting to Imlil. It's a lively roadside village with a handful of cheap cafés and one decent hotel, *Hôtel du Toubkal*, which boasts a pool, restaurant and bar. Rooms cost around 200dh for a double. The Saturday souq is worth exploring if you happen to be in Asni at the right time. But there is little reason to see Asni as anything other than a stopover en route to Imlil and for trekkers an inconvenient one at that. You will be approached by hustlers who will offer to arrange treks, guides and mules for you. Don't arrange anything in Asni; wait till you get to Imlil. Prices quoted in Asni will almost certainly be inflated and official guides make Imlil, not Asni, their base.

IMLIL (1740m/5707ft)

This busy and colourful trailhead serves trekkers well. There are plenty of cafés, places to stay and a strong contingent of guides and muleteers. Imlil is where most Jbel Toubkal ascents are planned and organised so you will find useful supplies in the shops and even copies of the 1:100,000 and 1:50,000 Toubkal maps. These go for 150dh; you might need to ask around to find a copy. When I last visited, Imlil was still awaiting telephone lines. Telephone numbers given below are generally in Marrakesh.

Locals will be keen to offer you their advice and, often, their mountain services as well. You should take time getting to know a guide before agreeing to be led by him – or, occasionally, her – so cut the deal over a glass or two of mint tea. Note that a guide is hardly necessary for a sim-

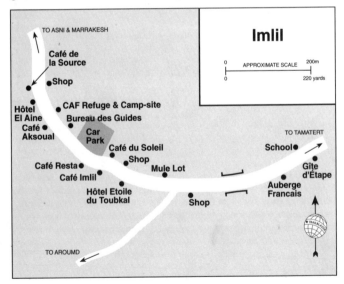

ple trek to the Jbel Toubkal summit and back to Imlil. You will pass others walking the same route and the path is reasonably distinct.

Services

The **Bureau des Guides**, opposite Café Aksoual, is the place to go to find a guide (there are about 50 based in Imlil) or for general advice about trekking in the Toubkal region. The bureau keeps a waiting list, so trekkers will be offered whichever guide is at the top of the list. These guides will only lead treks in the Imlil/Toubkal area. The staff there should also be able to tell you where to get a map.

Another place where people are always willing to give you advice or to chat about Toubkal trekking is the nearby **Club Alpin Français** (CAF) refuge. The gardien, Mohammed, is said to be the first and oldest guide in the Atlas. There's not much he doesn't know about the area. There are a number of **shops** selling groceries, drinks, tinned food and other useful supplies like matches, toilet paper and batteries. You can **change money** at the Etoile du Toubkal hotel.

Where to stay

Café du Soleil (☎ 04-48.45.90), recently rebuilt after it was washed away in the 1995 flood which swept through the Ourika valley, has four rooms at 80dh per room. Several people could sleep in each. A room with a shower is available for 100dh. Or you could sleep under the stars on the terrace for 15dh a night. The owner, Brahim, whips up a decent breakfast for 15dh. *Hôtel Etoile du Toubkal* (☎ 04-43.56.63) has eight rooms from 100dh, some look out over the street but the better ones at the back look over apple trees. There are hot showers. *Café Aksoual* has simple rooms for 25dh or you could sleep on the rooftop terrace for 15dh. Opposite, the *CAF refuge & camp-site* provides one of the better places to stay. It offers comfortable, clean dormitory accommodation for 20dh (CAF members) or 40dh (non-members) and use of its cooking facilities (including utensils) for an extra 5dh. There's also a small garden where campers can pitch their tents. *Hôtel El Aine* is good value with rooms for 30dh. There's a communal kitchen and TV room which residents can use. On the road out towards Tamatent there's a large *gîte* which sleeps about 11 people. It's a cut below the hotels just described, although it does boast great views of Toubkal. See the box on p129 for information about staying in the *Kasbah du Toubkal*.

Where to eat

All the places mentioned above serve food but, if you want a tagine or couscous rather than a simple omelette, you'll probably need to order several hours in advance. Dinner at *Hôtel El Aine* costs 30dh or 40dh for couscous and is pretty good. *Café du Soleil* and *Hôtel Etoile du Toubkal* are also recommended. The fact is, of course, that the very sight of Jbel Toubkal will make you hungry enough to eat almost anything.

❑ **Aroumd (1960m/6428ft)**
While Imlil is considered to be the main trailhead for Jbel Toubkal, Aroumd, a smaller village, is 45 minutes further along the Toubkal path by foot and so actually the last village before the Jbel Toubkal ascent. It can also be reached from Imlil by car but the road is terrible.

There are a number of decent places to stay in Aroumd and some trekkers will prefer to head here to avoid the more 'buzzy' atmosphere of Imlil. The French-run *Atlas Gîte* and *Café-Residence Aroumd* serve food. The gîte attached to the latter offers half-board accommodation with a hot shower for 80dh or rooms only for 30dh.

IMLIL-AROUMD-TOUBKAL (NELTNER) REFUGE [Map 1, p130]

Walk south through Imlil, past Café du Soleil on the left and Hôtel Etoile du Toubkal on the right, to a shady area where pack mules are kept. Turn right here on to the Imlil–Aroumd path. The path zigzags towards the Kasbah du Toubkal (see opposite page). Film director Martin Scorsese used the kasbah in *Kundun*, his movie about the Dalai Lama. The kasbah, which is now owned by British-based Discover Ltd and has been turned into trekkers' accommodation, made a fairly convincing Tibetan temple. Many of Imlil's locals made their screen debuts dressed as monks. Trekkers will no doubt agree with Scorsese that this part of the High Atlas has a lot in common with the Himalaya.

After 20 minutes' walking and having passed the kasbah, the path crosses a bridge before climbing to join a dirt road. Follow the road south for 25 minutes until you reach Aroumd (1960m/6428ft). From Aroumd follow the river bed south past a café. Find the path from Aroumd which leads along the left side of the river bed. The path then leads to a wide floodplain. After 15 minutes climb up the bank to the left past a small, walled orchard. (If you followed the path along the right-side of the river bed from Aroumd you cross the river bed, which might mean getting wet depending on the season) The path is reasonably distinct. Some 20 minutes later the path starts to climb steeply in a zigzag.

Follow the path to a small hut where a wrinkled but entrepreneurial character can usually be found selling soft drinks. There is a watercourse

---

(Opposite) Top: Descending from the summit of Jbel Toubkal which, at 4167m 13,670ft, is the highest peak in North Africa (see p131). **Bottom:** The route up to Tizi-n-Ouanoumss (see p132). (Photos © Richard Knight).

❏ The Kasbah du Toubkal

In 1995 British-based Discover Ltd (☎ +44 (0)1883-744392) restored the Kasbah du Toubkal, formerly a local Caid's summer residence, into one of the most exciting places to stay in or around Imlil. Local craftsmen transformed the kasbah into a Berber mansion using traditional techniques and hard manual labour; electricity arrived in Imlil in 1997 so, in 1995, there were no power tools. Materials were brought to the site by hand or mule. The kasbah, which offers great views from its elevated position, is now managed by husband and wife Arkia and Omar. There are pleasant gardens, three large public rooms, a gallery and even a hammam. A telephone line is due to reach the Kasbah soon. Inshallah. If it does, the number will be ☎ 04-48 56 11. Rooms are basic but clean and cost 50dh a night.

next to the hut. (You must purify the water, preferably with iodine – and this goes for all water sources.) After the hut, the path is lined by boulders which appear to have been placed deliberately. The path climbs steeply to the left after a further 45 minutes' trekking. There are large outcrops of rock on the valley side and, some minutes later, a waterfall.

A further 35-minute walk takes you to a split in the path; go right for the Neltner refuge or carry on for a couple of minutes to see Sidi Chamharouch, a marabout (tomb of religious importance), or to buy a drink from the small hut opposite. Trekkers can camp here but the few rooms available are reserved for Moroccans. There is a moussem (religious celebration) here in late September.

The Neltner path climbs steeply away from the shrine, crossing several springs (again, the amount of water on the path depends on the season), and passes an enormous rock buttress on the right (east) some two hours later. From here the path remains clear until the refuge is visible approximately one hour after passing the rock buttress. There is a large area leading up to the CAF Neltner refuge on which there are several flat camping spaces. Choose a sheltered one if you can; the wind here can be very strong.

The refuge (3207m/10,520ft) itself is one of the best in the Atlas but it's often overcrowded. It costs 30dh to sleep inside. The gardien can provide food (25dh), bottled water (10dh) and soft drinks. There is a gas stove

---

(Opposite) Top: Preparing a m'choui (see p76-7): whole lamb roasted in a sealed clay oven. **Bottom:** Shopping for provisions in Tabant (see p145). (Photos © Richard Knight).

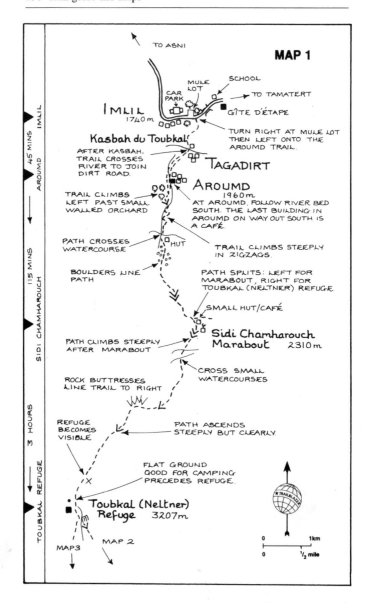

MAP 1

TO ASNI

SCHOOL

MULE LOT

CAR PARK → TO TAMATERT

IMLIL 1740 m

GÎTE D'ÉTAPE

TURN RIGHT AT MULE LOT THEN LEFT ONTO THE AROUMD TRAIL.

Kasbah du Toubkal

AFTER KASBAH, TRAIL CROSSES RIVER TO JOIN DIRT ROAD.

TAGADIRT

TRAIL CLIMBS LEFT PAST SMALL WALLED ORCHARD

AROUMD 1960 m

AT AROUMD, FOLLOW RIVER BED SOUTH. THE LAST BUILDING IN AROUMD ON WAY OUT SOUTH IS A CAFÉ.

PATH CROSSES WATERCOURSE

HUT

TRAIL CLIMBS STEEPLY IN ZIGZAGS

BOULDERS LINE PATH

PATH SPLITS: LEFT FOR MARABOUT, RIGHT FOR TOUBKAL (NELTNER) REFUGE.

SMALL HUT/CAFÉ

PATH CLIMBS STEEPLY AFTER MARABOUT

Sidi Chamharouch Marabout 2310 m

CROSS SMALL WATERCOURSES

ROCK BUTTRESSES LINE TRAIL TO RIGHT

REFUGE BECOMES VISIBLE

PATH ASCENDS STEEPLY BUT CLEARLY.

FLAT GROUND GOOD FOR CAMPING PRECEDES REFUGE.

Toubkal (Neltner) Refuge 3207 m

MAP 3   MAP 2

TRAILBLAZER

0   1km
0   ½ mile

IMLIL

45 MINS
AROUMD

115 MINS

SIDI CHAMHAROUCH

3 HOURS

TOUBKAL REFUGE

for general use if you can get near it. A small waterfall offers a cold opportunity to shower. Follow the stream south behind the refuge for five minutes to find it. The refuge was built with money raised by Louis Neltner, a distinguished French geologist and Atlas specialist who died in 1985.

TOUBKAL (NELTNER) REFUGE—JBEL TOUBKAL SUMMIT
[Map 2, below]

The route described here, the South Cwm ascent, is by far the most popular. Still, the loose scree makes the ascent difficult and the descent worse. Jbel Toubkal (4167m/13,670ft) is a graveyard for walking boots and none too kind to ankles. You should allow a day to get to the summit and back from the refuge, although it's feasible for walkers in a rush to reach the summit and return to Imlil in the same day. It is often very cold at the summit and there is no opportunity to refill water bottles en route.

Start from behind the Neltner Refuge and follow the gully south for five minutes until you reach a small waterfall. This is, incidentally, the place for showering in summer. Cross the stream in front of the waterfall to climb the scree path to the east. The path, which is in fact little more than a general direction and is not at all clear, scrambles over an expanse of large boulders. Small piles of stones mark the route, although, at this stage, you simply need to head upwards.

After 40 minutes, cross in front of a large and very obvious rock overhang (visible from the refuge) and walk back over the top of it to resume the climb. By now the path has degenerated into rather frustrating scree,

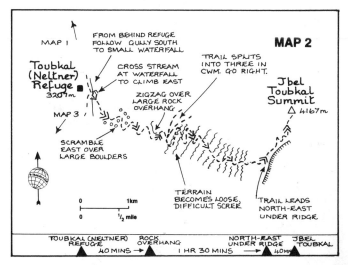

which will slow you down but is at least a little more clear to follow. In the dominant cwm of the mountainside the path splits into three; take the right-hand route (the others have worse scree and are more demanding). After a further 90 minutes' walking, the path climbs north just below a ridge which will have been visible for some time. The summit, which is marked by a tripod, is visible after a further 15 minutes. You should reach it some 25 minutes later.

Jbel Toubkal is the highest peak in the High Atlas and, indeed, North Africa at 4167m or 13,670ft. The views from here are magnificent; look for Jbel Sahro to the east, Jbel Siroua to the south and the Dome d'Ifni, which is connected to Toubkal by the Col d'Ifni, to the south-east.

Allow 120 to 150 minutes for the descent, which follows the same route as the ascent. I found 'scree running' the most effective method of dealing with the loose scree which makes the descent so difficult. It's a slightly risky approach but if you run in great hurdling strides you'll find your feet leave the scree before the dislodged debris carries you with it. To stop, bury your feet into the scree to come to a skidding halt in a cloud of dust. It takes a certain amount of confidence to descend in this manner, and you can expect to pick up one or two bruises.

TOUBKAL (NELTNER) REFUGE—TIZI-N-OUANOUMSS—LAC D'IFNI [Map 3]

This breathtaking walk offers great views from Tizi-n-Ouanoumss, a 3664m/12,017ft-high col, and a lengthy but rewarding descent to the serene Lac d'Ifni. It's a fairly long walk but you can take some comfort from the fact that any trekkers you meet travelling in the other direction are enduring one of the longest and most punishing ascents in the Atlas.

Set off from the Refuge in the same direction as for the Jbel Toubkal ascent; head south past the gully but, where the Toubkal path crosses in front of a small waterfall, continue south instead of turning east. After the waterfall, the path climbs fairly steeply for 15 minutes before levelling off into a beautiful square-bottomed valley. There is a waterfall and gorge to the left. The path then climbs again, weaving around a series of large rock outcrops, until it reaches a flat, grassy area which would make an outstanding camping site.

Continue for a further 20-25 minutes. The path then crosses the stream and zigzags steeply up the valley side to the east. After passing under a large overhang, the path continues to the col and is very easy to follow. You should reach the col, Tizi-n-Ouanoumss, some 45 minutes after heading east up the valley side. On a clear day, one can see all the way to the lake from here. It remains just out of sight during the descent.

The path descends sharply after the col and continues its downward thrust for a full 1500 metres (hence the agonised looks on the faces of

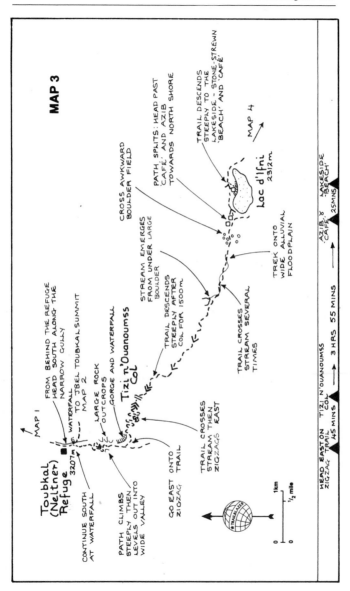

MAP 3

Toubkal (Neltner) Refuge 3207m.

CONTINUE SOUTH AT WATERFALL

PATH CLIMBS STEEPLY THEN LEVELS OUT INTO WIDE VALLEY

GO EAST ONTO ZIGZAG TRAIL

MAP 1

WATERFALL

FROM BEHIND THE REFUGE HEAD SOUTH ALONG THE NARROW GULLY

TO JBEL TOUBKAL SUMMIT MAP 2

LARGE ROCK OUTCROPS

GORGE AND WATERFALL

Tizi n'Ouanoumss Col

TRAIL CROSSES STREAM THEN ZIGZAGS EAST

STREAM EMERGES FROM UNDER LARGE BOULDER

TRAIL DESCENDS STEEPLY AFTER COL FOR 1500m.

TRAIL CROSSES STREAM SEVERAL TIMES

CROSS AWKWARD BOULDER FIELD

PATH SPLITS: HEAD PAST 'CAFÉ' AND AZIB TOWARDS NORTH SHORE

TRAIL DESCENDS STEEPLY TO THE LAKESIDE - STONE STREWN 'BEACH' AND 'CAFÉ'

TREK ONTO WIDE ALLUVIAL FLOODPLAIN

Lac d'Ifni 2312 m.

MAP 4

0   1km
0   ½ mile

HEAD EAST ON ZIGZAG TRAIL ► TIZI N'OUANOUMSS COL ► 45 MINS TIZI N'OUANOUMSS ► 3 HRS 55 MINS AZIB & 'CAFÉ' ► 25 MINS LAKESIDE 'BEACH' ascending trekkers!). Although the path is for the most part relatively easy to see, the steep hairpins demand concentration.

The stream emerges from under a large boulder some two hours later. At this point the path follows the water, crossing it several times (use the stepping stones). The path also starts to flatten out after the emergence of the stream. Some 90 minutes later the path drops down into a large, flat alluvial floodplain which leads to the lake, by now just visible. This is the first glimpse of Lac d'Ifni since the col. It doesn't look like it, but there are still 50 minutes to go before you reach the camp area.

Head left, to the north shore of the lake, across a rather awkward boulder field. There is a desolate *azib* (seasonal shelter for shepherds) to the left and, some 25 minutes after the lake came into view, a small hut, optimistically labelled 'café', which offers warm but welcome soft drinks. Follow the path to the left (north). It climbs away from the lake before descending very steeply to the right, to the lakeside, after some 20 minutes. This is the camp-site though in fact it is just a flat stretch of beach; on the plus side it's peaceful, there is another tiny café and you'll find plenty of rocks to use to weigh down your fly-sheet and shelter your tent from the wind.

Lac d'Ifni (2312m/7583ft) itself is a fine reward for the day's efforts. The café is run by a man named Mohammed, a Tom Sellick lookalike who serves soft drinks, bottled water and the occasional tagine. Since his customers are hardly in a position to argue, Mohammed charges above the odds; expect to pay 10-15dh for a bottle of water. One can normally order a tagine for 25-30dh per person.

LAC D'IFNI—AMSOUZERTE   [Map 4]

This relatively short and easy walk provides a chance to see cultivated valleys, small villages and traditional Berber life. This is the more colourful face of the Toubkal region and as such contrasts with the sharply spectacular but rather bleak scenes of the trek so far.

Take the path to the eastern end of the lake and traverse the east bank in a southerly direction. The path, which is fairly clear, passes the Sidi d'Ifni marabout after 25 minutes. A small moussem is held here in mid-August. Follow the path to the left of the marabout, past some rock buttresses and on to a small col after just five more minutes. Here, the path meets a dirt road or *piste* which offers a welcome rest for scree-battered feet.

Follow the road south-east; it zigzags all the way into the village of Aït Igrane. You can save time by cutting the corners but this means some scrambling over loose rocks, or you can take a leisurely stroll along the road. The view of the green, cultivated valley and its neat villages makes a wonderful sight.

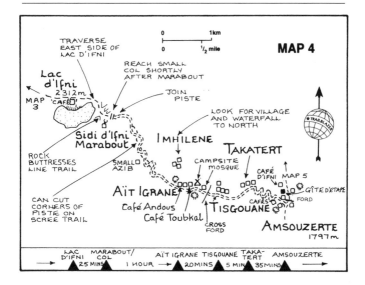

Approximately 30 minutes after joining the road you pass a small azib to the right. A further 30 minutes on, the road leads past walnut and silver birch trees into Aït Igrane. The terraced village of Imhilene and an impressive waterfall can be seen to the north.

Aït Igrane has two cafés, **Café Andous** and **Café Toubkal**, which one reaches in that order. The latter, owned by the Beläid family, offers cold drinks and snacks under the shade of a walnut tree. The Beläids also sell a limited range of everyday products such as toilet paper and soap. Attractive views across the family's cornfields help make this a pleasant place to relax. There is a shady camp-site complete with toilets and showers just past Café Toubkal. The price is a steep 30dh per night but, like most prices in Morocco, depends to some extent on the mood of the proprietor.

Continue downhill past a mosque to the left (where the time is always 3pm since the face of the clock is painted on) and cross a small ford. From here, the stream and path run more or less parallel. Another 20 minutes will take you to Tisgouane and, five minutes later, Takatert. After Takatert, the road hairpins downwards into Amsouzerte (1797m/5894ft). You'll pass several tiny cafés as you enter the village; there appears to be one for every villager. There's a gîte d'étape but it's a little difficult to find; walk through the village, crossing a ford, till you are almost out of the village. The gîte is on the left just before **Café Ifni** but you need to climb some steps and go through a large, bolted door to find it; it might be simpler to ask. The gîte, run by Omar, offers a very pleasant terrace, some rooms and cold showers and costs the standard 30dh per night.

Amsouzerte is not, in my opinion, the most attractive village in the area; it feels rather less welcoming than most. But it is a convenient place for a stopover and, if you've had enough, it's possible to get back to Marrakesh from here; ask about when to expect the next lorry or Landrover out of town. You might want to stock up on bottled water in Amsouzerte.

AMSOUZERTE—AZIB TAMENZIFT   [Map 5]

Leave the gîte through the backyard which leads onto a small path. Walk left along the path and follow it right at a stream. Climb alongside the riverbed to the north-north-east. The path starts to zigzag after the last house. Then take the high path heading west. After 30 minutes the path crosses an irrigation channel; follow it until the path climbs to the left on a steep, stepped route. It then climbs in a zigzag past a series of terraced fields and into a small village, reached some 55 minutes after leaving the gîte, which is neatly stacked against the hillside.

Continue upwards through the village after which the path leads onto a steep but open ascent towards a stunning saddleback ridge which will take a further hour to reach.The view from here, which stretches into the next valley and beyond, is fantastic. Follow the path to the north-east. You will reach a particularly disheartening false summit after a further one hour 30 minutes before, 30 minutes later, achieving the Tizi-n-Ouraï col (3109m/10,200ft), the highest point in this stage of the trek. A path from the right of the valley merges with yours not long before the col. Again, the views from this high point are deeply impressive.

After the col, the descent to the valley floor is rapid, about 20 minutes. In summer, this flat, grassy area is good for camping, taking a break or making lunch. In winter, it might be too wet. A water source emerges from the rocks on the west side of the valley.

From here the path becomes a good deal clearer. It winds north-north-east, then soon continues through a steep-sided gorge. After the long ascent and abrupt descent of the past few hours, this flat and clear trekking is a welcome respite. Walk for a further 90 minutes to a mini col. From here you can see a collection of huts and pens which make up the Tamenzift azib (2600m/8528ft). There are plenty of good places to camp around this area which you will reach after a further 20 minutes but, if you decide to plump for a patch anywhere near an azib, you should ask permission.

For a bracing shower, follow the stream west from here for about 40 minutes. You will hear the waterfall long before you see it; just when you begin to think you'll never reach the source of the splashing sounds, the

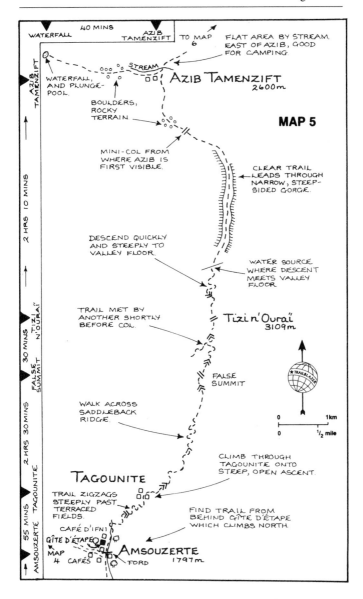

WATERFALL   40 MINS   AZIB TAMENZIFT   TO MAP 6   FLAT AREA BY STREAM, EAST OF AZIB, GOOD FOR CAMPING.

WATERFALL, AND PLUNGE-POOL.

STREAM

000 0 0

AZIB TAMENZIFT 2600m

AZIB TAMENZIFT

BOULDERS, ROCKY TERRAIN.

MAP 5

MINI-COL FROM WHERE AZIB IS FIRST VISIBLE.

CLEAR TRAIL LEADS THROUGH NARROW, STEEP-SIDED GORGE.

2 HRS 10 MINS

DESCEND QUICKLY AND STEEPLY TO VALLEY FLOOR

WATER SOURCE WHERE DESCENT MEETS VALLEY FLOOR

TIZI N'OURAÏ

TRAIL MET BY ANOTHER SHORTLY BEFORE COL.

Tizi n'Ouraï 3109m

30 MINS   FALSE SUMMIT

FALSE SUMMIT

WALK ACROSS SADDLEBACK RIDGE.

TRAILBLAZER

0   1km
0   ½ mile

CLIMB THROUGH TAGOUNITE ONTO STEEP, OPEN ASCENT.

2 HRS 30 MINS   TAGOUNITE

TAGOUNITE

TRAIL ZIGZAGS STEEPLY PAST TERRACED FIELDS.

FIND TRAIL FROM BEHIND GÎTE D'ÉTAPE WHICH CLIMBS NORTH.

CAFÉ D'IFNI

GÎTE D'ÉTAPE

MAP 4   CAFÉS

Amsouzerte 1797m

FORD

55 MINS   AMSOUZERTE

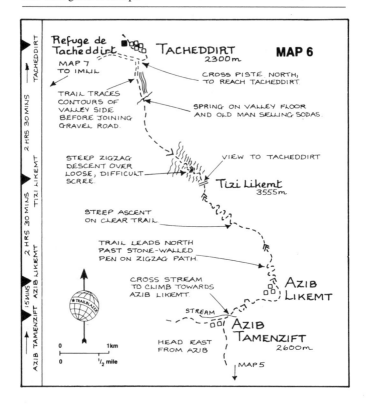

path opens onto it with its deep, icy plunge-pool. I defy any readers to stay in for more than a few seconds; it's incredibly cold!

If you decide to investigate the azib, exercise some tact. I went there planning to buy a chicken and was greeted by an attractive young Berber woman who seemed keen to show me round her home. She invited me to taste the thick, yoghurt-like drink which she had just made. But as we stood around exchanging smiles (neither of us understood what the other was saying) a young man raced into the yard in a cloud of dust and abused me roundly in Berber. He gestured wildly to the woman, to me and to the heavens before chasing me out. I gather he was jealous, although it had certainly not been my intention to make him so; but these azibs are very close-knit communities. No chicken that night.

AZIB TAMENZIFT—TACHEDDIRT [Map 6, opposite]

Cross the river and travel east from the azib. Follow the path over the opposite bank to another small azib and then bear left on a zigzag path past a stone-walled pen. The path which meanders in a north-westerly direction is clear. Follow it for a rather punishing 150 minutes to the col of Tizi Likemt at 3555m/11,660ft. Tizi Likemt is a well-trodden mule route, so the path is relatively easy to follow, but you must make sure you have plenty of water since there are no springs for some time. Cross the col and start a steep zigzag descent down the other side. You get a wonderful view of the Imenane valley floor from here, with villages huddled on each side.

The clear zigzag route leads down from here across a vast scree slope to the valley floor, across a river bed to a spring, after about 150 minutes, where there's normally an old timer selling sodas. From here, the path follows the contours of the slope to the right for a further 20 minutes before joining a gravel piste which leads on towards Imlil. Alternatively cross the road north to Tacheddirt (2300m/7544ft), a further 20 minutes walk, which is the village in sight from the piste. It is possible to make the trek from the Tamenzift azib to Imlil in one day but covering several cols over nine hours is a long slog. Better to break the journey in Tacheddirt.

Tacheddirt is a pleasant village, surrounded by a quilt of fields, with a small CAF refuge which is popular with trekkers. It is managed by a helpful gardien. Dormitory accommodation costs 40dh plus an extra 5dh for use of the kitchen. If the refuge is locked when you arrive, ask around for the gardien; often, however, he will be ready to greet you having seen you approach.

TACHEDDIRT—IMLIL [Map 7, p140]

Climb down to the Imlil piste, 10 minutes, which was crossed to reach Tacheddirt. The road heads west past a cluster of pine trees which you will pass after about 20 minutes. Continue uphill to a col, Tizi-n'-Tamatert (2279m/7475ft), which you should reach 60 minutes after joining the piste. Some 10 minutes later, look out for a small and strangely-located shop (in fact, little more than a hut) to the right of the route. Turn left here to follow a narrower mule-path down a tree-coated hillside.

This path zigzags steeply, so watch your footing, crossing the main piste twice as that route winds down towards Imlil. The path is for the most part clear. But if you do lose track of it, keep heading down until you pick it up again. Cross over the piste twice, 25 and then 30 minutes after turning left opposite the shop. You will then reach a river bed (dry in summer). Follow it right to pick up the piste again. Follow it downhill for five or 10 minutes before reaching a clear path to the left towards a village. Walk down through the village, Tamatert, to rejoin the road. Expect to

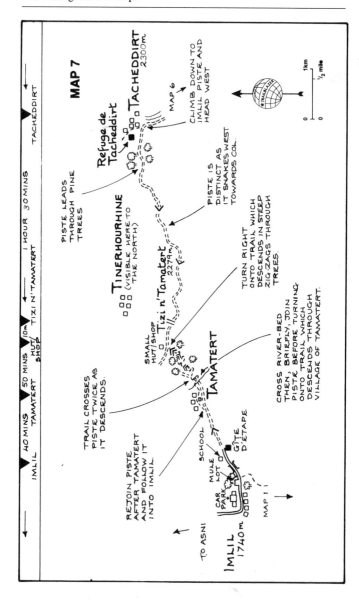

reach Tamatert some 50 minutes after leaving the main piste at the shop. Go west for a further 30 or 40 minutes to reach Imlil where, no doubt, you will feel you've earned a celebratory orange juice at Café du Soleil.

The M'goun region

M'goun is the second-most popular region in the High Atlas for trekking although it is quite different from Toubkal. While the climate here can be just as tough, and the peaks are only fractionally lower, M'goun has a softness and bright fertility which is lacking in the other Atlas regions described in this guide. One gets the sense here that life is perhaps just a little easier than it is in Sirwa or Sahro where the landscape appears more foreboding and dramatic. Without doubt, however, M'goun offers some of the most inspiring views in the Atlas and to reach the summit itself, at 4068m/13,343ft, is a truly rewarding challenge.

GETTING TO AZILAL

There are two **buses** a day from Marrakesh to Azilal (170 kilometres) from the main gare routière; one early and another after lunch. Check for specific times the day before you plan to go. The journey takes four or five hours and costs 40dh. Otherwise hop on a bus to Beni Mellal, a better-served transport hub. There are frequent services from Marrakesh to Beni Mellal; the journey time is a little less and the cost about the same. From Beni Mellal, three buses a day run to Azilal. However, once in Beni Mellal, it might prove simpler to find a way from there direct to the trail-head, Tabant, via Aït M'Hamed. The other option is to take a **grand taxi** from Marrakesh to Azilal. This should cost no more than 80dh per place.

AZILAL

Tabant is the trailhead for the M'goun treks described here. To reach Tabant from Marrakesh, however, travellers will pass through Azilal on the N8 road. While there isn't a great deal to recommend this small town on the grounds of aesthetics or history, Azilal is a pleasant enough place and a useful source of supplies. If you plan to visit the waterfalls at Ouzoud, which is well worth the time, you might find it convenient to break your journey in Azilal.

Services

Azilal has grown quickly over the past few years, partly because of the increasing number of trekkers who choose to tackle the M'goun massif.

❏ Cascades d'Ouzoud

This attractive waterfall, which plunges over brown, sun-scorched earth to a series of deep pools 100 metres below, is now firmly on the tourist's map of Morocco. The sheer gorge and powerful cascade make an impressive sight but the tacky cafés which have sprung up around it have diminished the effect just a little. Still, the Cascades d'Ouzoud are definitely worth a visit. Azilal is just 35 kilometres away and grands taxis regularly charge between the two for about 15dh per place. Azilal taxis are white.

There are two small hotels here: *Hôtel Dar Es Salaam* (☎ 03-45.96.57), run by the enthusiastic Abdullah, has double rooms for 70dh all of which share one cold shower. The nearby *Hôtel Vieux Moulin* is smaller but charges about the same. There are quite a number of camp-sites dotted around the falls most of which offer level pitches and great views.

The town itself is built along the road and so stretches quite some way from south-west to north-east (see map). This makes orientation easy although to walk from one end of town to the other would take 30 minutes. Visitors will find here: a **hospital**; **police station**; **téléboutiques**, several of which offer a fax and photocopying service; a **pharmacy**; a **Banque Populaire**; **food, stationery and hardware shops**; a **post office**; a **laundry**; a **tourist office**, although it's hard to imagine it does much business; a **petrol station**; an **ensemble artisanal**; and a **Thursday souq**.

The souq is one of the largest in the area so, if you can time it right, it's worth passing through Azilal on a Thursday to stock up for a long trek. Every sort of meat, vegetable and fruit is sold here, some so bizarre they look almost alien. You will also find here clothes, material, dodgy electrical goods, spices and hardware. The meat area of this sprawling tent-mall is a gruesome sight for many squeamish Westerners who find the animal debris strewn about quite off-putting.

Where to stay

There are quite a number of places to stay in Azilal. Budget-conscious travellers will have little difficulty finding somewhere to stay. Starting from the cheapest, the options are: *Hôtel Tissa*, not the best place in town, with rooms from 25-65dh and shared warm showers; *Hôtel Dadès* with singles/doubles for 30/60dh plus 5dh for a hot shower; *Hôtel Ouzoud* with the same charges; *Hôtel Souss*, the best value by far, with clean, recently-refurbished rooms from 35-70dh; and, Azilal's only 'up-market' hotel, the two-star *Hôtel Tanout* (☎ 03-45.87.87; 🖹 03-45.82.81) at the north end of town. The owner of La Mamounia in Marrakesh won't be

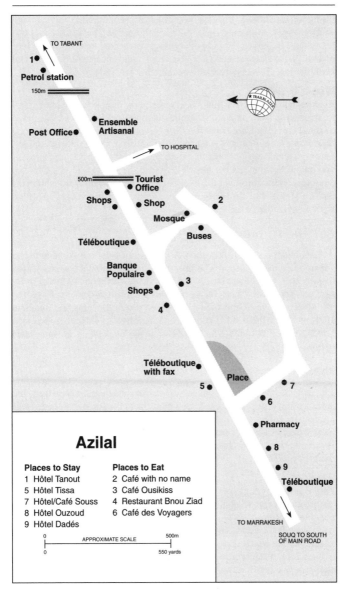

TO TABANT

1
Petrol station

150m

Ensemble
Artisanal
Post Office

TO HOSPITAL

500m Tourist
Office
Shops Shop

2

Mosque

Buses

Téléboutique

Banque
Populaire
Shops

3

4

Téléboutique
with fax

Place

5

7

6

Pharmacy

8

9

Téléboutique

TO TRAILBLAZER

Azilal

Places to Stay
1 Hôtel Tanout
5 Hôtel Tissa
7 Hôtel/Café Souss
8 Hôtel Ouzoud
9 Hôtel Dadés

Places to Eat
2 Café with no name
3 Café Ousikiss
4 Restaurant Bnou Ziad
6 Café des Voyagers

TO MARRAKESH

SOUQ TO SOUTH
OF MAIN ROAD

0   500m
APPROXIMATE SCALE
0   550 yards

losing too much sleep over the Tanout but it is comfortable, friendly and well-managed. All rooms are en suite with hot water 24 hours a day. If you really need to tighten the old purse strings, try asking to sleep on the roof of one of the cheaper hotels if you don't mind the possibility of there being insects. This can normally be done for just 15dh or so.

Where to eat

Epicurean travellers will find Azilal to be fairly disappointing but hungry trekkers fresh from M'goun will think the place is Morocco's last bastion of fine foods. Try *Café Ousikiss*, *Café Souss*, *Café des Voyageurs* or the *café with no name* near the tourist office. Each of these sells the ubiquitous tagine and couscous for the usual sort of prices. Order in advance if you can. Café Souss is the most lively of these places and you can also order omelettes, chips and the like. The café with no name probably wins the Azilal prix d'or for the best tagine. Expect to pay the usual 30-50dh for a main course in these places.

GETTING TO TABANT

A diabolical minibus makes the petrifying four-hour run from Azilal to Tabant everyday at 12pm. You need to get to the minibus, which leaves from beside the mosque (see Azilal map, p143), at about 10 am to make sure you get a seat. Places on the minibus are much in demand. Expect to pay 40dh each way. Otherwise take a grand taxi to Aït M'hamed for about 10dh and wait there for a camion or Landrover to Tabant. A ride in a Landrover will cost about 30dh so there is no financial advantage to this option.

TABANT

Tabant (1850m/6068ft) is one of the most appealing trailheads in the Atlas. A friendly, laid-back village which sits in the Aït Bou Guemez valley, Tabant offers outstanding views, the best of Berber hospitality and most essential services trekkers might need to prepare for a long trek. French trekkers have nicknamed Aït Bou Guemez *'la vallée heureuse'*, the happy valley.

Services

This is a small village but geographically, an important one since it acts as the administrative and economic focal point for a relatively densely-populated valley.

Tabant is further distinguished from surrounding villages by a solitary telephone line which occasionally connects it to the outside world. There is, therefore, a **téléboutique**. Trekkers will also find here a **post office**, **shops** (a butcher, hardware kiosk and general store) and **police** house. There is a lively **souq** every Sunday. **Guides and muleteers** are easily

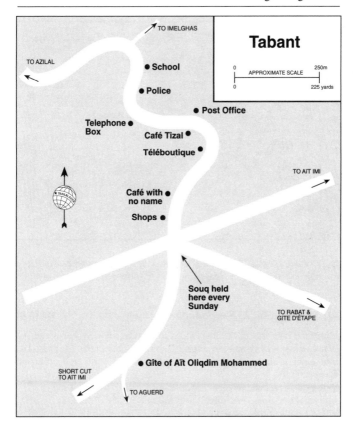

Tabant

TO IMELGHAS

TO AZILAL

● School

● Police

● Post Office

Telephone ●
Box

Café Tizal ●

Téléboutique ●

TO AÏT IMI

Café with ●
no name

Shops ●

Souq held
here every
Sunday

TO RABAT &
GÎTE D'ÉTAPE

● Gîte of Aït Oliqdim Mohammed

SHORT CUT
TO AIT IMI

TO AGUERD

0   APPROXIMATE SCALE   250m
0   225 yards

found here; just ask around at the gîtes. The Moroccan mountain guide training centre is situated in Tabant.

Where to stay

The *gîte* of Aït Oliqdim Mohammed (☎ 03-45.93.26) is central and clean. It charges 30dh (as in most High Atlas gîtes, guests must share large rooms). Showers are cold. Otherwise try the *gîte d'étape* a little way north of Tabant towards the next village, Rabat, which has similar facilities and, like almost all gîtes in the High Atlas, the same prices.

Where to eat

The gîte of Aït Oliqdim Mohammed supplies tasty tagines if enough notice is given. There are also two cafés: *Café Tizal*, behind the télébou-

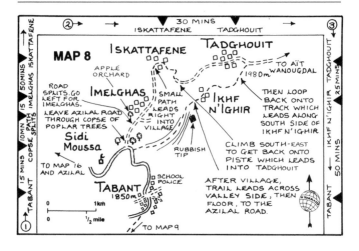

tique, which is quite lively; and the Berber *café with no name* adjacent to the shops. The latter is an interesting and friendly place and well worth a visit anyway.

AÏT BOU GUEMEZ: *Randonnée du Thé*   [Map 8]

This three-hour trek has been included to introduce new visitors to the Aït Bou Guemez valley and the gîtes d'étape available outside Tabant. The trek which is simply a circular tour of the villages north-west of Tabant makes a useful warm-up for the challenging stages ahead. Each village is slightly different and in each visitors can be sure to find themselves plied with mint tea, bread and olive oil in the true spirit of Berber hospitality. When I trekked this route I found it took six hours not three because of the incredible amount of tea I drank with the locals. I have, therefore, decided to label this short warm-up trek the Randonnée du Thé.

Leave Tabant (1850m/6069ft) on the Azilal road for 15 minutes at which point the Azilal road turns at right angles; leave the road and go straight on through a copse of poplar trees. After a further 10 minutes, the trail divides. Go left so that a village comes into view.

Head towards the village, past an apple orchard, which you should reach after a further 15 minutes. This is Imelghas. Go right (east) to the reach the centre of the village.

There is an excellent *gîte d'étape* here, owned by El Ouakhoumi Saïd, which has clean showers, a hammam, comfortable rooms and a well-lit common room with a good selection of books on the Atlas mountains and Berbers. Carry on through the village to find two more *gîtes d'étape* (both of which are pleasant enough); the first is owned by El Ouakhoumi Brahim ben Ichou.

Keep going along the piste until after 40 minutes a lesser path leads right towards another village, Iskattafene, which sits on the opposite side of a flat-bottomed valley. You'll reach the village 10 minutes later. Walk down into it until after five more minutes you find a *gîte d'étape* through a wooden door. It is signposted. This gîte is owned by El Ouassea Mohammed. There are three other *gîtes* in the village including that of Maskour Brahim; this is one of the better ones in Iskattafene though really they are all adequate and of a very similar standard.

Climb south-east to get back onto the piste which leads north-east to the next village of Tadghouit (1980m/6494ft) which you will reach after a further 30 minutes. This is the furthest extent of the loop which, after Tadghouit, leads along the south side of the valley for 25 minutes to Ikhf n'Ighir. There are two *gîtes d'étape* here including that of Imharken Mohammed which is clean, comfortable and the owner friendly. It also boasts a hammam. A third gîte is said to be on the way.

From Ikhf n'Ighir, climb down to the valley floor. Follow the indistinct trail west across the valley floor till the trail leads past an unpleasant rubbish tip 15 minutes later and, 15 minutes after that, leads into the treeline. Keep going for another 10 minutes to meet the Azilal road and, from there, it's a clear 10-minute walk back into Tabant.

M'GOUN: CIRCULAR TREK

Tabant—Aït Saïd—Azib n'Ikkis   [Map 9, p148]

Head west out of Tabant (1850m/6068ft) on the Azilal road but turn off left after five minutes to trek south-west across the neatly-cultivated fields of the valley floor on a narrow but clear path. After 20 minutes snaking through the fields the trail will lead through the quiet village of Aguerd n'Ouzrou after which the track descends into an attractive, wide valley which, in summer at least, is vivid green with crops and plants.

A further 15 minutes will take you through the village of Tamalout n'Aït Ziri, which isn't marked on the 1:100,000 Zawyat Ahançal map, after which the track leads along the left (south) side of the valley. The path at this stage is level and easy to see. After another 25 minutes the track leads past the village of Idoukaln which is clearly visible on the north side of the valley. Take a right turn (north-west) some 15 minutes later onto a wider stretch of path which leads to the middle of the valley floor. The villages of Talsnant and Agouti stand out on the north side of the valley at about this point.

Some 20 minutes later, the path leads onto a wide plain. Continue in a south-westerly direction; the actual path is quite hard to see. Start looking for a narrow piste after about 20 minutes. It leads south into the Assif

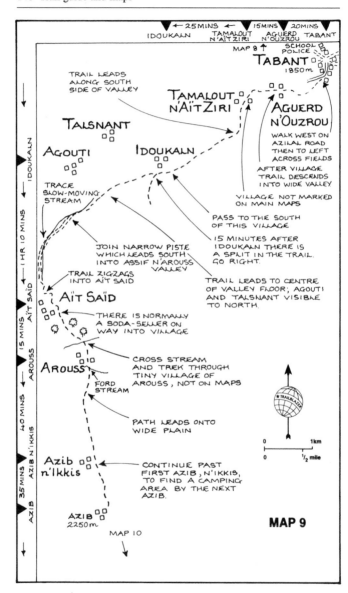

← 25 MINS ← 15 MINS 20 MINS
IDOUKALN   TAMALOUT AGUERD TABANT
             N'AÏTZIRI N'OUZROU

MAP 8 ↑
SCHOOL
POLICE
TABANT
1850m

TRAIL LEADS
ALONG SOUTH
SIDE OF VALLEY

TAMALOUT
N'AÏTZIRI

AGUERD
N'OUZROU

TALSNANT

WALK WEST ON
AZILAL ROAD
THEN TO LEFT
ACROSS FIELDS

AGOUTI   IDOUKALN

AFTER VILLAGE
TRAIL DESCENDS
INTO WIDE VALLEY

VILLAGE NOT MARKED
ON MAIN MAPS

TRACE
SLOW-MOVING
STREAM

PASS TO THE SOUTH
OF THIS VILLAGE

15 MINUTES AFTER
IDOUKALN THERE IS
A SPLIT IN THE TRAIL.
GO RIGHT.

JOIN NARROW PISTE
WHICH LEADS SOUTH
INTO ASSIF N'AROUSS
VALLEY

TRAIL LEADS TO CENTRE
OF VALLEY FLOOR; AGOUTI
AND TALSNANT VISIBLE
TO NORTH.

TRAIL ZIGZAGS
INTO AÏT SAÏD

AÏT SAÏD

THERE IS NORMALLY
A SODA-SELLER ON
WAY INTO VILLAGE

CROSS STREAM
AND TREK THROUGH
TINY VILLAGE OF
AROUSS, NOT ON MAPS

AROUSS
FORD
STREAM

PATH LEADS ONTO
WIDE PLAIN

Azib
n'Ikkis

CONTINUE PAST
FIRST AZIB, N'IKKIS,
TO FIND A CAMPING
AREA BY THE NEXT
AZIB.

0   1km
0   ½ mile

AZIB
2250m

MAP 9

MAP 10

IDOUKALN   1 HR 10 MINS   AÏT SAÏD   15 MINS   AROUSS   40 MINS   AZIB N'IKKIS   35 MINS   AZIB

n'Arouss valley and once you find it, it is easy to follow. Once in the valley, the piste traces a slow-moving stream. Carry on for another five minutes then leave the riverside and climb right (south-west) up a zigzag path which then wends generally south despite twisting and turning frequently. From here you can make out the mighty M'goun summit; which is the furthest peak to the south.

About 10 minutes later the trail leads into the small village of Aït Saïd where one can normally find some old fellow selling sodas cooled in buckets of stream water. Continue out of the village, leaving the shade of its trees, and follow the path to a gentle stream which should take another 15 minutes to reach. Moments later you will enter another, smaller village called Arouss which, again, is not marked on the main map.

The path leads from Arouss into a narrow valley after fording the stream in the village. Again the trail leads from the village south onto a wide, rolling plain on which sit several azibs. The plain here gives a real sense of the scale of the M'goun massif. Expect to reach the first of the scattered azibs after 40 more minutes of trekking.

This first azib is called the Azib n'Ikkis (2250m/7380ft). Keep heading south past here to find the best camping area and the end stage for this part of the trek. We've called this place 'Azib' because we were unable to find a more accurate name from either maps or locals. So, carry on south past Azib n'Ikkis to the next cluster of huts which you should reach after another 35 minutes. The views of the M'goun summit here are breathtaking. There is also water and soft, flat ground suitable for camping should you choose to break the trek at this stage.

Azib—Tarkeddid Refuge [Map 10, p150]
The trail continues from the azib in a south-westerly direction hugging the western bank of the valley. The actual path is at times quite hard to distinguish but the route is obvious and the terrain, though rocky, is not too difficult.

At this stage the trail is ascending steadily but gently. It quickly gets steeper however, until about 35 minutes into the trek, the valley meets another leading west. Head into this next valley which is thickly coated with bushes.

The path becomes clearer at this point as it zigzags steeply to a col, Tizi n'Oumskiyq (2909m/9541ft), reached 50 minutes into the trek, after which it continues to climb towards the south. Soon you will be able to see a second, higher col towards which you are heading.

As the trail gets closer to the col, Aghouwri Est (3400m/11,152ft), it becomes very steep. Expect to reach Aghouwri Est 110 minutes after passing over Tizi n'Oumskiyq. If you look back from the col you can see right back to the Azib n'Ikkis. The views from here really are magnificent in all directions. Look south from the col to see the M'goun summit.

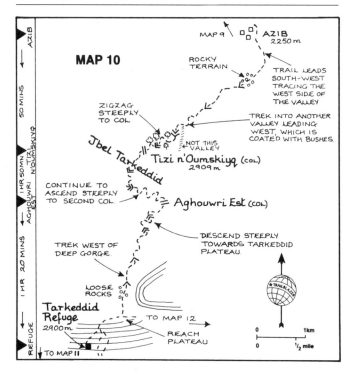

After crossing Aghouwri Est you have in fact traversed the Tarkeddid mountain which faces M'goun. The path then descends towards the Tarkeddid Plateau in tight zigzags in a generally south-south-westerly direction. Watch your footing. You will also see a deep gorge ahead of you; the trail actually leads to the right (west) of this.

The path continues to zigzag steeply downwards over loose rocks for 60 minutes before levelling out onto the plateau. After reaching the plateau look west where the refuge, in fair weather, is clearly visible. Walk across the flat, fertile plateau for 20 minutes in order to reach it.

The refuge is not the best; it is, in fact, little more than a dirty shell of a building. Since it can get very windy on the plateau, however, you might consider rigging up a tent inside the refuge if you plan to stay here. There are seldom more than a handful of other trekkers in the refuge. There are no facilities, except for a fireplace, and no supplies although, occasionally, you will find some astute local has loaded his mule with bottled water and sodas to sell on the plateau. There is a good water-source directly in front of the refuge, about 150 metres away. To me the Tarkeddid plateau is one of the finest sights in the Atlas mountains.

Tarkeddid Refuge—M'goun Summit—Tarkeddid Refuge [Map 11]
Poor weather can prevent trekkers from reaching the M'goun summit (4068m/13,343ft), the highest peak in the Atlas after Toubkal, even in summer. A bad day can often start out with calm weather and sunshine. If the weather is going to turn bad it often does so almost immediately after noon. The best advice, therefore, is to set out for the summit very early, perhaps 5am, in order to leave it by midday.

From the refuge walk east across the plateau towards its far bank and, five minutes later, take a path which clearly leads south up the bank at a right angle to the run of the plateau; there is another path, almost directly opposite the refuge, which seems to lead up between the largest two peaks visible from the plateau but don't take this path as it leads to a longer and less rewarding route.

The path on which you are trekking joins another then goes south-south-east. After 45 minutes the track levels out briefly before climbing again to the south-south-east towards an almost obscured col. You should expect to reach this small col some 20 minutes later. Then the path levels out again; it is at this stage fairly clear and easy to follow. Continue along the path as it zigzags steeply up the valley before again levelling out for an almost flat stretch that gives the impression of being a valley floor.

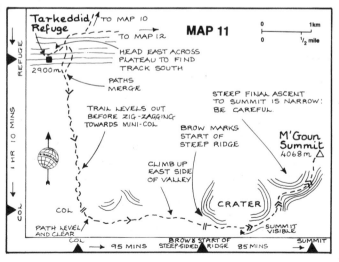

Keep going along this trail as it climbs gently but steadily for 50 minutes. At this point it quite suddenly starts to ascend very steeply as the path snakes up the east side of the enormous valley before reaching a false summit after another 20 minutes. The path here is distinct but loose-stoned and difficult; afterwards it becomes easier underfoot as it ascends more gently to the south-east.

Another 25 minutes will take you to a brow which also marks the start of a steep-sided ridge. Follow the top of the ridge, which at first leads south-east, around the rim of a massive crater. Be careful: the ridge is narrow and in high winds can be dangerous. The M'goun summit is clearly visible to the east as the ridge levels out after 15 minutes. There are magnificent views from here to the Anti-Atlas and the M'goun valley to the south.

Follow the ridge for a further 20 minutes when you'll begin a steep 20-minute climb to another brow. The ridge continues and the summit is still clearly visible, now to the north-east. This stretch of the trek is not for the faint-hearted; at some points the ridge is very narrow. Just 20 more minutes along it you come to a final steep section of ascent to the summit (4068m/13,343ft) which takes a further 10 minutes to reach. Follow the same route down for the descent and allow three hours.

Tarkeddid Refuge—Oulilimt Bivouac   [Map 12]
Setting out from the Tarkeddid refuge, head north-east across the plateau then east up the bush-covered incline at the far end. Climb over the bank and walk north-east around the edge of the huge Arouss gorge which, after crossing the bank, will appear to open up before you. Allow 15 minutes to reach this point from the refuge.

Continue to follow the south-east edge of the gorge until, 20 minutes later, you reach a steep zigzagged path which descends to the valley floor in which a stream, the Arouss, can be seen.

Climb down the zigzag path to reach the valley floor about 30 minutes later. Cross the stream and continue east to climb the bank up the other side. Just 10 minutes later the path leads into another section of flat-bottomed valley, also with a stream, which you should cross to climb north-east up the other side. From here the ascent is steep but the trail, despite snaking tightly, is quite easy to follow. Keep going up the path for 60 minutes in a generally easterly direction to reach the col, Tizi n'Oumsoud (2969m/9738ft). There are wonderful views from here into the wide Tinoughrine valley.

The trail, which remains distinct, then descends, steeply at first, to the north but quickly levels out to run east past a tiny azib on the right after 15 minutes. Rocks on either side of the path then form a narrow corridor for a short stretch before the path leads out onto the broad valley floor of the Oulilimt river. Continue trekking east enjoying easier terrain until, 35

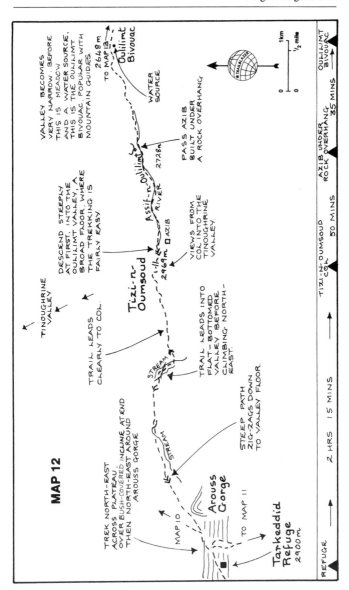

MAP 12

VALLEY BECOMES VERY NARROW, BEFORE THIS IS MEADOW AND A WATER SOURCE. THIS IS THE OULJIMT BIVOUAC, POPULAR WITH MOUNTAIN GUIDES.

2648 m
to MAP 13
Oulilimt Bivouac

WATER SOURCE

PASS AZIB BUILT UNDER A ROCK OVERHANG

2728m

Assif-n-Oulilimt RIVER

DESCEND STEEPLY AT FIRST, INTO THE OULIJIMT VALLEY, A BROAD FLOOR, WHERE THE TREKKING IS FAIRLY EASY.

TINOUGHRINE VALLEY

TRAIL LEADS CLEARLY TO COL.

Tizi-n-Oumsoud

2969m ☐ AZIB

VIEWS FROM COL INTO THE TINOUGHRINE VALLEY.

TRAIL LEADS INTO FLAT-BOTTOMED VALLEY BEFORE CLIMBING NORTH-EAST.

STREAM

STREAM

STEEP PATH ZIG-ZAGS DOWN TO VALLEY FLOOR.

TREK NORTH-EAST ACROSS PLATEAU, OVER BUSH-COVERED INCLINE AT END THEN NORTH-EAST AROUND AROUSS GORGE

MAP 10

Arouss Gorge

TO MAP 11

Tarkeddid Refuge 2900 m

0   1km
0   ½ mile

minutes later, you pass another small azib to the left. This azib has been built under a flat layer of overhanging rock which acts as a roof.

A further 35 minutes will take you to the point at which the valley suddenly grows very narrow, almost closing. Before this lies a wide, soft area of meadow at the centre of which springs a water-source. Although there is no shade, this is a great place to camp should you decide to stop here overnight; we've called it the Oulilimt bivouac because we've been unable to find a more specific name.

Oulilimt Bivouac—Refuge Aïn Aflafal [Map 13, opposite]

This short, attractive stage is easy to follow since it traces Oulilimt valley. Trek uphill from the valley floor on a path which leads left (east) of where the valley narrows. After 20 minutes, the path, having climbed briefly, goes down to a wide valley floor leading off at 90 degrees from the Oulilimt valley which, generally, the trail follows. Cross the wide valley and its stream to climb east back onto the side of the Oulilimt valley. The path ascends gently before levelling out after 10 minutes. Look out for a series of weird vertical rock formations around this area.

The trail then descends steeply in zigzags to arrive on the valley floor, heading east, after a further 15 minutes. Following the track and the stream some 20 minutes later you'll pass another azib built under a rock overhang. Some 20 minutes after that, the path climbs away from the valley to the east on its north side. The path leads away at 90 degrees from the Oulilimt river before continuing upwards very steeply for 40 minutes towards a low col.

After the col, the trail descends for 15 minutes in zigzags to another stream. Cross over and follow the stream east. The refuge Aïn Aflafal (2320m/7609ft), which sits between the river and a tributary, comes into view here and it takes just 20 more minutes to reach it.

Structurally, this refuge is identical to that of M'goun. Unlike the M'goun refuge, however, this one is clean and well-managed by a permanent gardien who also runs a small shop which sells essentials like canned food, matches and water. There are no other facilities, as such, since the refuge is little more than a shell of a building. Payment appears to be optional but offer 30dh per person.

Refuge Aïn Aflafal—Taghreft—Refuge Aïn Aflafal [Map 14, p156]

The refuge is a five-hour trek from Tabant. Before heading straight back to the Aït Bou Guemez valley, however, consider making a diversion east to the village of Taghreft. This is a pleasant and fairly easy trek which allows time to explore a series of relatively isolated Berber villages. The walking time from the refuge to Taghreft is two hours and thirty minutes so, if you decide to loop back to the refuge, allow five hours for walking. You should, in fact, allow a little more than five hours since, Berber hos-

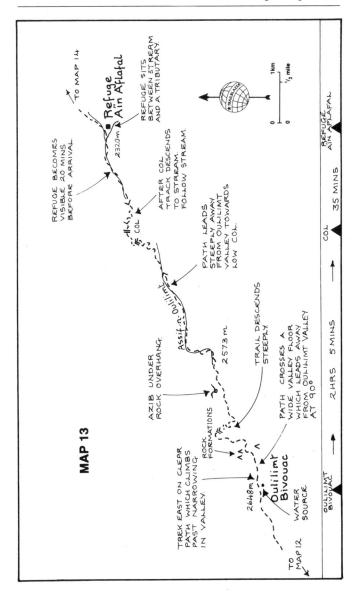

MAP 13

TREK EAST ON CLEAR PATH WHICH CLIMBS PAST NARROWING IN VALLEY.

ROCK FORMATIONS

AZIB UNDER ROCK OVERHANG.

2648m

Oulilimt Bivouac

WATER SOURCE

TO MAP 12

PATH CROSSES A WIDE VALLEY FLOOR WHICH LEADS AWAY FROM OULILIMT VALLEY AT 90°

TRAIL DESCENDS STEEPLY.

2573 m

Assif-n-Oulilimt

PATH LEADS STEEPLY AWAY FROM OULILIMT VALLEY TOWARDS LOW COL.

COL

AFTER COL TRACK DESCENDS TO STREAM. FOLLOW STREAM.

REFUGE BECOMES VISIBLE 20 MINS BEFORE ARRIVAL.

2320m

Refuge Aïn Aflafal

TO MAP 14

REFUGE SITS BETWEEN STREAM AND A TRIBUTARY.

1km
½ mile
0
0

OULILIMT BIVOUAC   2 HRS   5 MINS   COL   35 MINS   REFUGE AÏN AFLAFAL

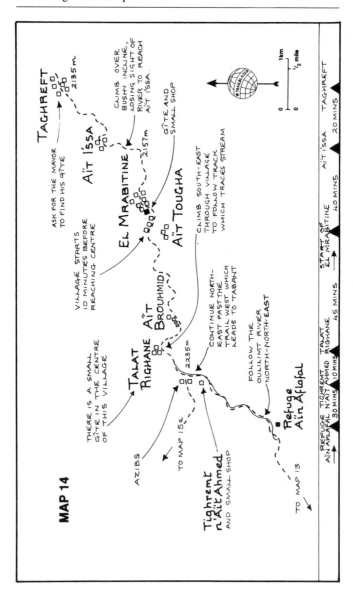

pitality being what it is, you will probably be invited to share tea once or twice along the way.

From the refuge, follow the river Oulilimt, which carves a route through the dominant valley in which the refuge sits, to the north-north-east. You might need sandals to follow this stretch of the river which, even in summer, could mean getting your feet wet. After tracing the river for 30 minutes look out for the Tighremt n'Aït Ahmed (2235m/7330ft), a bizarre, organic-looking dwelling which appears to have grown out of the floodplain. This giant sandcastle is no longer lived in but this is a popular camping area for trekkers and there is a small 'shop' nearby where the enterprising Mohammed Outfrit sells Cokes and so on.

Follow the valley to the north-west, past a route leading west towards Tabant, then north-east past some azibs on the left, and keep walking for 10 more minutes to get to the village of Talat Righane. There is a small *gîte d'étape* in the centre of the village which has cold showers, four large rooms with the usual mattresses and an attractive courtyard. The price is, as usual, 30dh per person. Ask for Aït Lehcen Brahim. The village itself looks out over neat and carefully-farmed fields which border the river as it wends its way out of sight to the south-east.

Climb down south-east through the village to follow the river in the same direction past the next village, Aït Brouhmid, which will take a further 20 minutes to reach. Shortly after Aït Brouhmid the trail zigzags steeply away from the river to the east. The path still parallels the river, only higher. Another 10 minutes will take you past a cluster of three dwellings, Aït Tougha, and, after 15 more minutes, to more buildings which mark the start of El Mrabitine. Walk for 10 minutes to find the village proper where Youss Aït Lehcen allows visitors to stay in his house for about 25dh per night. He can also whip up a pretty tasty tagine for a reasonable fee. There is a small shop next door.

Continue along the river until, after 15 minutes, the path climbs up and over a gentle bush-coated incline at which point you will lose sight of the river. Just 15 more minutes will take you to the village of Aït I'ssa and a further 20 minutes along the clear path is all it takes to reach the attractive, typically Berber village of Taghreft (2135m/7002ft).

Taghreft is a relatively large village with a population of about 800, and there is a *gîte d'étape* run by the mayor, Oligahouch Addi. It is sign-posted from the path but the signs stop a little short so you might need to ask around to find the right door. The gîte has cold showers and large shared rooms and the mayor is a great host. It also boasts a generator so is flooded with electric light long after the other locals have given up straining their eyes in candlelight.

As mayor of a fair-sized village, Oligahouch Addi also has a short-wave radio with which he could summon the helicopter from Marrakesh in an emergency.

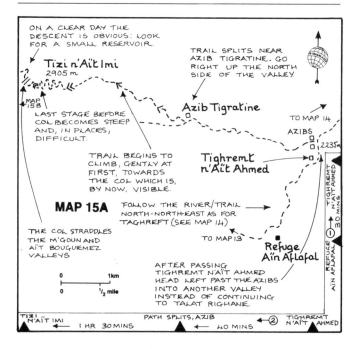

ON A CLEAR DAY THE DESCENT IS OBVIOUS: LOOK FOR A SMALL RESERVOIR.

TRAIL SPLITS NEAR AZIB TIGRATINE. GO RIGHT UP THE NORTH SIDE OF THE VALLEY.

Tizi n'Aït Imi
2905 m

MAP 15B

LAST STAGE BEFORE COL BECOMES STEEP AND, IN PLACES, DIFFICULT.

Azib Tigratine

TO MAP 14

AZIBS

2235 m

TRAIL BEGINS TO CLIMB, GENTLY AT FIRST, TOWARDS THE COL WHICH IS, BY NOW, VISIBLE.

Tighremt n'Aït Ahmed

MAP 15A

FOLLOW THE RIVER/TRAIL NORTH-NORTH-EAST AS FOR TAGHREFT (SEE MAP 14)

THE COL STRADDLES THE M'GOUN AND AÏT BOUGUEMEZ VALLEYS.

TO MAP 13

Refuge Aïn Aflafal

AFTER PASSING TIGHREMT N'AÏT AHMED HEAD LEFT PAST THE AZIBS INTO ANOTHER VALLEY INSTEAD OF CONTINUING TO TALAT RIGHANE.

0   1km
0   ½ mile

TIGHREMT N'AÏT AHMED 30 MINS

REFUGE AÏN AFLAFAL

TIZI N'AÏT IMI ← 1 HR 30 MINS

PATH SPLITS, AZIB ← 40 MINS ← ②

① TIGHREMT N'AÏT AHMED

Head back the same way to return to Refuge Aïn Aflafal; there is no quicker alternative route back to Tabant from Taghreft.

Refuge Aïn Aflafal—Tizi n'Aït Imi—Tabant [Maps 15a and 15b]

This varied stage includes a steep ascent to a 2905m/9528ft-high col and a long descent into the Aït Bou Guemez valley.

Follow the river north-north-east from the refuge, as for Taghreft, until, after 30 minutes, it leads to the strange Tighremt n'Aït Ahmed. At this point, instead of heading north-east towards Talat Righane, bear left (north-west) past the azibs into a smaller valley where the trail leads west. The col towards which you are trekking, Tizi n'Aït Imi, is clearly visible to the west.

Some 40 minutes later, at Azib Tigratine, the trail splits. Head right (north-north-west) up the fork which climbs the north side of the valley towards the col. The incline is at this stage fairly gentle. After about 15 minutes, the trail meanders more towards the north-west as it begins to zigzag more steeply. Continue to climb; it takes about 90 minutes to reach the col from where the path divides. Just before the col, the trail becomes very steep and quite difficult. When you finally reach Tizi n'Aït Imi

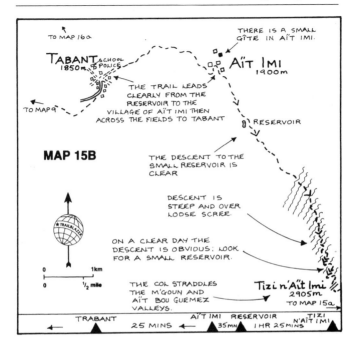

TO MAP 16a

THERE IS A SMALL GÎTE IN AÏT IMI.

TABANT 1850m SCHOOL POLICE

AÏT IMI 1900m

THE TRAIL LEADS CLEARLY FROM THE RESERVOIR TO THE VILLAGE OF AÏT IMI THEN ACROSS THE FIELDS TO TABANT

TO MAP 9

RESERVOIR

MAP 15B

THE DESCENT TO THE SMALL RESERVOIR IS CLEAR

DESCENT IS STEEP AND OVER LOOSE SCREE.

ON A CLEAR DAY THE DESCENT IS OBVIOUS; LOOK FOR A SMALL RESERVOIR.

★TRAILBLAZER

0   1km
0   ½ mile

THE COL STRADDLES THE M'GOUN AND AÏT BOU GUEMEZ VALLEYS.

Tizi n'Aït Imi 2905m
TO MAP 15a

TRABANT ← 25 MINS ← AÏT IMI 35mn RESERVOIR 1 HR 25 MINS TIZI N'AÏT IMI

(2905m/9528ft) you will see that from this great height you can look across both the M'goun and Aït Bou Guemez valleys. The views from here are exceptional and serve to illustrate the differences between them; Aït Bou Guemez seems far more fertile than M'goun. One can even make out Tabant, the goal, from here on a particularly clear day; then the descent is obvious.

If you can't make out Tabant itself, look for a small reservoir on the valley floor which is easy to see. Reach it by descending steeply straight down the mountainside. The terrain is loose scree, making it rather difficult but at least the route is clear. Allow 85 minutes to trek from the col to the reservoir.

From the reservoir, head north-north-west towards the bright, fertile valley floor in which Tabant sits. Some 35 more minutes will take you to the village of Aït Imi (1900m/6232ft) which spreads from some way into the valley. There is a *gîte d'étape* here, run by Imeghre Ahmed. Keep heading towards Tabant, which can be seen clearly now, across the cultivated fields of the Aït Bou Guemez valley. Expect to reach Tabant (1850m/6068ft) 25 minutes after leaving Aït Imi.

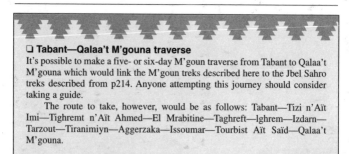

❏ **Tabant—Qalaa't M'gouna traverse**

It's possible to make a five- or six-day M'goun traverse from Tabant to Qalaa't M'gouna which would link the M'goun treks described here to the Jbel Sahro treks described from p214. Anyone attempting this journey should consider taking a guide.

The route to take, however, would be as follows: Tabant—Tizi n'Aït Imi—Tighremt n'Aït Ahmed—El Mrabitine—Taghreft—Ighrem—Izdarn—Tarzout—Tiranimiyn—Aggerzaka—Issoumar—Tourbist Aït Saïd—Qalaa't M'gouna.

M'GOUN TRAVERSE

Tabant—Agouti—Taghia—Abachkou
[Maps 16a and 16b, p162 and p163]

This is a long stage but the trekking is easy. Walk west from Tabant (1850m/6068ft) on the Azilal road. After 10 minutes, head south-west on a piste which leads across the cultivated valley floor to Sidi Moussa (see box opposite) which should take a further five minutes to reach. Carry on past Sidi Moussa to cross to the far side of the valley floor from Tabant where after another five minutes a path leads south-west back onto the Azilal road towards the village of Timit. Reach Timit after just a couple more minutes and continue along the trail through the village for 45 minutes to the next hamlet, Aït Ziri, where there are two *gîtes*. The piste at this stage is clear.

A further 25 minutes snaking gently south-west will take you to Talsnant (1952m/6402ft). There's a *gîte d'étape* in the centre of the village. Ask for the proprietor, Boukhayou Mohammed, to find it. Unlike most gîtes in this area, Mohammed's has hot showers.

Mohammed himself is something of a legend in the valley. He was caught in extreme weather on M'goun with clients who refused to follow his advice and descend. The helicopter had to be called but it was too late for one trekker. Such tragedies are rare in the Atlas but serve to highlight the importance of trusting local guides who know the area and are weatherwise. There is another *gîte* just five minutes further on in the adjacent village of Takhida. This one is owned by Jellou Brahim and his French

---

(Opposite) Top: Tighremt n'Aït Ahmed, (see p157). **Bottom:** En route to Taghreft see p157. (Photos © Richard Knight).

❑ Sidi Moussa

The Sidi Moussa agadir sits at 2008m/6583ft atop a perfectly pyramid-shaped hill north-west of Tabant. It can be seen for miles around and so is a straight-forward trek from Tabant. The views alone make it time well spent. An agadir is a traditional Berber granary fortified and used to hide food, animals and even people in times of tribal war.

The Sidi Moussa agadir is an excellent example; it is still visited and was partially restored between 1993 and 1996. This agadir is also a marabout, or tomb, devoted to the holy man Sidi Moussa. Local girls are taught to pray here for a husband, marriage and children. There is a ritual, occasionally still prac-tised, which requires a young girl to sleep outside the agadir on a Thursday night and then to kill and eat a cockerel. Other myths include one that claims mad people should be brought to the agadir in chains and left for three nights after which time they will be sane again.

Inside, the agadir follows the traditional format. There are store rooms and sleeping quarters for each family in the tribe, space for animals, a mill-stone, kitchen area and prayer mats. There are more rooms upstairs and four towers, one at each corner, for defence.

Tradition has it that visitors should make a pot of mint tea to leave for sub-sequent callers; you will always find some waiting for you but, since people climb up to Sidi Moussa less often these days, it might not be a very good idea to drink it.

wife. It is a friendly place with much better facilities than most gîtes including hot showers.

Continue on the distinct piste in a south-south-westerly direction to the village of Agouti which will take a further 20 minutes to reach. The *gîte* here, not quite so impressive, is run by Aït Ben Ali Mohammed. After Agouti the piste continues to wind west-south-west; it's very simple to follow and the terrain is largely flat and easy.

After an hour and 40 minutes of this, pass the village of Tighza (1819m/5966ft) to the south. The piste splits just 10 minutes later. Go left (west) remaining on a piste. Then, 20 minutes later, turn left (west) down a track which leads from the piste. A little further on, the piste will lead north towards Azilal but another branch will continue to trace the valley south-west. You will rejoin the piste later so taking this left turn is no more than a short cut. Simply stay on the piste if you would prefer but don't

---

Top: Lunch stop, M'goun Region. **Bottom:** The Berber village of Megdaz, see p170. (Photos © Richard Knight).

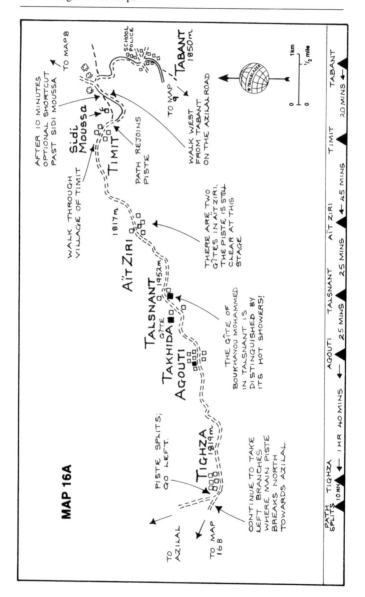

MAP 16A

TO MAP 8

AFTER 10 MINUTES
OPTIONAL SHORTCUT
PAST SIDI MOUSSA

SCHOOL
POLICE

TABANT
1850m.

1 km
½ mile

Sidi Moussa

WALK THROUGH
VILLAGE OF TIMIT

TIMIT

PATH REJOINS
PISTE

TO MAP 9

WALK WEST
FROM TABANT
ON THE AZILAL ROAD

AÏT ZIRI

1817m.

THERE ARE TWO
GÎTES IN AÏT ZIRI.
THE PISTE IS STILL
CLEAR AT THIS
STAGE.

1952m.

TALSNANT
Gîte

TAKHIDA

AGOUTI

THE GÎTE OF
BOUKHAYOU MOHAMMED
IN TALSNANT IS
DISTINGUISHED BY
ITS HOT SHOWERS!

PISTE SPLITS;
GO LEFT.

TIGHZA
1819m.

TO
AZILAL

TO MAP
16B

CONTINUE TO TAKE
LEFT BRANCHES
WHERE MAIN PISTE
BREAKS NORTH
TOWARDS AZILAL.

PATH SPLITS	◄	AGOUTI	◄	TALSNANT	◄	AÏT ZIRI	◄	TIMIT	◄	TABANT
TIGHZA 10 MIN	1 HR 40 MINS		25 MINS		25 MINS		45 MINS		20 MINS	

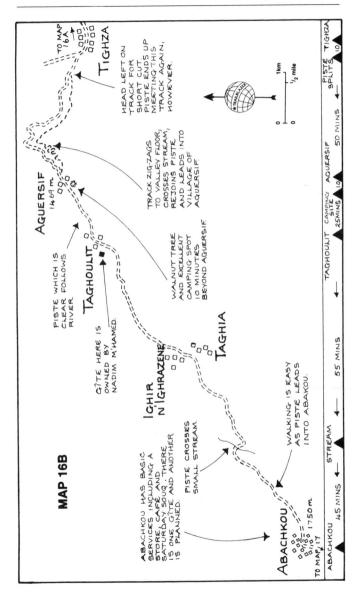

MAP 16B

ABACHKOU HAS BASIC SERVICES INCLUDING A STORE, CAFÉ AND SATURDAY SOUQ. THERE IS ONE GÎTE AND ANOTHER IS PLANNED.

ABACHKOU 1750 m.

PISTE CROSSES SMALL STREAM.

WALKING IS EASY AS PISTE LEADS INTO ABAKOU.

IGHIR N'IGHRAZENE

GÎTE HERE IS OWNED BY NADIM M'HAMED.

TAGHOULIT

PISTE WHICH IS CLEAR FOLLOWS RIVER.

TAGHIA

WALNUT TREE AND EXCELLENT CAMPING SPOT 10 MINUTES BEYOND AGUERSIF.

AGUERSIF 1469 m.

TRACK ZIG-ZAGS TO VALLEY FLOOR, CROSSES STREAM, REJOINS PISTE AND LEADS INTO VILLAGE OF AGUERSIF.

TIGHZA

HEAD LEFT ON TRACK FOR SHORT CUT. PISTE ENDS UP MEETING THIS TRACK AGAIN, HOWEVER.

TO MAP 16A

TO MAP 17

0   1km
0   ½ mile

ABACHKOU	STREAM	IGHIR N'IGHRAZENE	TAGHOULIT	CAMPING SITE	AGUERSIF	PISTE SPLITS	TIGHZA
45 MINS	55 MINS	55 MINS	25 MINS	10 MINS	50 MINS	10	

head north towards Azilal. The track zigzags, steeply at times, towards the valley floor. Watch your footing; the rocks here are loose.

Rejoin the piste 25 minutes later. Five minutes after that, the piste fords a stream and leads into the tiny village of Aguersif (1469m/4818ft). There is an excellent area for camping under some walnut trees by the stream some 10 minutes out of Aguersif. Don't forget always to ask permission before camping near a village. The piste follows the road and river to lead south-west into the next village, Taghoulit (1519m/4982ft), after a further 25 minutes. The *gîte* here is owned by Nadim M'hamed.

Keep going along the piste, making navigation simple, to trek past the villages of Ighir n'Ighrazene to the right and Taghia almost opposite to the left. After 55 minutes the piste will cross a gentle stream and a further 45 minutes of easy walking will take you into the larger village of Abachkou (1750m/5740ft). Abachkou has some services including a general store, a café and a Saturday souq. There is one basic *gîte*. It's the penultimate house in the village. Ask for Aït Benkoum Mohammed, the owner, who will show you to it. Another gîte is apparently being built by Tazazaout Mohammed. Call him on ☎ 03-45.93.19 to see whether it's ready yet. Otherwise, if you decide to break your trek in Abachkou, walk through the village to find a place to camp on the far side. Camping isn't great here but there are a few reasonable pitches if you hunt around.

Abachkou—Ghougoult—Ifira [Map 17]

Walk through Abachkou (1750m/5740ft) past the café and look for a trail which leads south-east towards the stream on the valley floor. Follow this path which, having reached the valley floor, doubles back to lead east past Abachkou. After five minutes, cross the stream to follow a path which zigzags up the opposite side of the valley to reach a wider path, easy to find, which leads under some trees.

About 30 minutes into the trek, the trail will lead past the village of Tazegzaout (1951m/6399ft), which sits on both sides of the valley, before swinging south. The trail remains distinct and relatively easy to follow; keep going for another 45 minutes at which point you will see an excellent camping area by an azib to the right of the path.

About 25 minutes later (or 70 minutes after Tazegzaout) the path splits. Take the higher route which leads south. Soon you will see the grey stone village of Aït Mallal, not marked on the 1:100,000 Azilal map, in the distance to the west. Continuing straight ahead after 20 minutes look out for the village of Ghougoult (1858m/6094ft). Just 10 minutes after this the trail leads through the village.

Climb south-south-west through the village as the path crosses to the other side of the valley. Follow the stream west, then west-south-west through the n'Doughour gorge as the valley in which Ghougoult sits leads away to the east. Keep following the gorge, which is easily traced, for one

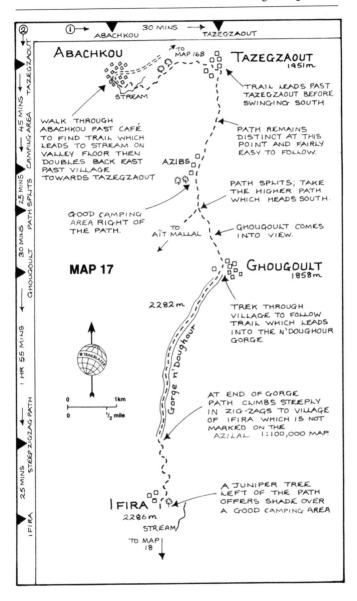

② ← TAZEGZAOUT ← 45 MINS CAMPING AREA ← 25 MINS PATH SPLITS ← 30 MINS GHOUGOULT ← 1 HR 55 MINS ← 25 MINS STEEP ZIGZAG PATH ← IFIRA

① → 30 MINS → TAZEGZAOUT
ABACHKOU

ABACHKOU

TO MAP 16B

TAZEGZAOUT
1951m

STREAM

TRAIL LEADS PAST TAZEGZAOUT BEFORE SWINGING SOUTH

WALK THROUGH ABACHKOU PAST CAFÉ TO FIND TRAIL WHICH LEADS TO STREAM ON VALLEY FLOOR THEN DOUBLES BACK EAST PAST VILLAGE TOWARDS TAZEGZAOUT

PATH REMAINS DISTINCT AT THIS POINT AND FAIRLY EASY TO FOLLOW.

AZIBS

PATH SPLITS; TAKE THE HIGHER PATH WHICH HEADS SOUTH.

GOOD CAMPING AREA RIGHT OF THE PATH.

TO AÏT MALLAL

GHOUGOULT COMES INTO VIEW.

MAP 17

GHOUGOULT
1858m

2282m

TREK THROUGH VILLAGE TO FOLLOW TRAIL WHICH LEADS INTO THE N'DOUGHOUR GORGE.

Gorge n'Doughour

★TRAILBLAZER

0   1km
0   ½ mile

AT END OF GORGE PATH CLIMBS STEEPLY IN ZIG-ZAGS TO VILLAGE OF IFIRA WHICH IS NOT MARKED ON THE AZILAL 1:100,000 MAP.

A JUNIPER TREE LEFT OF THE PATH OFFERS SHADE OVER A GOOD CAMPING AREA

IFIRA
2286m

STREAM

TO MAP 18

hour and 55 minutes. At this point, the trail starts to zigzag steeply to the right (south-west) away from the stream to the tiny village of Ifira (2286m/7498ft), 25 minutes further on. Ifira, too, is not named on the 1:100,000 Azilal map although one or two buildings are depicted in the right place just west of Jbel Tarkeddid.

There is a juniper tree to the left of the village, really just three buildings, under which there is a good camping area. If you do decide to stay here overnight, there is no alternative but to camp. So few travellers do stop that the handful of local children will form a semi-circle around your camp and stare at you non-stop until you leave. They are harmless if a touch disconcerting. There is a stream 10 minutes away, downhill to the east, in which one can wash; remember to throw used water well away from the stream. The most important feature of Ifira is the view across to Jbel Tarkeddid; watch the colours of the mountain change as the sun sets.

Ifira—Amerzi [Map 18]

The path from Ifira (2286m/7498ft) is difficult to make out but travel south through the village, then walk down to a stream, which can clearly be seen from this point. Expect to reach the stream 10 minutes after setting off. Follow the stream south for 30 minutes at which stage the trail climbs steeply to the south-east. Climb with it continuing in the same direction as the stream and its ravine, only higher. Some 20 minutes later the ravine quite suddenly widens out to reveal a gentle, sweeping valley. There's a tempting, grassy area 10 minutes further on, which would be ideal for camping; better, perhaps, than Ifira.

Keep ascending with the trail as it gets gradually steeper and the zigzags grow sharper. After a further 75 minutes of this the track leads onto a wide col, Tizi n'Rouguelt (2860m/9380ft), at the same time as another, higher path meets yours. Minutes later the track splits. The left (east) branch leads to the village of Tassawt n'Oufella and the Tarkeddid plateau. Ignore it. Take the right (south-west) branch which descends for 75 minutes along the west side of the valley to the village of Tasgaïwalt. After Tasgaïwalt the track zigzags steeply for about 10 minutes before snaking past a handful of buildings. After these, the trail leads onto a wider track, almost a piste, which runs for 45 minutes into Amerzi (2250m/7380ft).

If you plan to rest a night here, walk into the village and cross the stream to find a good camping spot away from its centre. There is a stream and shade here but, as in Ifira, trekkers will be a source of great amusement to the local kids. There are three small shops selling water, Cokes, matches and so on.

Follow the piste through the village then turn right just before the stream to find the only *gîte d'étape* in Amerzi. Otherwise ask for Aguemed Mohammed. Unfortunately, it's a damp, oppressive place with

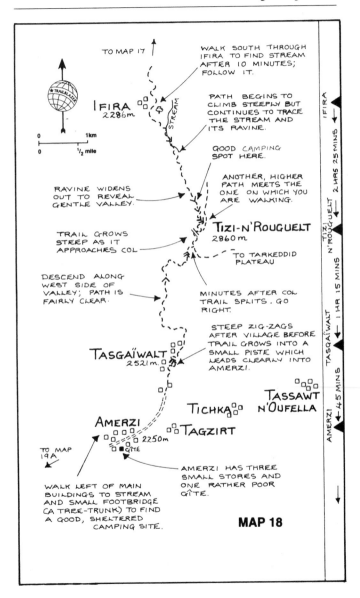

TO MAP 17

WALK SOUTH THROUGH
IFIRA TO FIND STREAM
AFTER 10 MINUTES;
FOLLOW IT.

IFIRA
2286m

STREAM

PATH BEGINS TO
CLIMB STEEPLY BUT
CONTINUES TO TRACE
THE STREAM AND
ITS RAVINE.

0   1km
0   ½ mile

GOOD CAMPING
SPOT HERE.

ANOTHER, HIGHER
PATH MEETS THE
ONE ON WHICH YOU
ARE WALKING.

RAVINE WIDENS
OUT TO REVEAL
GENTLE VALLEY.

TIZI-N'ROUGUELT
2860m

TRAIL GROWS
STEEP AS IT
APPROACHES COL

TO TARKEDDID
PLATEAU

DESCEND ALONG
WEST SIDE OF
VALLEY; PATH IS
FAIRLY CLEAR.

MINUTES AFTER COL
TRAIL SPLITS. GO
RIGHT.

STEEP ZIG-ZAGS
AFTER VILLAGE BEFORE
TRAIL GROWS INTO A
SMALL PISTE WHICH
LEADS CLEARLY INTO
AMERZI.

TASGAÏWALT
2521m.

TASSAWT
N'OUFELLA

TICHKA

AMERZI
2250m
TAGZIRT

TO MAP
19A

GÎTE

AMERZI HAS THREE
SMALL STORES AND
ONE RATHER POOR
GÎTE.

WALK LEFT OF MAIN
BUILDINGS TO STREAM
AND SMALL FOOTBRIDGE
(A TREE-TRUNK) TO FIND
A GOOD, SHELTERED
CAMPING SITE.

MAP 18

IFIRA

2 HRS 25 MINS

TIZI N'ROUGUELT

1 HR 15 MINS

TASGAÏWALT

45 MINS

AMERZI

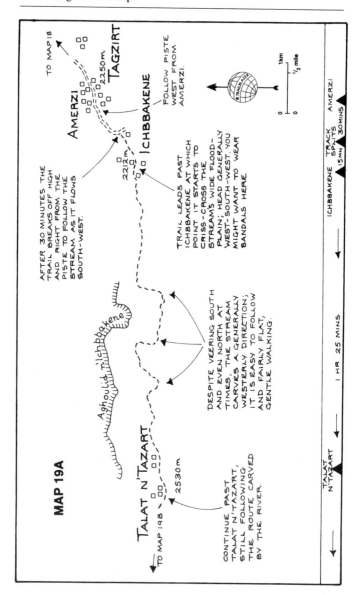

MAP 19A

TAGZIRT

AMERZI

2250m

TO MAP 18

FOLLOW PISTE WEST FROM AMERZI.

ICHBBAKENE

22/2m

AFTER 30 MINUTES THE TRAIL BREAKS OFF HIGH AND RIGHT FROM THE PISTE TO FOLLOW THE STREAM AS IT FLOWS SOUTH-WEST.

TRAIL LEADS PAST ICHBBAKENE AT WHICH POINT IT STARTS TO CRISS-CROSS THE STREAM'S WIDE FLOOD-PLAIN; HEAD GENERALLY WEST-SOUTH-WEST. YOU MIGHT WANT TO WEAR SANDALS HERE.

Aghoulid n'Ichbbakene

DESPITE VEERING SOUTH AND EVEN NORTH AT TIMES, THE STREAM CARVES A GENERALLY WESTERLY DIRECTION; IT IS EASY TO FOLLOW AND FAIRLY FLAT, GENTLE WALKING.

TALAT N'TAZART

2530m

TO MAP 19B

CONTINUE PAST TALAT N'TAZART, STILL FOLLOWING THE ROUTE CARVED BY THE RIVER.

1km
½ mile

0
0

TALAT N'TAZART — 1 HR 25 MINS — TRACK SPLITS — ICHBBAKENE — 15 MINS — 30 MINS — AMERZI

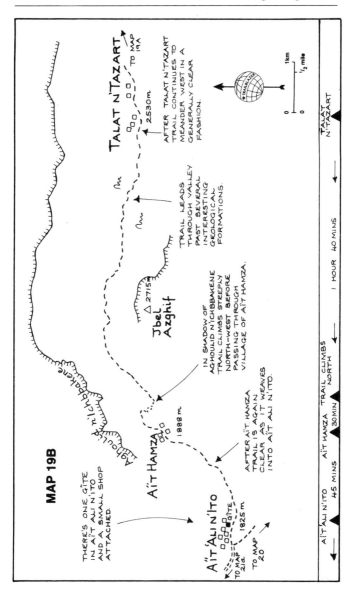

MAP 19B

THERE'S ONE GÎTE IN AÏT ALI N'ITO AND A SMALL SHOP ATTACHED.

Aghouid Nichbbakene

AÏT HAMZA
1888 m.

AÏT ALI N'ITO
1825 m.
GÎTE

TO MAP 21a
TO MAP 20

AFTER AÏT HAMZA TRAIL IS AGAIN CLEAR AS IT WEAVES INTO AÏT ALI N'ITO.

IN SHADOW OF AGHOUID NICHBBAKENE TRAIL CLIMBS STEEPLY NORTH-WEST BEFORE PASSING THROUGH VILLAGE OF AÏT HAMZA.

△ 2715 m
Jbel Azghif

TRAIL LEADS THROUGH VALLEY PAST SEVERAL INTERESTING GEOLOGICAL FORMATIONS.

TALAT N'TAZART

TO MAP 19A

2530 m

AFTER TALAT N'TAZART TRAIL CONTINUES TO MEANDER WEST IN A GENERALLY CLEAR FASHION.

TRAILBLAZE

0   1km
0   ½ mile

AÏT ALI N'ITO   AÏT HAMZA   TRAIL CLIMBS NORTH   TALAT N'TAZART
◄ 45 MINS ◄   ◄ 30MIN ◄   ◄ 1 HOUR 40 MINS ◄

only one decent room (back right) so, if you decide to stay the night in Amerzi, you are probably better off camping.

Amerzi—Aït Hamza—Aït Ali n'Ito
[Maps 19a and 19b, p168 and p169]

This stage of the traverse is fairly long, over five hours, but relatively easy both in terms of terrain and navigation. There are no demanding climbs or descents and the path is clear. That said, this is by no means a dull trek; there are fantastic views in all directions almost all the way. You will need to cross water several times so might want to keep a pair of sandals handy to avoid getting your boots wet.

Follow a wide path straight out of Amerzi to the west. After 30 minutes it will break off high and right to follow the stream as it flows south-west. Another 10 minutes will lead you down onto a wide, stony flood-plain which, again, continues to meander generally south-west.

Keep following the valley floor, past the village of Ichbbakene (2212m/7255ft), crossing and re-crossing from one side of the floodplain to the other to negotiate the many streams and rivulets which trace complicated paths across the valley floor. The valley leads briefly south before heading west again. Follow it and you can't go wrong.

Pass another village, Talat n'Tazart some two hours 10 minutes after setting out from Amerzi; the trail leads slightly further to the north before heading west again. You will then start another long slog along the valley floor. Weird rock formations punctuate the sensational surroundings and since there are few useful reference points from which to confirm your position, navigating your route adds to the interest. Keep going until, approximately 100 minutes after Talat n'Tazart, still nestling under the giant Aghoulid n'Ichbbakene ridge, the trail leads steeply right (north-west) up the side of the valley.

Stick with this trail as it makes its ascent until, 30 minutes later, it passes the village of Aït Hamza (1888m/6192ft). Aït Hamza, stacked neatly against the valley side, is exceptionally pretty. Keep going for another 45 minutes to reach the hamlet of Aït 'Ali n'Ito (1825m/6074ft). There is one *gîte d'étape* here, run by a rather unhelpful character called Bourchouk Abdellah, which has adequate shared rooms and a shower which occasionally runs hot. There is also a small shop attached and, I'm told, a telephone although I could find no evidence of it.

A motor road of sorts leads from Aït 'Ali n'Ito to Aït Tamlil. So transport, usually by camion, is irregularly available from here to Aït Tamlil from where one can get away to Azilal. Aït 'Ali n'Ito has a Saturday souq so Sunday is the best day to look for transport.

Aït Ali n'Ito—Megdaz—Aït Ali n'Ito   [Map 20, p171]

It would be a great shame to miss this short diversion from Aït 'Ali n'Ito. Megdaz is one of the most attractive Berber villages in the entire Atlas

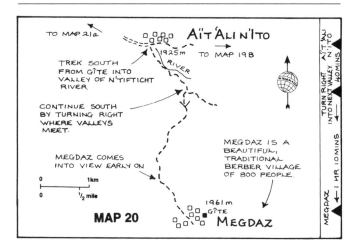

MAP 20

range. The trek to Megdaz takes a little under two hours so allow four hours to loop back to Aït 'Ali n'Ito. It is possible to make a longer, circular route from this diversion by trekking from Megdaz south, then west to Tagoukht, then north to Tasselnt and on to Ifoulou where one can pick up the trail to Aït Tamlil. This would be a full day's trek.

To get from Aït 'Ali n'Ito to Megdaz, however, trek south from the gîte d'étape into the valley of the n'Tifticht river which leads away at 90 degrees from the valley leading into Aït 'Ali n'Ito from the north-east. Some 40 minutes later, turn right (south-west) into another valley in which the trail begins to climb. The path is very distinct not least thanks to the mule dung which lines the way. This is a relatively busy route and you will no doubt pass a number of Berbers on donkeys journeying between Megdaz and Aït 'Ali n'Ito.

Megdaz itself will come into view 60 minutes later and, after trekking for just 10 more minutes, you will reach the first of its buildings. This is a large village of about 800 people with stout, square buildings stacked up against one another. Some of these mud mansions are up to 450 years old. Residents have to climb over each other's homes in order to reach their own front doors. The pale brown material used to build the village fades into the mountainside making the whole place look completely organic. It is quite a sight and a perfect example of traditional Berber architecture.

There is one enormous house in the centre of the village which stands out from the rest. It's almost a self-contained village for one extended family. Guests can stay here for about 25dh; there's a small unclassified *gîte* next door. The owner of this place, Hasou Nasser, is also the mayor.

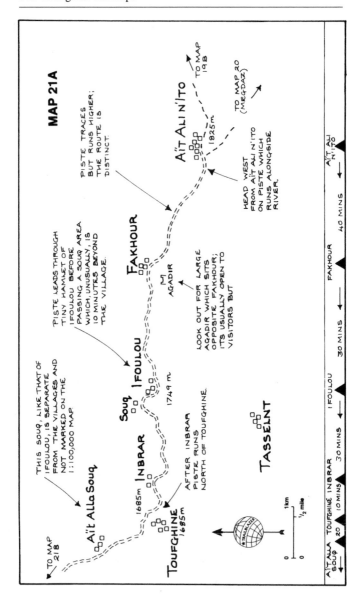

MAP 21A

TO MAP 19B

TO MAP 20 (MEG-DAZ)

AÏT ALI N'ITO

1825m

PISTE TRACES BUT RUNS HIGHER; THE ROUTE IS DISTINCT.

HEAD WEST FROM AÏT ALI N'ITO ON PISTE WHICH RUNS ALONGSIDE RIVER.

PISTE LEADS THROUGH TINY HAMLET OF IFOULOU BEFORE PASSING A SOUQ AREA WHICH, UNUSUALLY, IS 10 MINUTES BEYOND THE VILLAGE.

FAKHOUR

AGADIR

LOOK OUT FOR LARGE AGADIR WHICH SITS OPPOSITE FAKHOUR; ITS USUALLY OPEN TO VISITORS BUT

Souq IFOULOU

1749 m

THIS SOUQ, LIKE THAT OF IFOULOU, IS SEPARATE FROM THE VILLAGES AND NOT MARKED ON THE 1:100,000 MAP

INBRAR
1685m

AFTER INBRAR PISTE RUNS NORTH OF TOUFGHINE.

TASSELNT

AÏT ALLA Souq

TO MAP 21B

TOUFGHINE
1685m

1km
½ mile

0

0

*TRAILBLAZER

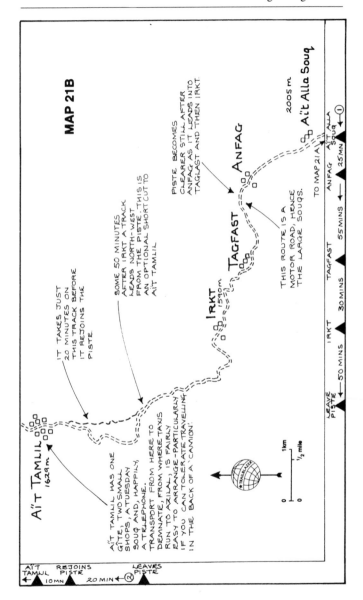

MAP 21B

Aït Alla Souq

2005 m

ANFAG

TAGFAST

IRKT
1590m

Aït TAMLIL
1629m

PISTE BECOMES CLEARER STILL AFTER ANFAG AS IT LEADS INTO TAGLAST AND THEN IRKT.

SOME 50 MINUTES AFTER IRKT A TRACK LEADS NORTH-WEST FROM THE PISTE. THIS IS AN OPTIONAL SHORT CUT TO AÏT TAMLIL

IT TAKES JUST 20 MINUTES ON THIS TRACK BEFORE IT REJOINS THE PISTE.

THIS ROUTE IS A MOTOR ROAD, HENCE THE LARGE SOUQS.

AÏT TAMLIL HAS ONE GÎTE, TWO SMALL SHOPS, A TUESDAY SOUQ AND, HAPPILY, A TELEPHONE. TRANSPORT FROM HERE TO DEMNATE, FROM WHERE TAXIS RUN TO AZILAL, IS FAIRLY EASY TO ARRANGE – PARTICULARLY IF YOU CAN TOLERATE TRAVELLING IN THE BACK OF A 'CAMION'.

TO MAP 21A

0   1km
0   ½ mile

AÏT ALLA SOUQ ①

ANFAG ◀— 25MN

TAGFAST ◀— 55 MINS

IRKT ◀— 30 MINS

LEAVE PISTE ◀— 50 MINS

AÏT TAMLIL ◀— 10 MN

REJOINS PISTE ◀— 20 MIN ② ◀—

LEAVES PISTE

The people of Megdaz are particularly friendly and welcoming; they are used to visitors but haven't changed the village to accommodate tourism. Five small shops dispense the usual essentials like toothpaste and water. Unless you plan to make the long loop round to Ifoulou, there is little alternative but to re-trace your steps back to Aït 'Ali n'Ito.

Aït Ali n'Ito—Aït Tamlil [Maps 21a and 21b, p172-3]

This long stage is, again, easily navigated; the trail follows the Tessaout valley almost all the way from Aït 'Ali n'Ito to Aït Tamlil. Set out from Aït 'Ali n'Ito on the piste which heads west parallel with the river. The trail leads higher than the river but keep tracing the valley for 40 minutes to the village of Fakhour which huddles on its north side. Opposite the valley stands an agadir. Trekkers can normally look round the inside of this large building but, at the time of writing, the stairs inside were in need of repair and the agadir was locked.

Some 15 minutes later the track swings sharply left to pursue the valley. Another 15 minutes will take you to the few buildings which form the village of Ifoulou (1749m/5736ft). As the path starts to ascend, keep going for 10 minutes, to trek past a purpose-built souq area. The Ifoulou souq is held every Monday.

The next village, Inbrar, will take 30 minutes to reach from Ifoulou and, beyond that, the trail passes to the north of Toufghine (1685m/5527ft) after a further 10 minutes. The souq of Aït Alla, which takes place every Monday, is 20 minutes past Toufghine on the right (north) side of the valley. The souq is not marked on the 1:100,000 Skoura map. The village of Anfag is 25 minutes beyond the souq. The path is very distinct for this whole stage which makes navigating straightforward.

Another 55 minutes and the piste, which grows wider and more distinct as it progresses west, leads through Tagfast and, 30 minutes after that, Irkt (1590m/5215ft). Look out for a steeper but smaller path which leads north-west from the piste some 50 minutes after Irkt. Follow it for 20 minutes after which the narrow track rejoins the wider piste for the final 10-minute walk into the Aït Tamlil (1629m/5343ft).

Aït Tamlil has one *gîte d'étape*, that of Ben Kezza ben Mohammed, and a two small shops. There is a souq on Tuesdays and a telephone. Aït Tamlil was, at the time of writing, home to a US Peace Corps project. Transport is available from here to Imi n'Ifri, where a bizarre natural bridge carries the road over a stream, and from Imi n'Ifri to Demnate. From Demnate, transport is available to Azilal. You might need to rely on a camion to get from Aït Tamlil to Imi n'ifri at which point there is a minibus service to Demnate. There are grands taxis at Demnate as well as three cheap hotels, téléboutiques, cafés, shops and an interesting kasbah.

The Sirwa region

Isolated and magnificent, Jbel Sirwa (3305m/10,840ft) offers some of the most exciting trekking in the Atlas mountains. The brooding, volcanic summit can be seen for many miles around and the trek to it is both varied and challenging. Sirwa bridges the High and Anti-Atlas ranges. Its peak is capped with snow almost all year round. The Berbers of this strange, charged landscape see fewer trekkers than those of Toubkal or Sahro. This remoteness makes trekking here difficult; paths can be hard to find and few locals speak English or even French. For this reason, the notes given here are particularly detailed. The circuit described here is a wide, circular route around the Sirwa region taking in the summit and some of the most fascinating villages and gorges found anywhere in the Atlas mountains.

TALIOUINE (984m/3227ft)

The sun-scorched village of Taliouine, surrounded by almond trees and overshadowed by a giant Berber kasbah, makes a great opening to the Jbel Sirwa trek. This is the main trailhead for reaching Jbel Sirwa and the last stop for supplies.

Since relatively few trekkers explore this harshly spectacular region Taliouine itself is not particularly geared to trekking, although some guides and muleteers do live here. However, you will find fresh supplies of fruit and vegetables and a reasonable range of other everyday goods; but it's probably better to stock up on essential gear and stores in Marrakesh or Ouarzazate where supplies are greater and prices lower.

The striking but collapsing kasbah is still lived in by Berber families, most of whom are descended from servants of past Berber leaders, and you will almost certainly find someone willing to show you round if you ask politely and appear interested.

Services

There's a Shell **garage** in the centre of the village with some **public toilets** opposite. Walking east from here along the main street will take you to the **Saffron Co-operative** (Taliouine is an important producer of saffron) and, just past the turning for the kasbah, a **téléboutique**. Heading west from the Shell garage along the main street will take you to a **vegetable market**, the **souq municipale** and the **Crédit Agricole bank**. You can **change money** here or at **Hôtel Ibn Toumert**. The bank doesn't change travellers' cheques and the hotel charges extortionate rates. Turn

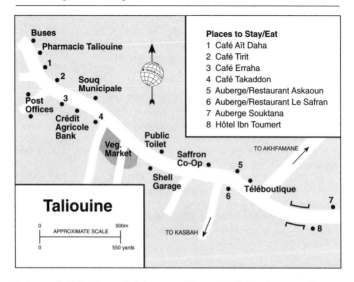

Buses
Pharmacie Taliouine

● 1
● 2   **Souq**
       Municipale
Post
Offices
● 3
  Crédit   ● 4
  Agricole
  Bank
       Veg.   **Public**
       Market   **Toilet**
                     ● **Saffron**
                        Co-Op ●   ● 5
                 Shell
                 Garage
                           ● 6   **Téléboutique**

Places to Stay/Eat
1 Café Aït Daha
2 Café Tirit
3 Café Erraha
4 Café Takaddon
5 Auberge/Restaurant Askaoun
6 Auberge/Restaurant Le Safran
7 Auberge Souktana
8 Hôtel Ibn Toumert

TO AKHFAMANE

                                         ● 7

                                      ● 8

Taliouine

0   500m
|———————————|
APPROXIMATE SCALE

0   550 yards
|———————————|

TO KASBAH

TO AKHFAMANE

left past Café Erraha to find the **post office** on the left and a **general store** on the right. Continue west on the main road to find a **pharmacy** on the right and, just a little further on, the main bus stop. A **souq** is held behind the kasbah every Monday.

Where to stay
Auberge Souktana (☎ 08-53.40.75; 🖹 08-23.14.11), on the east side of Taliouine near the bridge, offers satisfactory rooms for 70dh per person. It's a small place though, so call in advance. The auberge is run by Ahmed, a mountain guide, and his French wife. These are the people to talk to for trekking information. They can organise guides, mules and camping gear.

There's another auberge, *Askaoun*, a short walk further on towards the centre of the village. Try here if the Souktana is full. Otherwise, if you feel like splashing out for something a bit more up-market, try *Hôtel Ibn Toumert* which has double rooms from 360dh. The hotel has a bar and pool but it still seems rather over-priced.

Where to eat
Auberge Souktana dishes up reasonable meals of salad, brochettes and fruit for around 40dh. *Hôtel Ibn Toumert* has a reasonable *menu touristique* for 125dh and breakfasts for 39dh. There are a number of pleasant cafés scattered along the main drag serving the usual delights, tagines, couscous and so on; try *Café Takaddon*, *Café Erraha* or *Café Tirit*.

Getting to Taliouine and Akhfamane

A daily Taliouine **bus** leaves the gare routière in Marrakesh at 10am. Tickets, which are available from kiosk No 17, cost 60dh per person. It's a gruelling eight-hour journey with countless tedious stops.

Check whether the bus will take you all the way to Taliouine since it sometimes stops at Auolouz some 30km west. If you do end up in Auolouz, a full grand taxi to Taliouine will cost about 10dh per passenger. The bus journey itself might be tiring but it is also spectacular; near-vertical drops from the Tizi-n'-Test road, which reaches an altitude of 2100m/6888ft, hint at the dramatic scenes to come.

While it is possible to walk in under five hours from Taliouine to Akhfamane, the better starting point for Jbel Sirwa treks, many trekkers prefer instead to hop on the clapped-out minibus which regularly makes the journey. Ask at the Shell garage to find out when it's next expected. Unfortunately, the driver tends to demand a ridiculous fee from non-Moroccan passengers. While 30dh ought to be about right, the driver can ask for anything up to 200dh for a one-way journey; make out you would rather walk than pay over the odds and watch the price tumble.

TALIOUINE—AKHFAMANE

This is a straightforward and pleasant walk which takes between four and five hours. Most trekkers choose to skip this stage in favour of starting the trek from Akhfamane. There is motor transport from Taliouine to Akhfamane most days (see above) and the route becomes rather more interesting after Akhfamane. These notes and timings are approximate and based on local advice. There is no map for this section since, like most trekkers, I started the trek from Akhfamane.

Follow the main road (P32) out of Taliouine to the east. After 15 minutes you will pass a sharp right-hand turning to the village of El Qaçba. Look for a path which heads left (north-east) from the main road after a further five minutes or so. Take it. The path from here is very distinct and

❑ Akhfamane (1250m/4100ft)

There isn't a great deal to say about Akhfamane which is a typically small, dusty Sirwa village wedged between two flat-topped ridges. You will find a small kasbah, a few rooms for hire and a handful of friendly locals.

There are muleteers in Akhfamane; Lhoussaine Id-Ihya is particularly helpful and well worth talking to before heading out for Jbel Sirwa. His house is the first on the right as you enter the village.

climbs at a gentle rate. Keep the river bed to your left; the path more or less follows it from here through the village of Ighil-n-Imchguiln to Tirassat (1062m/3483ft) which you should reach about 90 minutes after leaving Taliouine.

After Tirassat, the path moves away from the river bed but then rejoins it 120 minutes later at the village of Timicha. Continue along the path and the river bed, which means crossing the tributary leading off to the south-east. You will then reach Tifourt approximately 20 minutes after leaving Timicha. Just outside Tifourt you will meet a wider road, large enough for vehicles, which forks left and right at the point at which you reach it. Take the right (south-east) fork and follow this road all the way into Akhfamane (1250m/4100ft) which you should reach some 40 minutes after leaving Tifourt.

There is an alternative to this route which is easier still to follow but makes less enjoyable walking. Walk out of Taliouine as before but take the left turn, a motor road, off the P32 before reaching the right turn to El Qaçba. This road follows the river bed all the way to Akhfamane. There's little difference between the two routes in terms of time. The latter route has the advantage that, should you regret deciding to walk, you could probably flag down a passing vehicle for a lift.

AKHFAMANE—MAZWAD—TI N'IDDR [Map 22]

Walk east through Akhfamane (1250m/4100ft) for about 500m until you reach a fork in the piste. Take the right fork which will take you up a gentle incline past the last few houses of the village. Keep following the piste, which is clear, as it continues its mild climb along the right (south) side of a gorge in an easterly direction. The river at the bottom of the gorge, the Tifrguene, is usually dry in summer.

Continue heading east until, 30 minutes after leaving Akhfamane, you reach a small azib on the right. This azib is used regularly so, depending on the time of year you visit Sirwa, you might find sheep or goats sheltering in it. Shortly after passing the azib, the piste turns left (north). Don't follow it. Instead, carry straight on and descend to the river bed where you will pick it up again. The route still heads generally east as it weaves between the river bed and the sides of the gorge.

Some 30 minutes beyond the azib, as you approach from the south-east, you will reach a series of dry ravines that fall away to your right every 200 metres or so. After a further 10 minutes, look to the north where a collection of terraced, stone-walled fields indicate the village of Aberniberka. Just 5 minutes beyond this, the route splits. Take the right (east) fork leaving the village to your left.

About 30 minutes later the piste will begin to climb into the hills, leaving the river bed behind. The landscape is barren and volcanic with

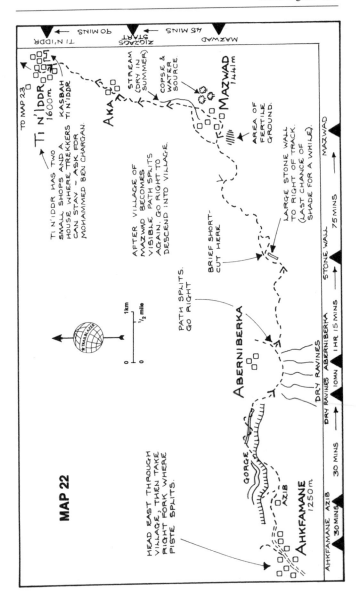

MAP 22

AHKFAMANE 1250m.

HEAD EAST THROUGH VILLAGE, THEN TAKE RIGHT FORK WHERE PISTE SPLITS.

GORGE

AZIB

PATH SPLITS. GO RIGHT

ABERNIBERKA

DRY RAVINES

BRIEF SHORT-CUT HERE

LARGE STONE WALL TO RIGHT OF TRACK. (LAST CHANCE OF SHADE FOR A WHILE).

AFTER VILLAGE OF MAZWAD BECOMES VISIBLE PATH SPLITS AGAIN. GO RIGHT TO DESCEND INTO VILLAGE.

AREA OF FERTILE GROUND.

MAZWAD 1441m

COPSE & WATER SOURCE

STREAM (DRY IN SUMMER)

AKA

TI N'IDDR 1600m

TO MAP 23

TI N'IDDR HAS TWO SMALL SHOPS AND A KASBAH WHERE TREKKERS CAN STAY – ASK FOR MOHAMMED BEN CHARGAN.

KASBAH TI N'IDDR

1km
½ mile
0

AHKFAMANE 30 MINS AZIB 30 MINS DRY RAVINES 10MIN ABERNIBERKA 1 HR 15 MINS STONE WALL 75 MINS MAZWAD

MAZWAD ◀ 45 MINS ZIGZAGS START ◀ 90 MINS TI N'IDDR

very little shade or animal life. Keep going for a further 30 minutes or so and you will come to a large stone wall to the right of the piste. Take advantage of the shade it offers as it's the last you'll see for quite a while. There is a small footpath at the wall which rejoins the piste a little later on, cutting out a few hundred metres. Follow this or stay on the piste. Either way, you will continue your gentle ascent for another 75 minutes in a generally north-easterly direction before the piste starts to descend.

At this point you should see an area of more fertile land to the south-east and some azibs across the valley. The route will start to snake and you will soon round a corner to see the village of Mazwad (1441m/4726ft) up ahead. As you approach the village, the route forks again. The right fork heads south, the left north-east. Take the right fork leading down into the village. Mazwad makes a good place to stop overnight or just for lunch. There are a few good patches of ground on which to pitch tents and a pleasant copse with a water source.

To continue on to Ti n'Iddr, take the left fork north-east. This stretch of track climbs at a steady pace. Soon the route will begin to follow another river bed, that of the Ti n'Iddr river, which is usually dry in summer. The river bed should be to your right some 150 metres below you. At about this time you should begin to notice that the route starts to head more north than north-east. Approximately 45 minutes after leaving Mazwad, the piste will start to zigzag through the foothills. Continue along the route, through the tiny village of Aka, ascending all the time as you walk. After a further 90 minutes of this you will reach Ti n'Iddr (1600m/5248ft). Walk down north through the village where you will find some good shade and a stream for fresh water should you plan to camp. There is also a house where trekkers can stay. Ask for Mohammed Ben Chargan. The village also has two small shops (both sell drinks and Butagaz) and an interesting kasbah.

TI N'IDDR—GUILIZ [Map 23]

Head north through the village for about a kilometre. You'll pass the kasbah on the right and some shops where you might want to take the opportunity to stock up on a few things. After 30 minutes, having left Ti n'Iddr behind, you will find yourself heading north along a sketchy path which climbs slightly. To the right (south-east) and left (north-west) you will see a series of beautiful ridges. Just before the right ridge you will see the Ti n'Iddr valley running north-east to south-west. After a further five minutes you'll come across a few houses; this is the start of the next village, Atougha, although the village proper is spread over some distance.

The path then begins to get steeper. Keep bearing left, ignoring any right forks and remaining close to the rock and houses on your left. Another five minutes will take you to a rounded house set in the rock to

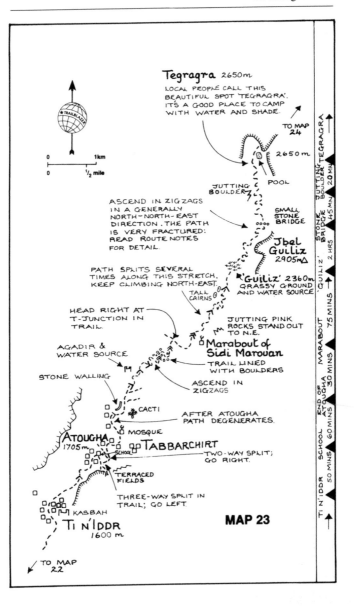

Tegragra 2650m

LOCAL PEOPLE CALL THIS
BEAUTIFUL SPOT 'TEGRAGRA'.
IT'S A GOOD PLACE TO CAMP
WITH WATER AND SHADE.

TO MAP
24

2650m

POOL

JUTTING
BOULDER

ASCEND IN ZIGZAGS
IN A GENERALLY
NORTH-NORTH-EAST
DIRECTION. THE PATH
IS VERY FRACTURED:
READ ROUTE NOTES
FOR DETAIL.

SMALL
STONE
BRIDGE

**Jbel
Guiliz**
2905m△

PATH SPLITS SEVERAL
TIMES ALONG THIS STRETCH.
KEEP CLIMBING NORTH-EAST.

'GUILIZ' 2360m
GRASSY GROUND
AND WATER SOURCE

TALL
CAIRNS

HEAD RIGHT AT
T-JUNCTION IN
TRAIL.

JUTTING PINK
ROCKS STAND OUT
TO N.E.

**Marabout of
Sidi Marouan**

AGADIR &
WATER SOURCE

TRAIL LINED
WITH BOULDERS

STONE WALLING

ASCEND IN
ZIGZAGS

CACTI

AFTER ATOUGHA
PATH DEGENERATES.

MOSQUE

Atougha
1705m

SCHOOL

Tabbarchirt

TWO-WAY SPLIT;
GO RIGHT.

TERRACED
FIELDS

THREE-WAY SPLIT IN
TRAIL; GO LEFT.

MAP 23

KASBAH

Ti n'Iddr
1600 m

TO MAP
22

0 ——— 1km
0 ——— ½ mile

*TRAILBLAZER

TI N'IDDR SCHOOL END OF ATOUGHA MARABOUT 'GUILIZ' STONE BRIDGE JUTTING BOULDER TEGRAGRA
50 MINS 60 MINS 30 MINS 75 MINS 2 HRS 45 MIN 20 MIN

the left. Just to the right there's another building with a small, blue door. Step inside and see some carpet-makers at work. Round the corner continue north along the path which begins to zigzag as it ascends more steeply. Look for more scattered and isolated houses to the left and a patchwork of terraced fields to the right.

Atougha proper (1705m/5592ft) will come into view about 15 minutes later. It makes an impressive sight. The houses are stacked neatly against the mountain with terraced maize and wheat fields spread out below. The path then bears right tracing the gorge and you will pass a school on the left. Keep right on the path which descends briefly and switches back south-east taking you across a small, dry gully before climbing again to lead through the rest of the village. You will meet a three-way split in your path about 30 minutes later. The right fork heads down, the middle fork straight on before disappearing and the left fork leads upwards. Take the left fork which soon passes some houses on the left and further on a mosque on the right.

Continue bearing left (east) for 50 metres until the path splits again. Go right: the left path moves sharply uphill over scree. Verify your position by looking for a cleanly terraced field which should be below you to your right.

The path then meanders through another section of Atougha, surely the longest village in the Atlas mountains. Look for a pink house with a green and lime metal door to your right. The route narrows as it passes by some wonderful stone buildings after which the ground underfoot becomes rocky for about 50 metres. You will pass some fine Berber wooden doors along this part of the path. These have recently become quite fashionable in more opulent Moroccan homes and they are beginning to sell for a small fortune. At this point you should be heading in a generally south-east direction until you round a corner which takes you east to a fork. Bear left uphill, although there is little difference between the two paths. The trek from Ti n'Iddr to Atougha takes some 105 minutes.

Atougha is the last village you pass through on your way to the Jbel Sirwa summit. After leaving the village you will find the path degenerates into a more rocky, dusty affair which is rather more difficult to trace. As you head east away from Atougha you will pass stone walling to the left and cacti to the right. The going is flat as you round one or two corners before seeing craggy peaks ahead to the east and more terraced fields. There's another village, Tabbarchirt, above the fields but this route does not reach it. The path splits some 100 metres further on. Bear left as you start to climb, then left again as the path switches back to cover the incline. You will now be heading west and Atougha will come back into view below. After another 100 metres, before you zigzag east, you will pass a large agadir and a water-source. It's a good idea to fill up your water bottles here but purify the water with iodine.

Continue the ascent, switching back between east and west as you go. Bear left after 50 metres to head west (look out for a stone wall on your right) then bear left after a further 50 metres. Again the path splits, go left (north). This sounds confusing but it isn't; just keep going up at every opportunity to avoid taking a mule path back down to the village. The path, which at this point is fairly clearly defined by big rocks and boulders either side, will get steeper the higher you go. As you climb you will again see Tabbarchirt to the right and a waterfall (dry in summer) will come into view to the north-east.

After a few more hairpins you will come to a T-junction. Head right (north) and after 50 metres you will reach a small square of bare ground after which the path divides again. Take the right path north-east and after 100 metres you should see the peaks ahead to the north and, just below on the left, the small marabout of Sidi Marouan. A small cairn on the right of the path will also help to verify your position.

Wind steadily up the mountain past some bizarre, jutting pink-coloured rocks to the north-east. You will soon reach the brow of a ridge where the path briefly disappears. Continue north-east to rejoin it. Again it disappears briefly, breaking off in all directions but take the middle way and soon enough you'll see a clear track winding up the incline. Approximately 75 minutes after leaving Atougha, having negotiated the splintering, zigzagging mess of the last stretch, you should find yourself at another clear fork in the path.

Take the smaller path to the right which leads north-east towards Jbel Sirwa. Five minutes later you'll see some jagged, broken rocks to the left about five metres from the path. A further 50 metres beyond these rocks the path splits again. Head left (north) and five minutes later you'll be on another brow of sorts. Jbel Guiliz, the furthest peak in view, stands to the north-east. The path continues north and soon Guiliz falls out of sight again. You will pass several tall cairns on the left 20 minutes later and again the path splits. Head right (north-east) to skirt round a hill, passing a stone wall on the left; again the path divides after some 200 metres. Head left, a switchback, going north-east to find yourself on more grassy ground about 30 minutes after the last time check and 215 minutes after leaving Ti n'Iddr. There's a good water-source here and some shelter. This is the best place to camp if you need to take a break before tackling the next stage. We've called this Guiliz, because Jbel Guiliz (2905m/9528ft) is the nearest peak, but it is really wilderness with no name. The altitude here is approximately 2360m/7740ft.

GUILIZ—TEGRAGRA   [Map 23, p181]

Retrace your steps to where the path splits (2360m/7740ft) and head east on the dirt path which follows the contours hugging the mountainside towards the north-east. Soon you will pass a large boulder on your left. After about five minutes you will see two sets of stacked boulders about 20 metres apart and, between them, an azib in the distance. Follow the path around the right set of stacked boulders until, after a further five minutes, several azibs come into view. These will be to your west as you walk past them; you will also see some scattered enormous boulders. At this point you will be climbing steadily. Some 30 minutes' trek from Guiliz the path will level out as you skirt around the mountainside in a north-easterly direction.

A gorge, dry in summer, will be visible to the right (south-east). More ridges carve patterns above the gorge. About 30 minutes later you will pass another huge boulder in the shade of which you might find Berber shepherds enjoying a tea break. Continue heading north-east and you will turn a corner to see a prominent peak ahead and to the north. Roughly 15 minutes after you will descend briefly to walk between two medium-sized boulders. You might be able to hear running water to the east and just a minute or two later you'll cross a gully. Head left for about 25 metres along the gully side, rounding a boulder on your right, to pick up the trail as it climbs. Climb for 20 metres to where the path divides. Go right so that you are walking parallel to the water source and again more azibs will come into view.

At this point the path is rock-strewn, wide and unclear but continue in the same direction for a further 50 metres until the path becomes framed briefly by two stone walls. Bear north-east from here and the path quickly become obvious again. The path will then start to ascend again before forking once more about 30 minutes after the last time-check. The smaller right branch clearly reaches down to the gully. Take the larger more distinct branch on the left. Be careful here; both paths appear to lead in the same direction at first. Consult your map with particular care.

Continue on this route and cross a dry gully littered with rocks, which runs north to south-east. There is another, smaller gully just 100 metres further on. The ground is flat and dusty over this stretch and interspersed with scrub and gorse. Gradually the terrain becomes more boulder-strewn and to the right you will pass a great, echoing gorge. To the left of the path here you will see pieces of jagged, fissured rock. Keep going until, 15 minutes after the last fork, you cross over a small stone bridge. Head north-east for 50 metres, weaving between more boulders, until the path becomes clear once more just five minutes further on. Keep the water to your left as you look for it. Again the path vanishes under the boulders and dust. Head south through the boulder field until you once more rediscover it, this time leading north-east. Look to your right for a marvellous view of the Guiliz summit (2905m/9528ft).

Keep on the path as it crosses a patch of mossy grass, along which runs a trickle of water (north-east to south-west), and aim around the left side of a giant, seamed boulder. After the path curves right and upwards. Continue east and up along a pebble-strewn and snaking gully then zigzag back to keep up the ascent. The path is visible because the stones underfoot are scuffed, light and compacted.

Some 15 minutes further on cross another mossy gully, this one descending from east to west, as you head in a generally northern direction. Immediately afterwards the path degenerates into loose scree and you need to negotiate a route between boulders to maintain your ascent and northern direction. Carry on like this until you reach a ridge. From here you will see Jbel Sirwa to the north while, to your right, you will see odd fissured, digit-like boulders. It's a little grassy underfoot and the path, once again, is not too obvious. Look out for animal droppings to help lead the way. You should aim for a generally east-north-easterly direction.

Another gully runs east to west some 20 metres below this point to the left. The path gradually descends to this gully, crosses it, and heads north. Just 50 metres further on you should find a pool of water and a source which, even in summer, offers a good chance to fill up water bottles but don't forget the iodine. Keep going north, past a deep ravine lined with jagged rock to the west. The path will curve around the ravine to lead north-west over scrubby terrain. It will slowly move to a more northerly route again. In the distance you will see Sirwa, the highest peak in sight at 3305m/10,840ft. A small azib will also be visible.

A strange three-metre-high formation of jutting boulders stands to the left of the path 30 minutes after the last time-check at the gully. Head to the right of this formation, crossing another gully, to carry on up through more boulders to the north-west. Aim more west when you see stone walls about 100 metres later. The path descends slightly as it passes these walled fields. When a gully appears to the left, head north. Use the water here to guide you; the path is thin, dusty and hard to see at this stage. After a further 10 minutes, still heading north, the ground becomes coated in larger boulders again and you should make out a small cairn to the right.The gully dries up almost completely at this point; cross it to the west side and carry on. Just 10 minutes more will take you to another pool (much larger than the last) and an excellent camping site set in a gorgeous valley and surrounded by steep, dramatic ridges. Locals call this spot Tegragra (2650m/8692ft).

TEGRAGRA—JBEL SIRWA SUMMIT—TIZGUI
[Map 24, p187]

This relatively long and demanding trek requires an early start both to allow time to make the summit and reach a good camping area in one stage and, in part, to avoid reaching the summit too late in the day; the weather can deteriorate after noon.

Note that you should use ropes for the final climb to the summit. The overall time given for this stage, therefore, doesn't include any time trekkers might want to spend climbing to the very top of Jbel Sirwa. Instead, the notes given continue from the point at which that rope climb would begin.

Head east up the ridge from the pool described at the end of the previous stage. An early morning start will allow you to follow the sun. As you walk you will pass an expanse of green, mossy ground to your left. The gully runs north-east to south-west across it. The going is steep from here; too steep, in fact, for mules. If you have one, your muleteer will want to go a separate route to meet you after you've achieved the summit.

A narrow trail leads up the ridge to join another, smaller gully further uphill. Follow the trail uphill until you pass the gully at which point the route turns to a more north-easterly direction. The path, which by now will be peppered with small stones and dust, leads between a number of large boulders. Allow about 15 minutes to cover this first ridge. At its peak, continue in a north-easterly direction. To your left you will see a huge mass of rounded, weather-worn boulders and rocks which form a mini-peak in their own right. Skirt round this feature to the north-east until, about 30 metres along, you find a gap in the boulders. Go through it and continue to climb steeply, flicking between a north-east and north-westerly direction as you trace the route upwards.

Adopt a generally north-westerly direction and look out for another peak of boulders 40 minutes after starting the trek. The ground by now will be thickly coated with gorse and boulders but it is at least flatter than the previous stretch. Head left (north-west) of the boulder peak and continue your ascent. After five minutes you will emerge at the top of another small ridge. Ahead you will see a short ascent to the north. Aim for this. When you reach the top, look for the flat-topped Jbel Tisfeldat (2918m/9571ft) standing out to the south-east. You should also be able to see another huge pile of boulders to the right (north-east) at the base of which springs a water source.

Head north-north-west, keeping these boulders to your right, until you pick up a more distinct footpath which leads north to a flatter ridge. The ground is again carpeted with gorse and boulders. While the path leads you north, look for another collection of big, craggy boulders which you will come across 10 minutes later. Make for these. A cairn will verify your position 60 minutes into the trek.

Ahead you should see another higher, craggier peak below which lies a flat expanse of gorse and rocks. Head north-north-west between a range of rocks; again a cairn will help you, leaving the previous stretch of path behind you to your left. The going again gets steep. After 10 minutes of sharp ascent, you should find the path leading you north-north-west along a narrow pass. Helpfully rocks line the route and those underfoot look

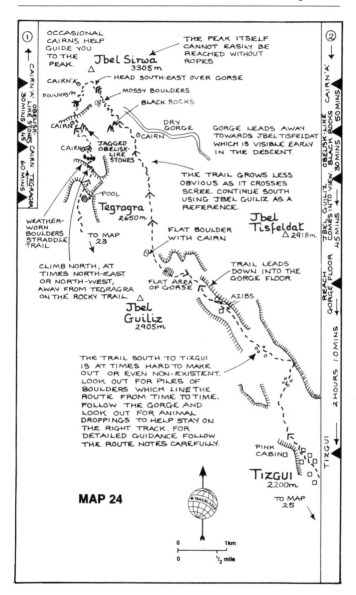

① OCCASIONAL CAIRNS HELP GUIDE YOU TO THE PEAK.

THE PEAK ITSELF CANNOT EASILY BE REACHED WITHOUT ROPES

Jbel Sirwa
3305m
△

CAIRN 'A' ○
HEAD SOUTH-EAST OVER GORSE

BOULDERS
MOSSY BOULDERS
BLACK ROCKS

DRY GORGE
○CAIRN

CAIRN
JAGGED OBELISK-LIKE STONES
CAIRN ○

GORGE LEADS AWAY TOWARDS JBEL TISFELDAT WHICH IS VISIBLE EARLY IN THE DESCENT.

THE TRAIL GROWS LESS OBVIOUS AS IT CROSSES SCREE. CONTINUE SOUTH USING JBEL GUILIZ AS A REFERENCE.

POOL

Tegragra
2650m

WEATHER-WORN BOULDERS STRADDLE TRAIL

TO MAP 23

FLAT BOULDER WITH CAIRN

Jbel Tisfeldat
△2918m

CLIMB NORTH, AT TIMES NORTH-EAST OR NORTH-WEST, AWAY FROM TEGRAGRA ON THE ROCKY TRAIL.

FLAT AREA OF GORSE

TRAIL LEADS DOWN INTO THE GORGE FLOOR.

AZIBS

Jbel Guiliz
2905m

THE TRAIL SOUTH TO TIZGUI IS AT TIMES HARD TO MAKE OUT OR EVEN NON-EXISTENT. LOOK OUT FOR PILES OF BOULDERS WHICH LINE THE ROUTE FROM TIME TO TIME. FOLLOW THE GORGE AND LOOK OUT FOR ANIMAL DROPPINGS TO HELP STAY ON THE RIGHT TRACK. FOR DETAILED GUIDANCE FOLLOW THE ROUTE NOTES CAREFULLY.

PINK CABIN○

MAP 24

Tizgui
2200m

TO MAP 25

② CAIRN 'A' 50 MINS
OBELISK-LIKE BLACK ROCKS 30 MINS
JBEL GUILIZ COMES INTO VIEW. 45 MINS
REACH GORGE FLOOR
2 HOURS 10 MINS
TIZGUI

① CAIRN 'A' 30 MINS
OBELISK-LIKE STONES 45 MINS
CAIRN 60 MINS
TEGRAGRA

★TRAILBLAZER

0   1km
0   ½ mile

worn. After five minutes the pass appears to peter out and you should then head right (north-north-east) towards another clump of rounded boulders. When you reach these, head north-east towards a small, neat line of boulders to the left. Walk along this line, a steep stretch, towards the next stack of obelisk-like boulders which will come into view in front of you.

Once you have reached these boulders, some 45 minutes after the 60-minute cairn, the path grows less distinct still. Be guided by a series of small, jagged and obelisk-like stones that jut upwards to the right (north-west) of the route. After five more minutes you will be through the boulders and onto very steep ground. Clamber straight up and over the rocks in front of you and suddenly the twin peaks of Jbel Sirwa (3305m/10,840ft) will appear to the north-north-east. Continue north to cross another 100-metre flattish area of short gorse. The peaks, your goal, will remain visible to the right.

The path will take you to the brow of another ridge and surprisingly soon the summit seems very close. Walk north-east along the top of the ridge for 10 minutes at which point the route will swing to the north, pointing directly at the peaks. Within minutes you will see an obvious cairn. Expect to reach this cairn 30 minutes after the boulders which were noted at the 105-minute stage. The final climb to the actual summit should, technically, be achieved from the cairn using ropes. Looking at it from the cairn, you will no doubt agree. It is actually relatively easy to do freehand but, unless you're very confident, you should settle for reaching the highest walkable point on Jbel Sirwa. This is no place to have an accident so don't take chances.

These notes, therefore, now move straight to the descent without giving timings or instructions for climbing to the summit. Whether you reach the very top or not, however, you will want to spend some time absorbing the magnificent 360-degree views from this mountain perch.

The descent
Head south-east over gorse along the same ridge. Keep left of the mossy boulders which line the ridge and start your descent down the mountainside. Walk south and soon you will see some five-metre-tall oblong rocks to your right (south-west). Continue down the mountain so that these rocks are above and behind you.

Five minutes later you will see Jbel Tisfeldat (2918m/9571ft) to the south-east and the dry gorge which spectacularly runs towards it. Still descending, stay parallel with some squarish boulders to your right. Straight ahead you will be able to make out a ridge, the route towards it is marked by a large cairn, towards which you are walking. The ground flattens at this stage. Just 50 metres on you will face some jagged slabs of black rock approximately 50 minutes after starting the descent. Go left of these and continue along the ridge with these slabs on your right. The path will, at this stage, become still less obvious as the ground turns to loose, difficult scree.

Aim south-east through another 100-metre-wide patch of gorse. The ridge slopes gently away on either side but looks increasingly steep to the right. After five minutes you will reach some smoothly-rounded boulders; stay left of these. Straight after these you will pass another cairn to the right. The ground is still flat. The route then starts to climb again, after five more minutes, towards a big rock-face ahead (south) on which sits another cairn. Walk toward this feature, climbing to its peak from the right, and once over the top you will see a collection of rounded boulders which, from this angle, look rather like crazy-paving. Again, the ground has become flat.

Continue south for another 10 minutes and you will see a large, round boulder with a sharper one perched upon it. Keep these to your right as you walk towards another patch of gorse-coated ground. Descend south-east and, about 80 minutes after leaving the summit, you will be able to make out Jbel Giuliz (2905m/9528ft) almost straight ahead and Jbel Tisfeldat to the east-south-east. To the left (east) you will see two rounded one-metre-wide boulders sitting next to each other. Head between these to the south.

After 50 metres a rock-face will appear to the left and more cairns to the right. Jbel Guiliz remains on the horizon straight ahead. Aim towards it. After 10 more minutes the ground starts to descend more steeply and the patches of gorse disappear. The gorge reappears to the east. Once you can see the gorge aim for it, not Jbel Guiliz which will be to the right of your view. Head south-south-east down towards the gorge floor, scrambling over boulders as you do so. Some 45 minutes after first making out Jbel Guiliz and Jbel Tisfeldat, you should have descended the east face of the ridge along which you had been walking to reach the gorge floor.

A pebbly trail runs along the west wall of the gorge. Follow it south. Look out for a massive, single boulder against the opposite wall to confirm your position. The trekking is flat. After five minutes you will pass an azib on the east bank and, after a further five minutes, another on your right. The dry gully which runs through the gorge will, depending on the season, yield water at some point along this path. Fill your water bottles when you find the spring which, in summer, will be about 30 minutes after reaching the gorge floor.

The path goes through a few ups and downs from here, crossing back and forth over the gully and starting to climb. It gets rockier as it does so. After 10 minutes of this the gully will be below you to the right, seemingly walled by the steep-sided gorge. The path divides about 15 minutes further on. Take the right fork which heads south-east and soon the path will become rockier still and, 30 minutes after finding the spring, the gorge goes out of sight.

Follow the path, which becomes surrounded by boulders, until the gorge gradually moves back into view. Here the path begins a steep descent, snaking north for 100 metres then sharply south. Look out for the gully to the west at which point the path levels out slightly. Behind you (north-east) a waterfall splashes the otherwise scorched scene. The path then divides 30 minutes after the last time-check. The right fork heads upwards but you should go left for five minutes to another split. This time take the right fork which goes straight on. This path starts to climb southwards after 100 metres. You will cross two stone-filled gullies and round a cor-ner but the route still meanders south. After a further 100 metres bear left alongside a stone wall and the path will descend. Continue south, ignor-ing another path which branches off to the north. The path widens almost to a piste 30 minutes after the last time-check.

The path descends now in a more south-easterly direction. Ahead and below you stands a pink cabin. Use this as a marker but don't head direct-ly towards it. Trek to the east of it; there is a gorge between it and your path. The cabin is a welcome sight, however, since it signals your approach to the village of Tizgui (2200m/7216ft). After a further five min-utes more houses will come into view. Shortly after this, the path divides. Follow the path into the village; it zigzags as it descends towards the houses, crossing the gorge, which previously divided you from the pink house, at its lowest point. If you carry on south from here for 50 to 100 metres, leaving the centre of the tiered village behind, you will come across some soft, terraced areas which make excellent camping points. There is a residence (not a gîte) at which trekkers can stay in Tizgui for about 35dh per person. Ask for Mohammed Mazouz Aznag.

TIZGUI—TAGOUYAM—TIZLIT   [Map 25]

Find the path which leads south-east from the village along the south-west side of the gorge in which the Tizgui sits. After five minutes you will pass a fascinating agadir set against the mountains. A further five minutes will take you to the bottom of the gorge where the path divides. One track heads right and up, the other left. Take the left track which starts to ascend slightly before gently rising and falling as it progresses. The series of peaks which had till now been overshadowing the route to the east starts to drop in height while below you, to the south-west, the village of Tagouyam (2000m/6560ft) comes into view about 45 minutes after leav-ing Tizgui.

At this point the path widens to a piste heading south-east and you will be upon Tagouyam quite quickly. Look for two minarets, one pink with grey edges, and head towards these. Within 10 minutes you will be in Tagouyam, a village which leads almost continuously into another, Assara. You will pass a water-source on the left. There is also a *house* in

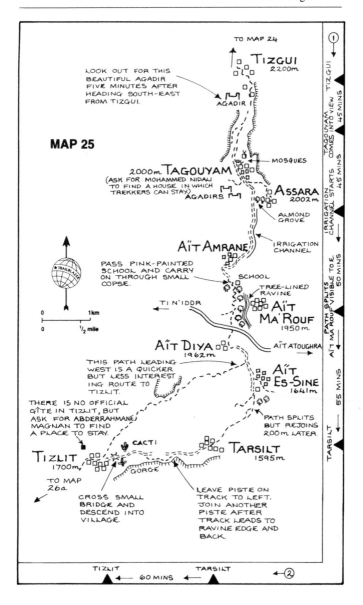

MAP 25

TO MAP 24

TIZGUI 2200m

LOOK OUT FOR THIS BEAUTIFUL AGADIR FIVE MINUTES AFTER HEADING SOUTH-EAST FROM TIZGUI.

AGADIR I

2000m TAGOUYAM
(ASK FOR MOHAMMED NIDAI TO FIND A HOUSE IN WHICH TREKKERS CAN STAY)
AGADIRS

MOSQUES

ASSARA 2002m

ALMOND GROVE

Aït AMRANE

IRRIGATION CHANNEL

PASS PINK-PAINTED SCHOOL AND CARRY ON THROUGH SMALL COPSE.

SCHOOL

TREE-LINED RAVINE

TIN'IDDR

Aït MA'ROUF 1950m

Aït DIYA 1962m

AÏTATOUGHRA

THIS PATH LEADING WEST IS A QUICKER BUT LESS INTERESTING ROUTE TO TIZLIT.

Aït ES-SINE 1641m

THERE IS NO OFFICIAL GÎTE IN TIZLIT, BUT ASK FOR ABDERRAHMANE MAGNAN TO FIND A PLACE TO STAY.

PATH SPLITS BUT REJOINS 200m LATER.

CACTI

TARSILT 1595m

TIZLIT 1700m

TO MAP 26a

GORGE

CROSS SMALL BRIDGE AND DESCEND INTO VILLAGE

LEAVE PISTE ON TRACK TO LEFT. JOIN ANOTHER PISTE AFTER TRACK LEADS TO RAVINE EDGE AND BACK.

TRAILBLAZER

0   1km
0   ½ mile

TAGOUYAM COMES INTO VIEW TIZGUI   45 MINS

IRRIGATION CHANNEL STARTS   45 MINS

PATH SPLITS VISIBLE TO E.   50 MINS

AÏT MA'ROUF   55 MINS

TARSILT

TIZLIT   TARSILT
◄— 60 MINS ◄—

Tagouyam in which people and mules can stay. Ask for Mohammed Nidali. Continue through the village until the piste divides. Take the left fork which descends south. Ahead you will see two flattened peaks very close to each other. On top of these sit two agadirs. The piste leads past an attractive almond grove to the left and a village, Agoulzi, can be seen further to the east.

An irrigation channel starts to run along the left-side of the route 90 minutes into the trek. The route also becomes flatter at this point and, to the right, you will see a rocky area. Clamber over these rocks, heading south-west for 20 metres and the village of Aït Amrane appears. Bear left, staying flush with the irrigation channel, and walk into the village. As you do so the piste will bear right over some white rocks and continue south-west past the houses. Follow the path, leaving Aït Amrane behind. This route will take you temporarily north but soon you will walk past, on your right, a school, decorated as always with pictures of Pluto and Mickey Mouse. Continue on for five minutes following the piste as it bears left to a stream bed. The path then leads through some trees, heading south-east, before rising out of the small gorge onto a boulder-strewn and irregular path. A stone wall to the left is a useful guide.

After a short while the track will start to descend. At this point, ignore the path that leads down to the field and head upwards, or south-south-east, for a couple of minutes over some worn boulders. Check your position at this point by noting a village which should be in sight. To the left, north-east, on the far side of a tree-coated ravine, stands Aït Ma'rouf (1950m/6396ft). At 50 minutes after meeting the irrigation channel, the path divides again. Go left. The path crosses a big piste, which runs from Ti n'Iddr to Aït Atoughra and leads down to a copse surrounded by a stone wall. There is a water-source here; look for a pipe supported by rocks.

Head south-south-east along the path which leads past the small water-pipe. After five minutes you will pass through the village of Aït Diya and 50 metres further on join a piste. To the left (north-east), across a gorge, is a small cluster of buildings which is another school. After another five minutes the dusty piste becomes chalky and you will soon cross a bouldered gully which goes over a small dip.

About 100 metres further on there is another gully at which point the route switches back west. Look across the gully and you will see another path leading south-south-east. Follow it by walking across the dry gully. Note that here you will see another path which hugs the rocks to the west; this is a quicker route to Tizlit but it misses out the impressive gorge.

(**Opposite**): Muleteer and family, Ahkfamane, Sirwa Region. (Photos © Patrick Maguire).

Follow the first path for 200 metres to where the piste reappears heading south-east. Take it and, within a few minutes, you'll see another village, Aït es-Sine.

Soon after this you will reach a crossroads of sorts. Go south-east, so avoiding the route into Aït es-Sine, unless you want explore the village. A minute later, some 20 minutes after leaving the water-source, the piste divides. Take the right fork; again the alternative leads into Aït es-Sine.

Heading downhill you will soon pass some houses on the left and again the path divides. Bear left over some very rocky ground and down towards some trees. The path is distinct and, when you reach the trees, there is a big rock which stands out. The continuing path is lined by red, jagged stones. Cross over 200 metres of red rock to where it divides again. Take either fork as they rejoin 200 metres later. Follow the path which is now quite flat although there are some difficult rocky sections.

After walking for 25 minutes from the turning to Aït es-Sine you will note a shiny rock-face and to the left of this a peak. Behind it lies the village of Tarsilt. After five minutes the shiny rock-face comes properly into focus and at this point the path heads south-west. Check your position by looking for a small brick hut which is just visible straight ahead. From here the path leads to Tizlit but, if you're with a mule, it's better to leave the path to head west over pebble-strewn ground. There is a very faint path over this section.

An azib will appear to the south-south-west and you should cross a dry, winding gully that heads towards it. Bear west over what has become flat, red and gorse-covered ground. After five minutes the main path will come back into view. There are fissured rocks to either side of it. Join the path, which is becoming wide enough to be considered a piste, as it starts to rise a little. It is heading west.

The path divides but take either side since they join again in 200 metres or so. At that stage, however, you should break from the path to head south-west. Directly ahead but very distant, you will see a pointed mountain peak. Use this as a guide since the path will by now have disappeared again. To the left there is an ever-deepening rock-sided ravine. Keep right of this and 35 minutes after noting the shiny rock-face, you will pick up the clear path again.

Follow this and note that the ravine becomes a fantastic gorge littered with weird-shaped boulders which appear almost to have been hand-sculpted. There are some attractive camping spots along this stretch but the piste itself will lead into the village of Tizlit (1700m5576ft) in about

---

(Opposite) Top: The view from Sirwa summit, 3305/10,840ft (see p188). Bottom: Terraced fields, Sirwa Region. (Photos © Patrick Maguire).

25 minutes. If you decide to camp in the bottom of the gorge you should consider there could be a danger of flash floods.

After five minutes, with the gorge on your left, the route will head up over splintered, rocky ground covered in cacti. Keep going for 200 metres until you round a corner to see a small bridge. Cross it and head left towards the village. The fields help to guide you in the right direction. Ten minutes later you will see the amazing and ancient village, its buildings carved into the rock itself. There is a house in which trekkers can stay but no official gîte. Ask for Abderrahmane Magnan. It is the furthest and highest house from the point at which you enter Tizlit.

TIZLIT—IFRANE—TINFAT [Maps 26a and 26b, p195 and p196]

This 21-kilometre-long stage has the benefit of being fairly easy going almost all the way. Break the trip at Ifrane if it seems too long for one comfortable stage. Leave Tizlit west from the house of Abderrahmane, descending 50 metres, and you will see the gorge wall to the south-east and a concrete hut close by to the west. Below this hut is a path which you should pick up and follow to the south-west. A few minutes later you will pass two azibs to the left shortly after which you will reach a small brow from where you will see the path stretching away across the south side of the mountain. The path itself is heading west. The gorge is to the left at this stage, running parallel with the path.

After walking from Tizlit for 20 minutes look for a massive and pre-cariously-perched boulder threatening to roll into the gorge. This should help confirm your position. Walk for a further five minutes and you should see a white mosque appear in the distance to the south-west. Soon after this sighting, the path heads west and crosses a dry gully. The ground is flat and stony. Keep going for 10 minutes, starting to climb slightly, and you'll see the beginning of a ravine on your left. To the right (north-west) there will be a ridge with finger-like fissures. Another five minutes will take you onto a flat patch south of which stands a tiny stone building. The path is rocky and difficult here but with care you can still make it out. Continue west until, 40 minutes after the precarious boulder, you see an azib and terraced fields to the left (south).

Some 10 minutes later, as you descend across fairly difficult terrain, the path again becomes quite hard to follow. By the time you have nego-tiated a patch of particularly prickly cacti, however, the village previous-ly indicated by the distant mosque comes properly into view. Continue along the path, which is joined by another from the north-west, as it begins to climb west up the mountainside running parallel to a fertile gorge populated by talkative toads. There's a man-made gully on the right but after 50 metres it becomes obscured by plants. At this stage head down

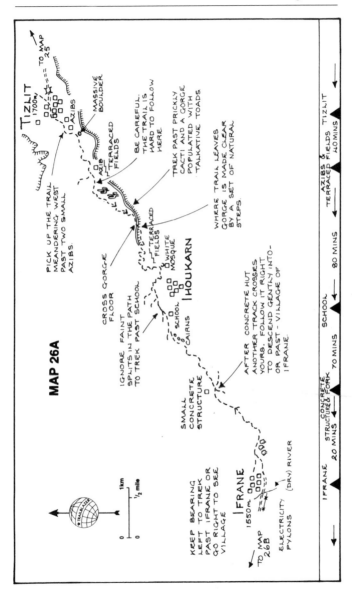

MAP 26A

TIZLIT □ 1700m

TO MAP 25

AZIBS

MASSIVE BOULDER

PICK UP THE TRAIL MEANDERING WEST PAST TWO SMALL AZIBS.

AZIB

TERRACED FIELDS

BE CAREFUL. THE TRAIL IS HARD TO FOLLOW HERE

TREK PAST PRICKLY CACTI AND A GORGE POPULATED WITH TALKATIVE TOADS

CROSS GORGE FLOOR

TERRACED FIELDS

WHITE MOSQUE

HOUKARN

WHERE TRAIL LEAVES GORGE IS MADE CLEAR BY A SET OF NATURAL STEPS

IGNORE FAINT SPLITS IN THE PATH TO TREK PAST SCHOOL

SCHOOL

CAIRNS

SMALL CONCRETE STRUCTURE

AFTER CONCRETE HUT ANOTHER TRACK CROSSES YOURS. FOLLOW IT RIGHT TO DESCEND GENTLY INTO OR PAST - IFRANE

1km
½ mile

★ TRAILBLAZER

IFRANE □ 1550m

KEEP BEARING LEFT TO TREK PAST IFRANE OR GO RIGHT TO SEE VILLAGE

TO MAP 26B

ELECTRICITY PYLONS

(DRY) RIVER

IFRANE — STRUCTURE & FORK 20 MINS — CONCRETE 70 MINS — SCHOOL 80 MINS — AZIBS & TERRACED FIELDS 40 MINS — TIZLIT

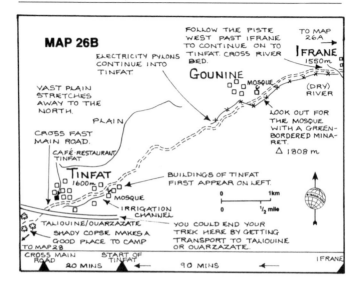

MAP 26B

FOLLOW THE PISTE WEST PAST IFRANE TO CONTINUE ON TO TINFAT. CROSS RIVER BED.

TO MAP 26A →

IFRANE 1550m

ELECTRICITY PYLONS CONTINUE INTO TINFAT.

GOUNINE

MOSQUE

(DRY) RIVER

VAST PLAIN STRETCHES AWAY TO THE NORTH.

LOOK OUT FOR THE MOSQUE WITH A GREEN-BORDERED MINA-RET.

PLAIN

△ 1808 m

CROSS FAST MAIN ROAD.

CAFÉ-RESTAURANT TINFAT

TINFAT 1600m

BUILDINGS OF TINFAT FIRST APPEAR ON LEFT.

0   1km

MOSQUE

0   ½ mile

IRRIGATION CHANNEL

TALIOUINE/OUARZAZATE

SHADY COPSE MAKES A GOOD PLACE TO CAMP

YOU COULD END YOUR TREK HERE BY GETTING TRANSPORT TO TALIOUINE OR OUARZAZATE.

TO MAP 28

CROSS MAIN ROAD   START OF TINFAT
20 MINS   ▲ ←   90 MINS   ←   IFRANE

a narrow zigzag to the gorge floor and cross it in a south-westerly direction to pick up a pebbly piste on the opposite side. The start of this piste is marked by obvious natural steps.

One or two other faint paths lead from the main piste 90 minutes into the trek. Ignore these and continue to climb up through some terraced fields in sharp zigzags. Head towards the white mosque. The ascent is short and the path quickly straightens out near the village, Ihoukarn, before dividing. Head right. This path, which is now quite chalky, as it leads past some houses before another split will take you left towards the school which you should reach 30 minutes after the last time-check.

Go left past the school after which you should pick up a piste heading south-west up the mountainside. After 10 minutes the path divides. Fork left. Continue south-west past a number of cairns for 60 minutes until you reach a small concrete structure to the right. Just after this another path crosses yours running east to west.

Follow the new path right, towards the village of Ifrane (1550m/5084ft) which will shortly come into view. The path will split about 100 metres short of Ifrane. Bear left (south-south-west) along a tiny gully towards some trees. Go past the trees and the path twists west past Ifrane. Keep bearing left so that you avoid Ifrane until you reach a well and a piste which runs past the rest of the houses. Follow this piste west, crossing a dry river as you do so.

Keep following the piste which moves to a west-south-westerly direction. Electricity pylons start running alongside the piste. After a further 10 minutes you will see a mosque with a green-bordered minaret to the north-west. This is the village of Gounine. Keep going along this piste for 70 minutes when some houses will appear to the left while, to the right, a vast, flat and arid plain comes into view. The houses mark the start of Tinfat (1600m/5248ft).

Follow the direction of the overhead cables; you'll pass a mosque and there are houses on both sides of the piste. Unexpectedly, some 20 minutes later, you cross a main road! It leads east to Ouarzazate and west to Taliouine. Cross over the main road past *Café-Restaurant Tinfat* and carry on for 100 metres to find a shady copse which makes an excellent camping spot. If you need to find a room for the night ask at the café; expect to pay 30dh. You can, of course, end your trek here by getting transport to Taliouine or Ouarzazate.

TINFAT—MIGGARN—AKHFAMANE   [Map 27, p198]

Walk out of Tinfat on the main road towards Taliouine. After 15 minutes you will see a road sign indicating that you are 222 kilometres from Agadir. Another, 10 minutes later, tells you Taliouine is 24 kilometres away. Some 100 metres after this second sign, cross to the north side of the road and look for a piste heading west towards a souq area. The actual souq takes place every Tuesday. You will pass the souq area after 10 more minutes. You might need to ask someone to show you the way to the souq since there are a number of buildings in this area and it can be a little confusing. By the time you pass the souq, the piste leads north towards the mountains. Keep following it, ignoring any other paths which cross it.

The piste divides after 60 minutes. Take the left fork north towards the village of Ighrem. After 10 minutes, at which point Ighrem will be to the right, your piste will be crossed by another. Carry on if you don't have a mule; if you do, the muleteer will probably want to head left to rejoin the piste a little further on. These notes follow the latter route since most trekkers do employ muleteers. Continue for 30 minutes, passing an azib on the left. When you pass a solitary palm tree to the right, the path starts to descend into a valley. After a further 20 minutes you should be more or less in the valley bottom. To the right lies a fertile area filled with trees. Keep on the piste as it crosses the valley floor, passing a water-source, and leading to the north-west. The few houses scattered around here make up the start of the village of Miggarn (1250m/4100ft) which you will reach about two hours 40 minutes into the trek.

Continue up the main piste to reach the village proper. You will pass a school on your way into the village. Follow the route north-north-west into the valley once more. Note that in winter the valley could be too wet

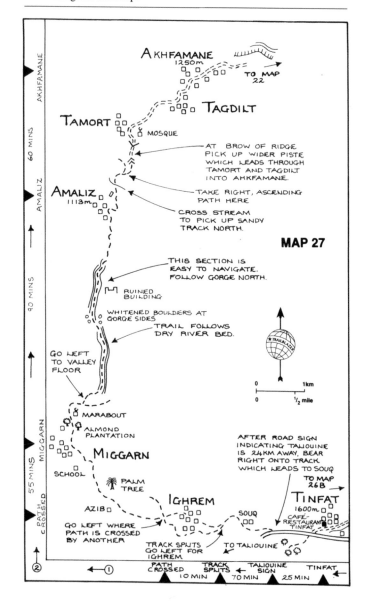

AKHFAMANE
1250m
TO MAP 22

TAGDILT

TAMORT

MOSQUE

AT BROW OF RIDGE
PICK UP WIDER PISTE
WHICH LEADS THROUGH
TAMORT AND TAGDILT
INTO AKHFAMANE.

TAKE RIGHT, ASCENDING
PATH HERE

AMALIZ
1113m

CROSS STREAM
TO PICK UP SANDY
TRACK NORTH.

MAP 27

THIS SECTION IS
EASY TO NAVIGATE.
FOLLOW GORGE NORTH.

RUINED
BUILDING

WHITENED BOULDERS AT
GORGE SIDES

TRAIL FOLLOWS
DRY RIVER BED.

GO LEFT
TO VALLEY
FLOOR

★ TRAILBLAZER

0   1km
0   1/2 mile

MARABOUT

ALMOND
PLANTATION

MIGGARN

SCHOOL

PALM
TREE

AFTER ROAD SIGN
INDICATING TALIOUINE
IS 24KM AWAY, BEAR
RIGHT ONTO TRACK
WHICH LEADS TO SOUQ

TO MAP
26B

TINFAT
1600m

CAFÉ-
RESTAURANT
TINFAT

IGHREM

SOUQ

AZIB

GO LEFT WHERE
PATH IS CROSSED
BY ANOTHER

TRACK SPLITS
GO LEFT FOR
IGHREM

TO TALIOUINE

Left margin (top to bottom): AKHFAMANE | 60 MINS | AMALIZ | 90 MINS | MIGGARN | 55 MINS | PATH CROSSED

② ←①
PATH
CROSSED
10 MIN
TRACK
SPLITS
70 MIN
TALIOUINE
SIGN
25 MIN
TINFAT

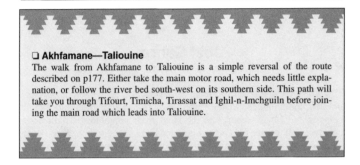

❏ Akhfamane—Taliouine

The walk from Akhfamane to Taliouine is a simple reversal of the route described on p177. Either take the main motor road, which needs little explanation, or follow the river bed south-west on its southern side. This path will take you through Tifourt, Timicha, Tirassat and Ighil-n-Imchguiln before joining the main road which leads into Taliouine.

in which case you must take a higher alternative route in the same direction. This should be relatively easy if you make sure you trace the line of the gorge. The path will then lead through an almond plantation before passing a marabout on the right after just 10 minutes or so.

At this point a smaller path breaks left from the route you have been following. Take this smaller path which will eventually lead down to the very bottom of the valley. Go north-north-west through the valley, walking under a rusty water pipe and heading towards a ruined building up ahead. Some whitened boulders at the sides of the gorge will also help to check your route once you have been walking for 45 minutes from Miggarn.

Continue along the same route for 30 minutes to the village of Amaliz (1113m/3650ft) past a fascinating sequence of weird plants as the valley becomes more fertile. The path will take you east-north-east around the edge of Amaliz. Ten minutes after the village, the path divides but take the dominant route.

After five more minutes you will cross a stream, so you might need sandals, to pick up a sandy stretch of the piste heading north. Some 15 minutes further on a small, rocky path joins the piste from the right. Follow this smaller path up in a north-north-easterly direction. This is the last ascent of the stage and it does get quite steep for about 10 minutes.

When you reach the brow of the ridge over which you are climbing, head north-east to rejoin the wider piste as it meanders towards a mosque. This marks the village of Tamort. From here the piste snakes past dusty houses and mad turkeys for 10 minutes into the village of Tagdilt. Just 10 more minutes and the path winds into Akhfamane. From here one can get motor transport back to Taliouine where, no doubt, the cold beers of Hôtel Ibn Toumert will beckon. Others might prefer to extend their trek by continuing to Taliouine on foot.

Jbel Sahro

This awesome and beautiful range of stark peaks, formidable gorges and isolated communities stretches north-east from Ouarzazate and Zagora between the Sahara desert and the High Atlas mountains. Bright oases punctuate an otherwise forbidding landscape. Nomadic Berbers roam vast, barren valleys beneath strangely-formed and tangled peaks. This is also the land of the infamous Aït Atta tribe, warrior Berbers who resisted French control until 1933.

Tourism has hardly begun to develop here and trekking is still new. This makes Sahro a highly rewarding area in which to travel but also a difficult one. The trails, like those of Jbel Sirwa, are often unclear. Accommodation is scarce and supplies need to be carried. Summers are scorching, winters freezing and water can be hard to find. But trekking in Sahro is an exhilarating adventure. You will feel like an explorer and your efforts will be rewarded by coming across fascinating communities and epic views; such treasures are all the more exciting for being hidden from the gaze of most visitors to Morocco.

JBEL SAHRO: TRAVERSE

N'Kob

N'Kob (sometimes Nekob), a quiet oasis where many of the Aït Atta tribe of 'white Berbers' live, is a convenient trailhead for Jbel Sahro treks. It might feel like the end of the world, framed as it is by bizarre mountains and harsh terrain, but if you are sensibly equipped you will find all your basic needs are met.

There are three places to stay: *Kasbah Salamat Dauod* with rooms for 30dh per person which includes use of the shower; *Kasbah Bahba*, a touch more up-market, with en suite rooms from 150dh and a traditional Berber tent. A place in the tent which sleeps 12 costs 50dh; and *Gîte Bahba*, next door has rooms from 60dh.

Eating opportunities are fairly limited. *Café-Restaurant Bab n'Ali* does a good tagine and salad, enough for three or four people, for 50dh. You might need to order in advance. There is also a **post office**, **hammam**, **shops**, a **Sunday souq** and two **téléboutiques**. For information about **mule and guide hire**, ask for Maarir Hussaine at Café-Restaurant Bab n'Ali.

Getting to N'Kob Buses rarely go direct to N'Kob except on Saturdays in preparation for the Sunday souq. Catch the M'Hamid bus east from

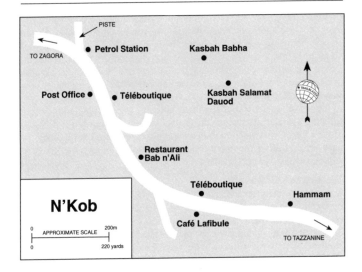

Ouarzazate on the N9 and ask to be dropped at Tansikht. This should take about two and a half hours and will cost 25dh per person. From Tansikht you will need to find a grand taxi to take you north-east to N'Kob. Expect to pay 15dh per place in the taxi for a journey which will last under an hour.

N'Kob—Tifdassine
N'Kob makes a good base from which to organise a traverse of Jbel Sahro but Tifdassine, connected to N'Kob by motor road, is deeper into Sahro trekking country; most trekkers prefer to start walking from there.

Brief notes are given below should you wish to walk this section. The route follows the motor road so, if you set out for Tifdassine on foot but change your mind, you should be able to hitch a lift in a passing vehicle. You should leave a full day to walk from N'Kob to Tifdassine.

Walk out of N'Kob west towards Zagora for 500 metres until you reach a petrol station. A piste leads north from the left side of the petrol station. Take it. There are a few smaller trails off the piste but you should ignore these.

The land is flat and pebble-strewn. After five kilometres, the piste divides. Take the right fork north through a scattered village called Alminewakta.

Two kilometres later, the piste forks again; bear left (north) for 200 metres at which point it splits in several directions. Take a sharp right turn (north-east) past a school.

Continue for another 300 metres until you are walking parallel with a dry river bed for 200 metres. The piste will take you past more houses. zigzag up past them until you reach another divide in the route. Go right and after 50 metres right again so that you are heading north. After a further 50 metres you will arrive at another split. Go right and head towards a clump of palm trees. Pass to the left of these and follow the piste which by now stands out clearly as a major route.

You will snake across dramatic hills of jagged, flinty rock before reaching a plateau after which the piste descends. Suddenly, over the brow of the ridge, a vast valley will open up before you. Head north along the piste, which leads across the west side of the valley, through the village of Aigai to Tifdassine (1210m/3968ft).

Tifdassine—Boilouz   [Map 28]

Descend onto the piste which divides where you join it. Take the right fork (generally north-east) immediately crossing a dry river bed. Look for several cairns to the right to verify your position. After 100m cross another dry bed and at this point leave the piste to head north-east across boulder-strewn terrain. In the distance to the north-east you will see an enormous, sheer rock-face. It's flat on top but scooped at the corner.

After 10 minutes you will ascend a gentle slope to find yourself on sparsely cultivated ground. Keep heading north, with the rock-face on your right side, and after another five minutes a piste will come into view. Head right (north-east) along it until, after 100 metres, it dwindles to a path. Five minutes later it widens to a piste again before dividing. Take the trail to the right and head north-east over rocky ground worn away by previous travellers.

Some 45 minutes into the trek, the path is bisected by another, smaller track. Go left (north-east). You will see to the left (north) a piste leading up a mountainside. Ignore it. To the right are extraordinary, sculpted cliff faces. Soon you'll start to descend gently. The whitened rock under foot will guide you down, but don't go right down to what is a small valley bed. Keep midway between the rocks and the bed. The path is clear. A cluster of organic-looking boulders to your left will verify your position. Bab n'Ali, a huge, towering rock which stands out clearly even from this distance, is now visible to the east. Beneath you lies a wide valley.

The village of Irhazzoun n'Imlas will come into view towards east-south-east 40 minutes after the last time-check. The path, leading east, flattens as it becomes less defined towards the valley floor. Keep going south-east and you will just be able to trace it. It helps that, at this stage, the village is straight ahead. After 15 more minutes you will see a fertile expanse on the left (north-east) while the village is further on. The path comes and goes to some extent but bear south-east along it so that the village is directly in front of you. When you reach a stone wall bear left

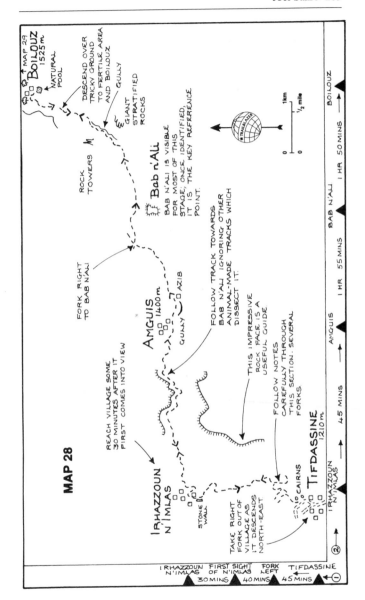

MAP 28

Boilouz 1525m.

MAP 29

NATURAL POOL

DESCEND OVER TRICKY GROUND TO FERTILE AREA AND BOILOUZ

GULLY

GIANT STRATIFIED ROCKS

ROCK TOWERS

Bab n'Ali

BAB N'ALI IS VISIBLE FOR MOST OF THIS STAGE; ONCE IDENTIFIED, IT IS THE KEY REFERENCE POINT.

TRAILBLAZER

0 1km
0 ½ mile

FORK RIGHT TO BAB N'ALI

FOLLOW TRACK TOWARDS BAB N'ALI IGNORING OTHER ANIMAL-MADE TRACKS WHICH DISSECT IT.

AMGUIS 1400m.

AZIB

GULLY

THIS IMPRESSIVE ROCK FACE IS A USEFUL GUIDE

REACH VILLAGE SOME 30 MINUTES AFTER IT FIRST COMES INTO VIEW

FOLLOW NOTES CAREFULLY THROUGH THIS SECTION. SEVERAL FORKS

IRHAZZOUN N'IMLAS

STONE WALL

TIFDASSINE 1210m.

CAIRNS

TAKE RIGHT FORK OUT OF VILLAGE AS IT DESCENDS NORTH-EAST

IRHAZZOUN N'IMLAS 45 MINS

FIRST SIGHT OF N'IMLAS 30 MINS

FORK LEFT 40 MINS

TIFDASSINE 45 MINS

IRHAZZOUN N'IMLAS

AMGUIS 45 MINS

BAB N'ALI 1 HR 55 MINS

BOILOUZ 1 HR 50 MINS

(north-east) along a less rocky path and you will see a small range of rocks to the right (now south-east). Stay parallel with these and ascend a small ridge ahead of you (east-south-east). The trail joins a piste halfway up the ridge. Head south-east across the scattered village which you will reach about 30 minutes after it first came into view.

Continue south-east through the village and cross a wide, dry river bed after which the path swings east-south-east over a small brow. Keep on heading towards Bab n'Ali. After 10 minutes you'll be going east and 20 minutes later you will have ascended to a north-easterly route. There is a valley to the left (north) lined with huge, rounded cliff faces. Shortly afterwards a village, Amguis (1400m/4592ft), will appear almost straight ahead. Carry on north-east along the path ignoring others which cross it.

The trail leads to a dry gully some 15 minutes after Amguis. Cross it to continue east along the path which will trace the gully. After 15 minutes or so you will pass an azib to the right (south). Bab n'Ali is getting closer all the time. After 20 minutes the path will ascend a small ridge. Follow the whitened rock which denotes the trail across rocks. Carry on for 35 minutes until a splash of green plants tells you there is a water-source along this stretch of path. In the wetter seasons you will be able to trace its flow but in the dry season you will be forced to clamber over a steep rock-face to a find a fig tree and, just beyond it, the water.

Carry on along the rocky path towards Bab n'Ali, climbing steadily for about 10 minutes until you reach a stone-coated plateau. Trek across the plateau for 10 minutes until the path divides; go right, towards Bab n'Ali. After 100 metres the path is crossed by another which runs west to east. Ignore it. Bab n'Ali will be on your right side (east) about 10 minutes later and after a few more minutes the track will have led into a dry gully. Head north-east towards another massive rock formation and pick up the trail north as it leads out of the gully. This second rocky area is now to your right. The path comes and goes but keep going north.

Giant stratified rocks will appear to your right some 15 minutes after Bab n'Ali. Climb north, taking care not to lose the path which is hard to follow over the rocky terrain. To the right is a steep but shallow gorge. The path rises and falls fairly gently for the next 10-15 minutes. An impressive system of valleys and peaks will gradually come into view. Carry on for another five minutes to reach a small ravine which descends east-north-east. The path goes down (north) between two rock-faces. The rock itself forms deep steps at the bottom of this stretch of track as it leads onto a valley floor. It then ascends north over a small ridge, weaving an ill-defined track upwards.

Around 30 minutes after the giant stratified rocks, look out for a huge fissured gorge to the north. You are heading east towards Igli at this point, before correcting north-east down a gentle scree slope. The trail leads along a dry gully running north-east until it breaks east over a small ridge which overlooks a valley. Look left to see some gargantuan, free-standing rock towers. Descend east-north-east. In the distance you might be able to see a vivid green fertile area. This is your goal.

Some 55 minutes after the last time-check the track descends over rocky ground to a dry river bed which leads north-east towards that fertile land and, 10 minutes later, you will reach it. This tiny community, really no more than a few huts, is called Boilouz (1525m/5002ft). Walk three minutes south-east to find a natural pool which is dry in the summer. Trekkers regularly camp here.

Boilouz—Tassigdelt   [Map 29, p207]

Walk west-north-west from Boilouz (1525m/5002ft) to pass a cluster of small buildings sitting on a ridge to the left (south) at which point correct to head north-west. Far ahead to the west you will see a series of massive, square peaks. Keep heading north-west as the path which leads in that direction become more distinct. The going is flat and the ground strewn with loose rocks and pebbles.

After five minutes, pass between some boulders where the ground becomes sandy. There is a small stone wall on the right side of the path. After a further five minutes, cross a dry, stony river bed. Head west along it for 50 metres until you find a vague path. There are a couple of buildings ahead and steeply jagged rocks on either side. Soon this little hamlet will be to your left (south-west). Bear right around the rocks to head north-north-west. Continue along a stony path which runs for 50 metres between tiered fields before gently curving up and around a hill in zig-zags, staying parallel with the fields.

The path divides 50 minutes into the trek. Go right heading north-west, and after two minutes you will see an azib on the right. Just before you reach it, leave the path and head north for 100 metres to another azib, this one more ramshackle than the last.

At this point head north-east over rocky ground to where an indistinct path will appear. Follow it, ignoring another path which appears soon after. This track ascends to the north. Quite suddenly you'll see a valley to the north-east. Keep winding along the path for 10 minutes until you reach the end of a gorge. Here, 35 minutes after the last time-check, pick up a path ascending north-west. It describes wide zigzags, but stick with it.

It gets hard to trace the path along this stretch. Sometimes it is marked by a run of straight stones, sometimes it runs over rounded boulders. Keep an eye out for mule droppings; they help to mark the route. After 15 minutes, the path leads to a small brow. To the north, on the next ridge, you will see some jutting cliff faces. Head towards these. After 20 minutes you will have negotiated your way up and around the ridge to a gentle descent. Look out for the village of Igli at the bottom of the valley to the west.

Trek north up the next ridge then descend for five minutes over the other side crossing smooth rock before the ascent starts again. This time head north-north-west towards a mass of flat-topped cliff-faces.

Reaching the next ridge 50 minutes after the last time-check, you will see that the ground ahead is strewn with huge obelisk-like boulders. Climb north, tracing the trail through this strange boulder field. After five minutes the path leads north-east, skirting around the right side of the flat-topped rocks which you saw from the last ridge. The path is rocky and the climbing steep. Head north past this rock formation and carry on north for another 30 minutes until you come to a small azib. Some cairns help lead you to it. This is Tassigdelt (2256m/7219ft), a decent camping site with a water-source and an empty azib for shelter. Expect to reach Tassigdelt some 60 minutes after the last time-check on the ridge. Depending on the time of year, it might take some effort to find the water-source; look for a fertile patch of green plants.

Tassigdelt—Tizi n'Ouarg [Map 29]

Follow a stone wall north-east to find the trail which will immediately ascend north-north-east in zigzags. Climb over some dense black rocks and boulders but continue north-east though you might lose sight of the path here; after which you will begin a gentle descent. The terrain is pebbly and the rocks a reddish colour. You can discern the path whitening the red.

Some 30 minutes into the trek the path leads onto a plateau. Look north to see a valley and to the north-north-east to see a huge, jutting rock. Walk east-north-east, keeping this rock to your left, before descending towards the valley. Cross over a dry, flat river bed to head north-north-west over a gorse-coated ridge. After a few more minutes you will see some azibs to the right (north-east).

Keep going along the left side of a dry gully and you will find a path which takes you over a small ridge towards the north-west. After 100 metres it breaks off to the north. Don't follow it. Instead, ascend north-west to reach another ridge. Then descend over some gorsy ground before ascending again north-north-west over featureless ground towards some strange, sharp and black rock formations. Keep these on your left side until a gap appears where you can cross over them (north-west).

Once up and over these rocks, 30 minutes after reaching the plateau, a path appears running north over flat ground. Follow it as it descends into a valley. There are azibs to the left. Ascend north-north-west for 15 minutes until the path leads north-east. After a further five minutes you will reach a plateau, 80 minutes into the trek, then a gentle descent. Keep heading north-east along this track for 30 minutes at which point you will cross a narrow gully.

The path then goes upwards again, this time north-west, taking you to some black rocks which will force you north-east for a short while. A lone

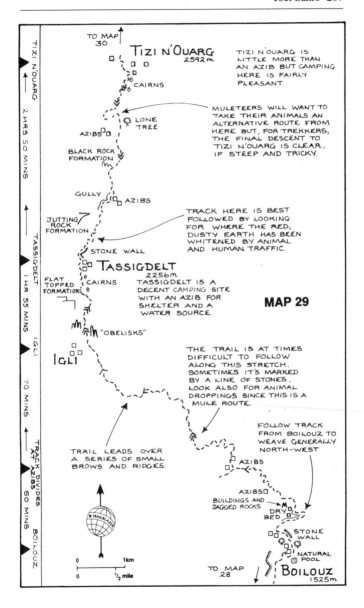

TIZI N'OUARG 2592m

TIZI N'OUARG IS LITTLE MORE THAN AN AZIB BUT CAMPING HERE IS FAIRLY PLEASANT.

TO MAP 30

CAIRNS

LONE TREE

AZIBS

BLACK ROCK FORMATION

MULETEERS WILL WANT TO TAKE THEIR ANIMALS AN ALTERNATIVE ROUTE FROM HERE BUT, FOR TREKKERS, THE FINAL DESCENT TO TIZI N'OUARG IS CLEAR, IF STEEP AND TRICKY.

GULLY

AZIBS

JUTTING ROCK FORMATION

TRACK HERE IS BEST FOLLOWED BY LOOKING FOR WHERE THE RED, DUSTY EARTH HAS BEEN WHITENED BY ANIMAL AND HUMAN TRAFFIC.

STONE WALL

TASSIGDELT 2256m

FLAT TOPPED FORMATIONS

CAIRNS

TASSIGDELT IS A DECENT CAMPING SITE WITH AN AZIB FOR SHELTER AND A WATER SOURCE.

MAP 29

"OBELISKS"

IGLI

THE TRAIL IS AT TIMES DIFFICULT TO FOLLOW ALONG THIS STRETCH. SOMETIMES IT'S MARKED BY A LINE OF STONES. LOOK ALSO FOR ANIMAL DROPPINGS SINCE THIS IS A MULE ROUTE.

FOLLOW TRACK FROM BOILOUZ TO WEAVE GENERALLY NORTH-WEST

TRAIL LEADS OVER A SERIES OF SMALL BROWS AND RIDGES.

AZIBS

AZIBS

BUILDINGS AND JAGGED ROCKS

DRY BED

STONE WALL

NATURAL POOL

BOILOUZ 1525m

TRAILAZIZ

0   1km

0   ½ mile

TO MAP 28

TIZI N'OUARG ← 2 HRS 50 MINS ← TASSIGDELT ← 1 HR 55 MINS ← IGLI ← 70 MINS ← TRACK DIVIDES AT AZIBS ← 50 MINS ← BOILOUZ

tree to the north-north-east will verify your position. After a couple more minutes, the path leads north-west to a small plateau then descends again over a gorse-coated mountainside.

If you have a mule, the muleteer will want to leave you at this point to meet you after this next stretch which is difficult for mules. Head west over a small ridge, which comes into view where the patch of gorse ends. The path then makes a very sharp descent. Far below you'll see the path meandering north-north-west through a wide valley. The mule, meanwhile, makes a longer but easier descent.

After making it down this steep face, 60 minutes after the last time-check, pick up the clear track running north-north-west over sparse, flat land. There are fantastic views along the valley to either side. Some 20 minutes later, another valley will meet yours from the left (south-west). There are several azibs dotted around the point where the two valleys adjoin. To the right stand a series of one-metre-high cairns. This is Tizi n'Ouarg (2592m/8501ft).

Tizi n'Ouarg—Isk n'Iferd—Tislit n'Ouzarzam—Tagdilt [Map 30]
Walk behind the azib heading west across a gorsy incline. The path isn't clear at first but, after five minutes, you will find one zigzagging steeply up the incline. After 20 minutes the track reaches the ridge at which point the path becomes much rockier.

Another five minutes will take you onto a plateau and over a shallow decline. Look out for azibs straight ahead. The peak to the north-east is Isk n'Alla (2569m/8426ft). The path will take you across a small valley and north between two tall rock masses. Over this stretch the path becomes ill-defined as it crosses dusty, rocky ground. Keep ascending steadily to the north-north-west.

Look for a small copse 45 minutes into the trek and head towards it. The path describes lazy zigzags across boulders and gorse. Within 10 minutes you will be in the copse and a few minutes later the path will lead onto a mini-plateau heading north-west. The path at this point is sandy and dusty. After a 10-minute descent you should be able to see a vast valley and plateau region stretching away to the north-west.

Twenty-five minutes later, walking north-north-west along the trail, you will reach a shallow valley littered with tumbledown azibs. Leaving the valley to the left, the path switches back towards the azibs. Before reaching them, it crosses a depression to ascend smoothly for 10 minutes. It then descends slowly north. Ahead stand some amazing peaks of splintered, fissured rocks. In a valley below, to the north-east, lies Tislit n'Ouzarzam. The path winds around the east side of the bizarre rocks before descending steeply in zigzags over and around large rocks and boulders.

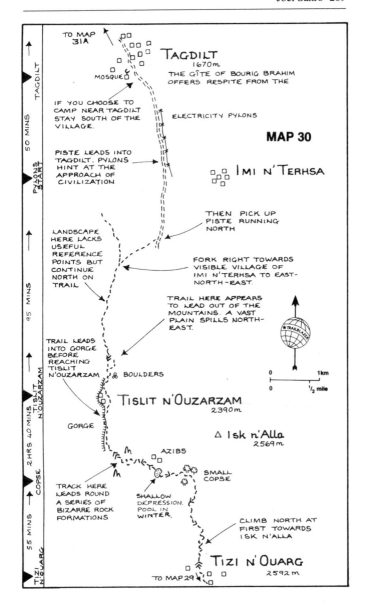

TO MAP 31A

TAGDILT
1670m
THE GÎTE OF BOURIG BRAHIM
OFFERS RESPITE FROM THE

MOSQUE

IF YOU CHOOSE TO
CAMP NEAR TAGDILT
STAY SOUTH OF THE
VILLAGE.

ELECTRICITY PYLONS

MAP 30

PISTE LEADS INTO
TAGDILT. PYLONS
HINT AT THE
APPROACH OF
CIVILIZATION

IMI N'TERHSA

THEN PICK UP
PISTE RUNNING
NORTH

LANDSCAPE
HERE LACKS
USEFUL
REFERENCE
POINTS BUT
CONTINUE
NORTH ON
TRAIL

FORK RIGHT TOWARDS
VISIBLE VILLAGE OF
IMI N'TERHSA TO EAST-
NORTH-EAST.

TRAIL HERE APPEARS
TO LEAD OUT OF THE
MOUNTAINS. A VAST
PLAIN SPILLS NORTH-
EAST.

TRAIL LEADS
INTO GORGE
BEFORE
REACHING
TISLIT
N'OUZARZAM

& BOULDERS

★ TRAILBLAZER

TISLIT N'OUZARZAM
2390m

0   1km
0   ½ mile

GORGE

△ Isk n'Alla
2569m

AZIBS

SMALL
COPSE

TRACK HERE
LEADS ROUND
A SERIES OF
BIZARRE ROCK
FORMATIONS

SHALLOW
DEPRESSION.
POOL IN
WINTER.

CLIMB NORTH AT
FIRST TOWARDS
ISK N'ALLA

TIZI N'OUARG
2592m

TO MAP 29

TAGDILT

50 MINS

PYLONS START

95 MINS

TISLIT N'OUZARZAM

2 HRS 40 MINS

COPSE

55 MINS

TIZI N'OUARG

It will take about 40 minutes to get clear of this rocky stretch. Continue to descend so that you are trekking north-west across a short plateau. The trail then snakes down towards the valley which flicks in and out of sight

After 35 minutes of descent, it leads past a tight flower-filled gorge. Continue north with the gorge to the left as the track leads away from it to a ridge. Then take the path which leads down into the gorge and head north to an azib which you should expect to reach about 40 minutes after first seeing the flowery gorge. This is Tislit n'Ouzarzam (2390m/7839ft). If you decide to camp here in the wet season, climb to high ground to find a safe site.

Climb north-east away from the gorge towards several piles of large boulders. The gorge will then be to the left. You will see that it peters out into flat ground. After five minutes pick up a path leading north over flat, rocky ground. After a further 10 minutes you will cross a dry river bed as the path continues north. At this stage you appear to be almost out of the mountains. A giant plain spills north-east and, on the horizon, another mountain range claws at the sky. The terrain here changes from boulder-strewn to dusty. It's punctuated by winding gullies and river beds. Trek in a generally north-easterly direction.

After 40 minutes, as the path heads north, look for the village of Imi n'Terhsa (1650m/5412ft) to the east-north-east and the track which leads to it. Take this path and descend over a dry gully before reaching a piste. Pass the village to your right (east) and follow the piste north. Imi n'Terhsa is widespread so it takes some time to get clear of the last houses.

About 40 minutes after the last time-check, electricity pylons join the road to the right as you trek north-west towards Tagdilt (1670m/5477ft). Use these to guide you and after 20 more minutes you will have left Imi n'Terhsa and the power lines behind. At this point Tagdilt is visible straight ahead. When you reach the mosque, some 30 minutes later, you will know you have arrived.

There is a well-kept *gîte* in Tagdilt (40dh per person) which is man-aged by Bourig Brahim. If you plan to camp, pitch your tent before you actually reach the village on the flat land which surrounds it to the south. You can get motor transport from here to Boumalne from where you can catch a bus back to Ouarzazate.

Tagdilt—Aït Yassine   [Maps 31a and 31b, p211 and p213]

This stretch of the trek covers markedly different terrain. Having left the peaks behind, the going is flat and the views more desert-like. The route is beautiful, however, and serves to illustrate the great diversity across the Moroccan Atlas.

Follow the piste west from Tagdilt until it veers left (north-west) by the mosque. After five minutes walking on level ground you will see a couple of houses ahead. Bear left, avoiding the track which leads to them.

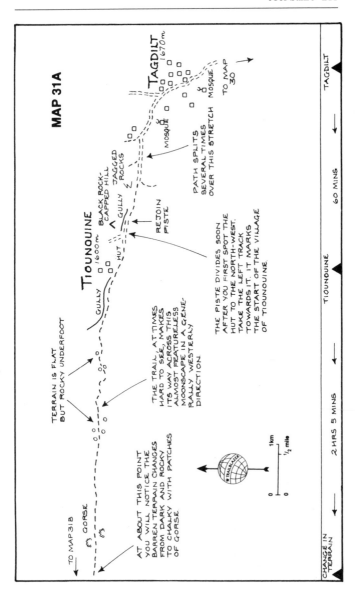

MAP 31A

TAGDILT 1670m

TO MAP 30

TIOUNOUINE 1600m

BLACK ROCK-CAPPED HILL

JAGGED ROCKS

GULLY

HUT

GULLY

RETJOIN PISTE

MOSQUE

MOSQUE

PATH SPLITS SEVERAL TIMES OVER THIS STRETCH

TERRAIN IS FLAT BUT ROCKY UNDERFOOT

THE TRAIL, AT TIMES HARD TO SEE, MAKES ITS WAY ACROSS THIS ALMOST FEATURELESS MOONSCAPE IN A GENERALLY WESTERLY DIRECTION

THE PISTE DIVIDES SOON AFTER YOU FIRST SPOT THE HUT TO THE NORTH-WEST. TAKE THE LEFT TRACK TOWARDS IT. IT MARKS THE START OF THE VILLAGE OF TIOUNOUINE.

TO MAP 31B

GORSE

AT ABOUT THIS POINT YOU WILL NOTICE THE BARREN TERRAIN CHANGES FROM DARK AND ROCKY TO CHALKY WITH PATCHES OF GORSE

1km
½ mile
0

CHANGE IN TERRAIN   2 HRS 5 MINS   TIOUNOUINE   60 MINS   TAGDILT

After 30 minutes the piste divides, bear left to the west. Some 10 minutes later you will pass some elevated, jagged rocks to the right. The piste bifurcates again at this point. Bear right (north-west) across a narrow, dry gully. After a short while the piste dwindles to a path heading north-west over rocky ground. Carry on for another 10 minutes until clear of the rocks, and the path, which by now is somewhat intermittent, is leading west-north-west. Look for a low ochre hill capped by black rock in the distance and trek towards it for a few minutes. You will then be able to rejoin the piste which runs past the black-capped hill to the north-west.

Soon a wide gully will appear to the right, snaking west. Trace it until a tiny hut appears to the north-west. The piste divides again some 50 metres after you spot the hut. Go left and head towards it. You will see now that there are several dwellings. This hamlet is called Tiounouine (1600m/5248ft). You should reach it 60 minutes after leaving Tagdilt.

Keep following the trail north-west past the village to what seems to be the definition of nowhere. After 10 minutes you will see the large gully to your right again. Continue north-west until, after another 10 minutes, the trail winds towards the west. After a further 25 minutes you will leave the gully behind as the track leads west but the gully continues north-west. Five more minutes will take you to another shallower river bed. Cross it and pick up the path again. After 100 metres you will cross another river bed but maintain a westerly direction. The trail, which is often just discernible, makes its way across this at times almost featureless moonscape for another two hours.

You will notice, some 125 minutes after the last time-check, that the terrain, still completely flat, changes from being dark and rocky to chalky with patches of gorse. At about this point you should be able to pick out a ridge to the west with agadirs built atop it. Continue west, ignoring a piste leading north-west which crosses the path. After a further 15 minutes you will cross another wide, dry bed. Carry on west. A further 15 minutes will bring you to a point where the agadirs can clearly be seen. Head towards them then west-south-west along the indistinct trail which leaves the agadirs to your right.

The track gradually widens to a piste as it meanders west then south-west. Look west for a clear patch of fertile land 30 minutes later. This is Aït Yassine (1453m/4765ft). At this point the piste divides. Go left to find the village which you should reach after approximately four hours 15 minutes' walking. It sits by the floodplain of the Dadès river. While there is little to recommend Aït Yassine itself, although the views in every direction are striking, you might choose to break your trek here.

Aït Yassine—Tassouit [Map 31b, opposite]

The piste runs clearly to the south-west from Aït Yassine. With the ridge, river bed and village to the right (west), the piste continues to wend south-

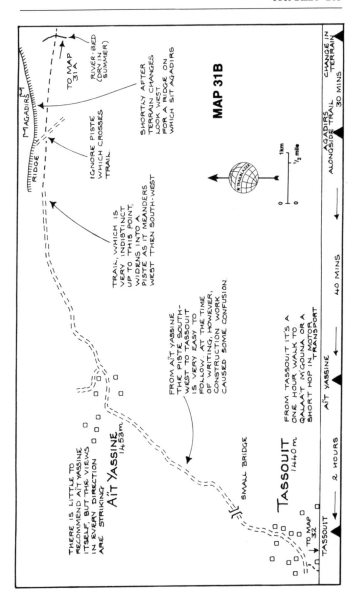

MAGADIRS

TO MAP 31A

RIVER-BED (DRY IN SUMMER)

SHORTLY AFTER TERRAIN CHANGES LOOK WEST FOR A RIDGE ON WHICH SIT AGADIRS

MAP 31B

RIDGE

IGNORE PISTE WHICH CROSSES TRAIL

TRAIL, WHICH IS VERY INDISTINCT UP TO THIS POINT, WIDENS INTO A PISTE AS IT MEANDERS WEST THEN SOUTH-WEST

FROM AÏT YASSINE THE PISTE SOUTH-WEST TO TASSOUIT IS VERY EASY TO FOLLOW. AT THE TIME OF WRITING, HOWEVER, CONSTRUCTION WORK CAUSED SOME CONFUSION.

1 km
½ mile
0

THERE IS LITTLE TO RECOMMEND AÏT YASSINE ITSELF, BUT THE VIEWS IN EVERY DIRECTION ARE STRIKING

AÏT YASSINE 1453 m.

FROM TASSOUIT IT'S A ONE HOUR WALK TO QALA'AT M'GOUNA OR A SHORT HOP IN MOTOR TRANSPORT

SMALL BRIDGE

TASSOUIT 1440 m.

TO MAP 32

CHANGE IN TERRAIN
30 MINS
AGADIRS ALONGSIDE TRAIL
40 MINS
AÏT YASSINE
2 HOURS
TASSOUIT

west. After 40 minutes, the piste becomes confusing because of the unfin-
ished construction work. You will come to a man-made gully. Cross over
a small bridge and continue south-west along the piste. Tassouit
(1440m/4723ft) will come into view soon after crossing the bridge.
Simply follow the piste all the way to it. Allow two hours to trek from Aït
Yassine to Tassouit.

The village itself is quiet and uninspiring but one can normally find
limited supplies, and a place to stay for a 30dh charge. Since there is no
official gîte you will need to ask around. *Camping* is possible outside the
village. From here is just a one-hour walk north-west across the floodplain
through Zawyat to the town of Qalaa't M'gouna (sometimes called El
Kelâa M'gouna) which is described in more detail below. One can normally find motor transport to Qalaa't M'gouna either by grand taxi or
camion. Expect to pay about 15dh per person.

Qalaa't M'gouna (El Kelâa M'gouna)

Fields in the Dadès are defined not by hedges but by roses. In spring the
roses are harvested to make rose-water and Qalaa't M'gouna, an otherwise unexceptional but pleasant town, is the centre for this process. A
colourful rose festival is held at harvest time in May; it is made all the
more appealing by the women of the Aït Atta tribe of Berbers, said to be
the most beautiful women in Morocco, who bring roses to the town from
the surrounding valleys. Hundreds of tonnes of rose petals are then made
into rose-water at a factory based in an old kasbah. It is shipped from
Morocco to Grasse in southern France where it is used as a basic ingredient in a whole range of perfumes. The sweet-smelling water is also used
for washing hands across the Islamic world.

Qalaa't M'gouna offers all the services trekkers might need after a
challenging Jbel Sahro trek. There are three places to stay. The most
expensive, *Les Roses des Dadès* (☎ 04-88.38.07), has fine views, a pool
and stables. It costs around 400dh for a double room. *Auberge Pont
d'Almou* (☎ 04-83.69.13) is about four kilometres out of town to the west.
It's a small, attractive place with mid-range prices. Budget travellers
should try *Hôtel du Grand Atlas* (☎ 04-88.38.37), on the main road
through the town, which charges about 70dh for basic but adequate rooms.

Services include a Wednesday **souq**, a handful of shops (all of which
sell rose-water), a **bank**, **téléboutiques** and a **Bureau des Guides**. Head
straight for the Bureau des Guides for trekking information or to find a
guide or muleteer. There's a **hammam** in Hôtel du Grand Atlas.

JBEL SAHRO: CIRCULAR TREK

Qalaa't M'gouna and Tassouit

Qalaa't M'gouna is the trailhead for this circular trek although the walking proper starts from Tassouit. Both places mark the end of the Jbel Sahro

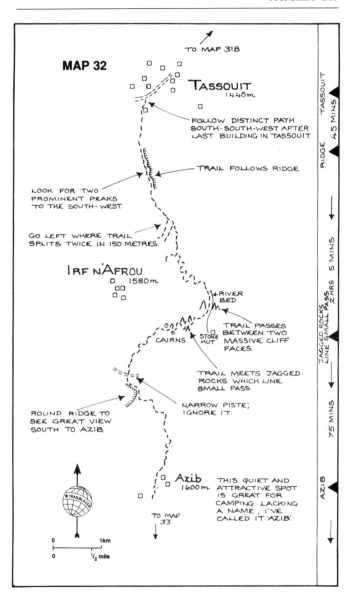

MAP 32

TO MAP 31B

TASSOUIT
1440m

FOLLOW DISTINCT PATH
SOUTH-SOUTH-WEST AFTER
LAST BUILDING IN TASSOUIT.

TRAIL FOLLOWS RIDGE.

LOOK FOR TWO
PROMINENT PEAKS
TO THE SOUTH-WEST.

GO LEFT WHERE TRAIL
SPLITS TWICE IN 150 METRES.

IRF N'AFROU
1580m

RIVER
BED

TRAIL PASSES
BETWEEN TWO
MASSIVE CLIFF
FACES.

CAIRNS
STONE
HUT

TRAIL MEETS JAGGED
ROCKS WHICH LINE
SMALL PASS.

ROUND RIDGE TO
SEE GREAT VIEW
SOUTH TO AZIB.

NARROW PISTE;
IGNORE IT.

Azib
1600m

THIS QUIET AND
ATTRACTIVE SPOT
IS GREAT FOR
CAMPING. LACKING
A NAME, I'VE
CALLED IT 'AZIB'.

TO MAP
33

0   1km
0   ¹/₂ mile

★ TRAIL N° AZ.31

TASSOUIT

RIDGE 45 MINS

JAGGED ROCKS
LINE SMALL PASS 2 HRS 5 MINS

75 MINS

AZIB

traverse described over the previous few pages. You could walk to
Tassouit from Qalaa't M'gouna in about an hour. The route is fairly clear.
Or you could take a grand taxi or camion for about 15dh per person. These
route notes pick up the trek from Tassouit. Although this trek is described
here as a circular route (*boucle*), it really ends not in Qalaa't M'gouna but
in Boumalne du Dadès. The towns are close, however, so the route is
almost a complete circle.

Tassouit—Azib [Map 32, p215]

Walk south-west through Tassouit (1440m/4723ft) until you reach the last
house in the village. If you are continuing straight on from the traverse,
this will be about where you had got to at the end of that trek. At the edge
of Tassouit head south-south-west and you will quickly walk clear of the
village and onto a distinct path which will take you over some rocks
towards smoothly-rounded hills. The terrain is pebble-strewn. The trail
then averages a south-south-easterly direction up and down a series of
arid slopes.

Two prominent peaks can clearly be seen to the south-west about 45
minutes into the trek as the trail leads along a ridge to the south-west. A
series of craggy peaks stand out to the south and a valley lies to the right
(south-west); gullies run into it from the ridge. Heading south-south-east
you will pass the craggy peaks to the right after some 15 minutes. As you
do so you will descend for a small stretch and the piste will meander
between some jagged rocks for 50 metres. Keep on the piste, averaging
south-south-east.

Some 45 minutes later you will pass another stretch of valley to the
right (south-west) and the track divides. Go left (south-east) and another
dry valley will appear. After 150 metres a path will branch right from the
trail to take you away from the valley to the left. Follow it to another piste
which leads west around a hill until it faces south.

At this point another path branches off to the south-west. Follow it as
it carves a snaking descent towards a fertile valley lying west-south-west.
The path leads generally south-west. You will then see a village to the
right (west) called Irf n'Afrou (1580m/5182ft). At this point the path
swings to the south-east to trace a river bed. Walk along the river bed,
heading south, to pass between two massive rock-faces. To the south-
south-east you will see a little stone hut. Carry on south-west, heading
away from the river bed, to follow the path as it ascends steeply to a ridge
before leading along a narrow pass framed by jagged rocks. The trail at
this point, 65 minutes after the last time-check, is marked by cairns.

The path will start to run south-west up a rocky gully as it ascends
towards another ridge which is again capped by jagged waist-high rocks
which form a pass. After 10 minutes you will descend to the south-west.
Straight ahead is a sharp peak that looks like a walnut whip. The path

heads to the right of this (south-west) and across some fissured rocks. After another five minutes the path crosses a narrow piste. Ignore this and continue south-west over flat ground engraved by little rivulets.

After another 10 minutes you will round a ridge to be confronted with a great view into a valley. Look to the south-west where a lone azib stands in this green fertile place. Continue along the path until you find yourself trekking south over a dry river bed and you pass the azib to the right. You will see now that there are some other huts to the left (south-east) and, straight ahead, as well. To the south-west there is a hut built into the rocks and to the north-west some cultivated fields. We were unable to find a name for this beautiful and tranquil spot, perfect for camping, so have simply called it azib (1600m/5248ft). Expect to reach this azib about 50 minutes after reaching the cairns.

Azib—Tafoughalt [Map 33, p219]

Trek south-south-west from the azib (1600m/5248ft) along the valley floor. You will pass a low stone wall to the left. Where this ends a path appears to the left. Take it. After 50 metres it crosses the river bed to lead south-south-west. After just five minutes the path bifurcates. Bear left over flat ground to stay more or less parallel with the river bed. The valley sides are crowned by sharp peaks. There is little vegetation. Gradually the path veers almost due south. A series of low, rounded peaks in the distance makes a useful marker. Carry on for another 10 minutes to make a short ascent.

Follow the path as the terrain becomes loose and rocky. Keep heading south, making a short descent onto another stretch of dry river bed. Cross over it and climb again. Look out for a small house set into the hill to the left of the path. A low wall runs to the right. Keep flush with the wall and bear right to follow a trail which ascends south-south-west.

After 40 minutes trekking the path divides into three. Bear left (south-east) and upwards (the middle path is flat, the one to the right descends). The left path leads across gentle hills and ridges south-south-east. Look out for an azib to the south-east. At this point the path divides. Bear left and after five minutes you will see to the south-south-east a peak with a deep ravine running north-north-west across it.

Cross a shallow gully and continue south. The track will start to ascend in zigzags. The few small huts around this point form the hamlet of Tidghit. There are some huts on the slope facing you. To your left (south-south-east) stands an impressive sequence of summits and to the west-south-west one peak encircled by a gorge. Head south-south-west keeping the huts to your right. The rocks on the track are black and shiny, gleaming in contrast to the golden gorse.

You should reach a water-source to the right some 30 minutes after the path divides into three. The trail then descends to a river bed which wends south-south-east to a path which leads south-south-west. That path, which you should follow, ascends gently. After 10 minutes you will pass a large boulder blocking a left turn from the trail. The terrain here is a little more sandy. Another 15 minutes will take you south on a steep ascent over some large boulders after which the boulders give way to a broad view into a valley. There is an azib to the right just a little further on. Continue along the path bearing left, off which minor forks lead.

The path continues to another dry river bed 45 minutes after the water-source. At this stage the ground flattens out and ahead, south-west, you will see a small hut. As you approach you will see more azibs and fields to the right. Pass these, keeping left, and continue south-south-west. Although this turning is hard to see after 100 metres the path branches right from the river bed to pass over whitened rock.

Just 15 minutes later, the path recrosses to the left side of the river bed to lead south to a huge, jagged boulder which sits precariously in the centre of the river bed. Some 20 metres later the path again crosses the river bed to trace a route towards the south-east. There is some water here. The path then begins to zigzag clearly and steeply towards the mountain peaks. This area is still Tidghit. After 10 minutes a ravine comes into view to the left (north) and a massive, sharp peak stands ahead (east). Keep climbing up the mountainside. After another 10 minutes you will pass over a ridge to face south once more.

Carry on south until you see a valley straight ahead. This is Tafoughalt (2050m/6724ft). Head down over the rocks towards an expanse of verdant land and a collection of huts. There is a wonderful pool here at this natural *camping* area. To find the pool go north-west up a shallow, flower-filled gorge for five minutes. Then clamber over some rocks to reach it. Follow the river bed east for five minutes to find a source for drinking water. You should reach Tafoughalt after a total trek of about 180 minutes.

Tafoughalt—Tizi n'Tagmout—Assaka n'Aït Ouzzine   [Map 33]

Trek south-south-east, leaving the dry river bed behind, as the trail leads between two huts about 100 metres apart towards a walled orchard of almond trees straight ahead. Go left of the orchard, past a water point, towards another small orchard 100 metres ahead.

Follow the path towards these trees but go west as you reach a wall to the left and some rocks to the right. This direction leads towards another valley. After 50 metres go left from the path onto boulder-strewn ground, then south for 100 metres before correcting south-west across an incline which leads away from the valley. Continue south-west over a series of small ridges until you see to the left (south-south-east), a tall range of stratified summits. The terrain here is reddish and rocky. Straight ahead

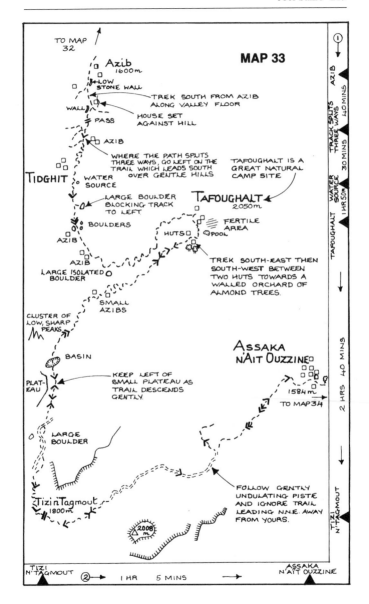

MAP 33

TO MAP 32

Azib 1600m

LOW STONE WALL

TREK SOUTH FROM AZIB ALONG VALLEY FLOOR

WALL

HOUSE SET AGAINST HILL

PASS

Azib

WHERE THE PATH SPLITS THREE WAYS, GO LEFT ON THE TRAIL WHICH LEADS SOUTH OVER GENTLE HILLS

TAFOUGHALT IS A GREAT NATURAL CAMP SITE

TIDGHIT

WATER SOURCE

LARGE BOULDER BLOCKING TRACK TO LEFT.

TAFOUGHALT 2050m

FERTILE AREA

BOULDERS

HUTS

POOL

AZIB

TREK SOUTH-EAST THEN SOUTH-WEST BETWEEN TWO HUTS TOWARDS A WALLED ORCHARD OF ALMOND TREES.

AZIB

LARGE ISOLATED BOULDER

SMALL AZIBS

CLUSTER OF LOW, SHARP PEAKS

ASSAKA N'AIT OUZZINE

BASIN

PLATEAU

KEEP LEFT OF SMALL PLATEAU AS TRAIL DESCENDS GENTLY.

1584m

TO MAP 34

LARGE BOULDER

TizinTagmout 1800m

2008 m

FOLLOW GENTLY UNDULATING PISTE AND IGNORE TRAIL LEADING N.N.E. AWAY FROM YOURS.

AZIB 40 MINS

TRACK SPLITS THREE WAYS 30 MINS

TAFOUGHALT WATER SOURCE 1 HR 50M

2 HRS 40 MINS

TIZI N'TAGMOUT

(south-west) you will see a cluster of low peaks. Expect to see these some 35 minutes into the trek.

As you get close to these peaks, the track modifies to a south-south-westerly course so that you pass to the left of them. Then pick up a path heading south which goes upwards in lazy zigzags. After 15 minutes cross a ridge, heading west. In the distant south-west stands is a wide, flat section of the range called Tagmout. Keep following the trail until as it swings to point south again, an enormous, rectangular rock mass comes into view. Descend steeply south-west from here until the path flattens and leads south-south-west. This whole area seems to have been whittled into a vast array of peaks and ridges, clusters of strange black rock and sheer cliff faces.

Some 80 minutes into the trek will see the track lead into a sort of basin. Continue south-west and cross a narrow gully. The path ascends for just 50 metres before descending towards a small plateau. Keep to the left of this, sticking to the path. After 10 minutes the track will curve briefly east. At this stage you will see a steep peak ahead and, to the right of it (south-south-east), a sharp, jagged rock-face. Keep on the path, which leads south now, towards the jagged rock-face. Just five minutes later an epic view will suddenly open up to reveal a vast valley and mighty stretch of mountains running west-north-west to east-south-east. These are the Tagmout mountains. A big, isolated boulder stands in the foreground. Follow the track west-south-west now, going towards the valley.

Cross a dry gully, which runs south into the valley, 30 minutes after reaching the basin. The trail at this stage leads south-west. You will see from here that there are some houses and trees in the valley. Head south along flat ground, bearing left, and after 15 minutes you will find the path swings south-east away from the valley. After a few more minutes walk the path joins a piste. Go left (south-east) and then briefly east. Then, 200 metres later, pick up the path, which is on the left of the piste, heading east-south-east between rocks. To the left is a huge, craggy rock and to the right long, flat mountains.

After another five minutes the path fades into a dry gully, heading east. Follow it for five minutes until you see an azib ahead. Here rejoin the path which leads out of the gully and past the azib. After another 10 minutes pick up the piste which steers over a col, Tizi n'Tagmout (1800m/5904ft), which you should expect to reach some 160 minutes into the trek. At the col you will see to the left, running north-east to west, a long, craggy range. To the right, running north-east to south, a flatter, steeper range.

Continue north-east along a gently undulating piste for about 30 minutes reaching a dry, rocky river bed. The piste leads north-east, to negotiate a rock mass, then south-east. Another trail, ascending north-north-east, meets yours. Ignore it. After five minutes the piste starts a descent into an impressive valley, walled by fissured rock. Cross over a dry river bed, that of the Oued Assaka, before climbing the opposite side of the valley. Keep on following the trail for another 30 minutes to reach Assaka n'Aït Ouzzine (1584m/5195ft). This is a particularly attractive little village. Follow the winding track north-east through it, past some almond trees, to find the pleasant camping area. There is water here; remember to use your iodine.

Assaka n'Aït Ouzzine—Irhissi   [Map 34, p222]

Walk 200 metres north-east from the last building in Assaka n'Aït Ouzzine to find a path which climbs a rock-face running parallel with an almond orchard. Ascend north-east in wide zigzags until, after 10 minutes, the village has been left behind. To the left (north-west) another path runs along the opposite side of the valley. Continue north-east, negotiating the occasional ascending switchback.

Look down to the left 35 minutes into the trek to see another area of tiered fields lush with green vegetation. About five minutes later a plateau comes into view straight ahead. Keep going east-north-east. Imposing, flat-topped volcanic peaks stand out to the north-east. This is Tine Ouiayour (2129m/6983ft). The land along this stretch is mostly flat and covered with gorse and small boulders. After 20 minutes you will descend into a low valley where you will see azibs and walled fields to the left (north-east). Leave the path and pass to the right of these fields to head north-east directly towards Tine Ouaiyour. Then, 30 minutes after reaching the low valley, pick out a clear path heading east.

Follow this path as it descends gently crossing a small gully and swinging to face east-north-east. After 10 more minutes the path will wind east into another dry gorge. Walk to the right (south-east) side of the gorge to find a path which ascends out of the gorge to the east-north-east. Tine Ouaiyour will be to the left.

Some 35 minutes later the path will have passed around the east side of Tine Ouaiyour and another series of huge, strange summits (to the east-north-east), Jbel Amlal (2447m/8026ft) comes into view. Follow the path for a further 15 minutes, now heading north, to pass an azib and some strange rock formations to the right (east-north-east). Another 15 minutes will take you to an azib on the left. As you pass these, look due north to see an amazing, sheer gorge. The track descends west, then north towards the gorge. Clamber down the right (east) side of the gorge in zigzags.

You should reach the floor of the gorge 20 minutes later and you'll see a stone wall. This gorge is Irhissi (1625m/5330ft). Continue zigzagging along the gorge, following the path, until, after 10 minutes, it crosses a small stream. The gorge floor has by now become green and fertile. The depth of water in the gorge will, obviously, depend on the season. After 10 more minutes, the path crosses the stream again. At this point bear right

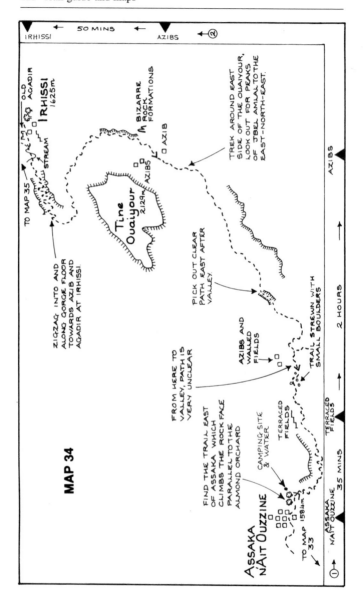

MAP 34

IRHISSI ◄— 50 MINS ◄— AZIBS ◄—Ⓝ

OLD AGADIR
IRHISSI 1625m

STREAM

TO MAP 35

ZIGZAG INTO AND ALONG GORGE FLOOR TOWARDS AZIB AND AGADIR AT IRHISSI.

BIZARRE ROCK FORMATIONS

□ AZIB

Tine Ouaiyour 2124m

AZIBS □

TREK AROUND EAST SIDE OF THE OUAIYOUR, LOOK OUT FOR PEAKS OF JBEL AMLAL TO THE EAST-NORTH-EAST.

PICK OUT CLEAR PATH EAST AFTER VALLEY

FROM HERE TO VALLEY, PATH IS VERY UNCLEAR

AZIBS AND WALLED FIELDS

TRAIL STREWN WITH SMALL BOULDERS

AZIBS ◄

FIND THE TRAIL EAST OF ASSAKA WHICH CLIMBS THE ROCK FACE PARALLEL TO THE ALMOND ORCHARD

CAMPING SITE & WATER

TERRACED FIELDS

ASSAKA N'AIT OUZZINE 1584m

TO MAP 33

①—► N'AIT OUZZINE 35 MINS ◄ TERRACED FIELDS ◄ 2 HOURS —► AZIBS

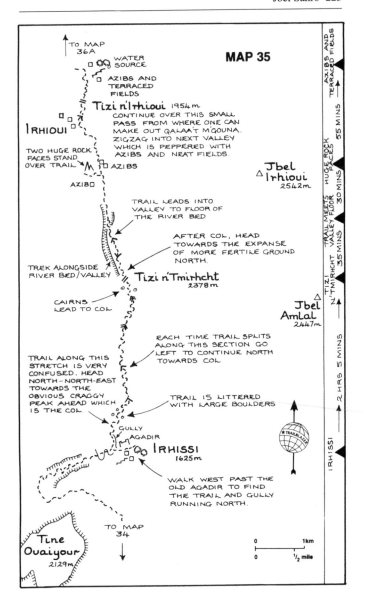

TO MAP
36A

WATER
SOURCE

AZIBS AND
TERRACED
FIELDS

MAP 35

Tizi n'Irhioui 1954m
CONTINUE OVER THIS SMALL
PASS FROM WHERE ONE CAN
MAKE OUT QALA'AT M'GOUNA.
ZIGZAG INTO NEXT VALLEY
WHICH IS PEPPERED WITH
AZIBS AND NEAT FIELDS.

IRHIOUI

TWO HUGE ROCK
FACES STAND
OVER TRAIL

AZIBS

△ Jbel
Irhioui
2542m

AZIBO

TRAIL LEADS INTO
VALLEY TO FLOOR OF
THE RIVER BED

AFTER COL, HEAD
TOWARDS THE EXPANSE
OF MORE FERTILE GROUND
NORTH.

TREK ALONGSIDE
RIVER BED/VALLEY

Tizi n'Tmirhcht
2378m

CAIRNS
LEAD TO COL

△ Jbel
AmLal
2447m

EACH TIME TRAIL SPLITS
ALONG THIS SECTION GO
LEFT TO CONTINUE NORTH
TOWARDS COL

TRAIL ALONG THIS
STRETCH IS VERY
CONFUSED. HEAD
NORTH-NORTH-EAST
TOWARDS THE
OBVIOUS CRAGGY
PEAK AHEAD WHICH
IS THE COL.

TRAIL IS LITTERED
WITH LARGE BOULDERS

GULLY
AGADIR

IRHISSI
1625m

★ TRAILBLAZER

WALK WEST PAST THE
OLD AGADIR TO FIND
THE TRAIL AND GULLY
RUNNING NORTH.

TO MAP
34

Tine
Ouaiyour
2129m

AZIBS AND TERRACED FIELDS
55 MINS
HUGE ROCK FACES
30 MINS
TIZI N'TMIRHCHT TRAIL MEETS VALLEY FLOOR
35 MINS
2 HRS 5 MINS
IRHISSI

0   1km
0   ½ mile

(north-east) for five minutes. A hut and some cultivated terraces come into view to the left. The path then leads past an old agadir on the left; this is a good *camping* spot where almond trees offer shade and there is water. Find higher ground in the wet months. Again, you could choose to bivouac here if you so desired.

Irhissi—Tizi n'Tmirhcht—Tizi n'Irhioui   [Map 35, p223]

Walk west behind the agadir for 150 metres to find a trail and gully running north towards Tizi n'Tmirhcht. It is difficult to follow the trail as it winds north. First it leads west for 200 metres at which point a separate path crosses a small mound after which it re-joins the gorge floor. Cross over and head north-north-east to find a path on the right which zigzags up. After 10 minutes the path will take you back across the gorge floor to head north-east.

All the time the trail is gradually ascending north-north-east. The terrain is boulder-strewn and sandy. There is a tall, craggy peak directly ahead. This is where the trek leads. Go on ascending in zigzags; each time the path seems to bifurcate continue to head north.

The ascent take some 90 minutes which, when combined with the initial gorge-walking, means the path reaches Tizi n'Tmirhcht (2378m/7799ft) 125 minutes into the trek. Some cairns mark the col which is anyway fairly distinct. To the north far ahead you will be able to see a plain and a town. This is Qalaa't M'gouna. Trek north along the boulder-strewn and heather-coated track. There is a small river bed to the left. Continue north as the path leads down to a fertile valley. Go along its right side.

The path reaches the valley's dry river bed 35 minutes after passing over the col. Ascend gently along the left (west) face of the valley until the path leads north for 30 minutes to some massive, rock-faces which stand closely together. The path branches right (north) 200 metres before reaching these to lead over a low, rocky ridge. Continue north past some azibs, as the path leads across the same dry river bed and then ascends in zigzags.

You will pass some huts on the left about 25 minutes later. This is Irhioui. Carry on until you reach another small pass, Tizi n'Irhioui (1954m/6409ft), from where you will again be able to see Qalaa't M'gouna. Follow the path as it winds into another valley which is peppered with azibs and neat fields. There is an obvious water-source here. Keep on the main track as it runs along the right side of a dry ravine, some almond trees and terraced plots. This is the place to camp if you

---

(Opposite) Top: A long descent in the Jbel Sahro region. **Bottom:** Rock formations at Tassigdelt, see p206. (Photos © Patrick Maguire).

decide to break your trek here. Expect to find this area 30 minutes after reaching the first huts of Irhioui.

Tizi n'Irhioui—Boumalne du Dadès
[Map 36a and 36b, p226 and p227]

Get onto the path and head north down the ravine. The path is clear but bear left if faced with any deviations to remain alongside the ravine floor. The terrain is loose and rocky. Maintain a northerly direction. After 10 minutes you will pass a small farm to the right. Stick with the ravine which itself guides you in the right direction: north. After 20 minutes the track crosses the ravine (a small stone wall will confirm your position), to lead north-north-east while the ravine winds away north-north-west. The trail then grows almost to a piste which can clearly be seen wending its way north over increasingly flat and low-lying ground. This route is called Imi n'el Louh.

Climb a small ridge, 45 minutes into the trek, to see a small plain behind which foothills rise to the High Atlas. The piste winds north-east around the ridge. After a few minutes it meets a tiny path heading across the boulder-strewn plain towards the north. Bear left, following this path, allowing a hut just ahead to guide you. Pass to the right of the building, heading off the path as you do so, to cross another river bed. Shortly after this, pick up a double piste which leads north past a stone-walled field. The piste divides soon after.

Keep going straight (north), ignoring the left (west) branch which runs parallel to the wall. After two minutes the track disappears although you will pass another running east to west. Continue north until, after 10 minutes, you pass another small farm to the right after which the path becomes clear again.

By now the foothills seem close; when you see a large, rocky hill, deviate from the path (north-east) to rejoin another stretch of it running north. As you pass over a small sandy bed you will lose it and cross a tiny plateau peppered with rounded rock formations before coming to some more stone walls to the left. The path again becomes clear, leading north.

The track divides 75 minutes into the trek. Go right (straight on) into the foothills. Follow the track as it ascends gently over whitened rocks and gritty ground. After 10 minutes it swings north-east and ahead stands a steep black slope. At this point break from the path to head north once more. This direction will lead you down to another path which crosses a (dry) river bed heading north-north-west over flat, rocky ground before climbing a little.

(Opposite): The final push across the plateau towards Boumalne du Dadès, Jbel Sahro region. (Photo © Patrick Maguire).

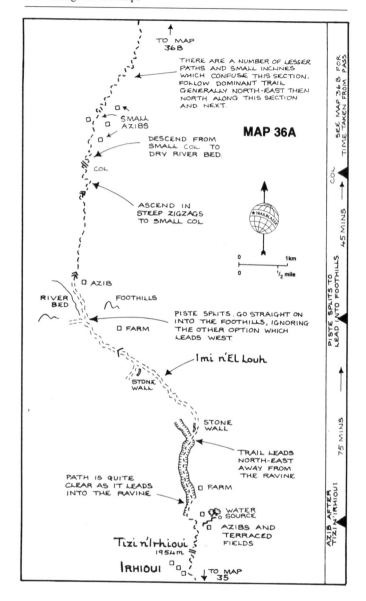

TO MAP
36 B

THERE ARE A NUMBER OF LESSER
PATHS AND SMALL INCLINES
WHICH CONFUSE THIS SECTION.
FOLLOW DOMINANT TRAIL
GENERALLY NORTH-EAST THEN
NORTH ALONG THIS SECTION
AND NEXT.

SMALL
AZIBS

DESCEND FROM
SMALL COL TO
DRY RIVER BED.

MAP 36A

COL

ASCEND IN
STEEP ZIGZAGS
TO SMALL COL

★ TRAIL AZIB

0 _____ 1km

0 _____ ½ mile

AZIB

RIVER
BED

FOOTHILLS

FARM

PISTE SPLITS. GO STRAIGHT ON
INTO THE FOOTHILLS, IGNORING
THE OTHER OPTION WHICH
LEADS WEST

Imi n'El Louh

STONE
WALL

STONE
WALL

TRAIL LEADS
NORTH-EAST
AWAY FROM
THE RAVINE

FARM

PATH IS QUITE
CLEAR AS IT LEADS
INTO THE RAVINE

WATER
SOURCE

AZIBS AND
TERRACED
FIELDS

Tizi n'Irhioui
1954m

Irhioui

TO MAP
35

COL

SEE MAP 36 B FOR
TIME TAKEN FROM PASS

45 MINS

PISTE SPLITS TO
LEAD INTO FOOTHILLS

75 MINS

AZIB AFTER
TIZI N'IRHIOUI

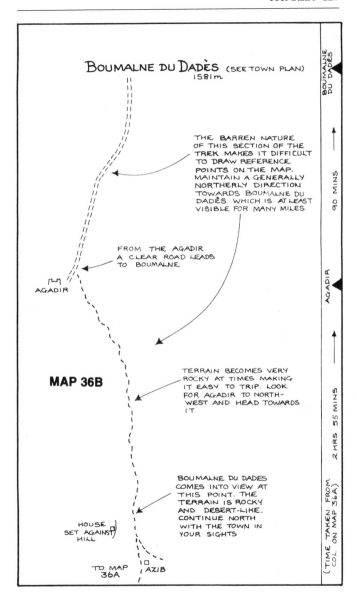

BOUMALNE DU DADÈS (SEE TOWN PLAN)
1581m

THE BARREN NATURE
OF THIS SECTION OF THE
TREK MAKES IT DIFFICULT
TO DRAW REFERENCE
POINTS ON THE MAP.
MAINTAIN A GENERALLY
NORTHERLY DIRECTION
TOWARDS BOUMALNE DU
DADÈS. WHICH IS AT LEAST
VISIBLE FOR MANY MILES.

FROM THE AGADIR
A CLEAR ROAD LEADS
TO BOUMALNE.

AGADIR

MAP 36B

TERRAIN BECOMES VERY
ROCKY AT TIMES MAKING
IT EASY TO TRIP. LOOK
FOR AGADIR TO NORTH-
WEST AND HEAD TOWARDS
IT.

BOUMALNE DU DADES
COMES INTO VIEW AT
THIS POINT. THE
TERRAIN IS ROCKY
AND DESERT-LIKE.
CONTINUE NORTH
WITH THE TOWN IN
YOUR SIGHTS

HOUSE
SET AGAINST
HILL

TO MAP
36A

AZIB

BOUMALNE
DU DADÈS

90 MINS

AGADIR

2 HRS 55 MINS

(TIME TAKEN FROM COL ON MAP 36A)

Dip to cross a small plateau, heading north, and then another dry river bed. Look for an azib ahead and to the right and keep to the left of it as the track climbs a steep ridge in zigzags. Ascend for 20 minutes to a col, then descend to a dry river bed. Continue along the river bed for 10 minutes until, five minutes later, the track leads past a small azib to the right.

Just after this break away from the river bed to maintain a northerly direction up a small incline where the path again becomes more obvious. Look to the left to see another stone azib just before which the trail leads up an incline to a ridge. Trek up and along the ridge for 10 minutes until the path divides. Bear right over a small hill. After five minutes cross another (dry) river bed (there is a well here) and carry on north.

Pass another small azib to the right 10 minutes later. Another 15 minutes will take you past another azib to the right. Just after this the track joins another as it leads north through a narrow valley. After 15 minutes the path crosses to the right side of a (dry) river bed which also runs north. Cross it to pick up a small path heading north-north-west over the brow of a hill; now trekking in a more northerly direction you leave the path as it passes a stone house set into the hill. At this point Boumalne du Dadès comes into view and the terrain quickly becomes rocky and desert-like.

Head north for ten minutes, north-east for ten minutes and then east-north-east for ten minutes until the track crosses a hill and another dry river bed. Boumalne is now in your sight making it hard to go wrong. Stumble over difficult, rocky ground (it's easy to trip here) for another 40 minutes until the trail crosses a piste. Ignore the piste and continue north. Look across the plateau where an agadir stands left of Boumalne. Trek to the agadir which is further away than it looks; it will take another 35 minutes to reach it. From the agadir the piste leads clearly north to Boumalne du Dadès (1581m/5185ft) town. It will take around 90 minutes to go from the agadir to Boumalne.

Boumalne du Dadès

Boumalne du Dadès is a rather more attractive town than Qalaa't M'gouna which lies about 20 kilometres west. There is a peaceful, laid-back air here which trekkers will no doubt appreciate after a demanding Sahro circuit. Boumalne is a small community but one which offers a useful range of services.

Services There's a **Banque Populaire**, a **post office**, **bus station**, **tabac**, **petrol station**, basic **shops**, **hammam** and several places to stay or eat.

Places to stay *Hôtel Adrar* (☎ 04-83.03.55), near to the CTM office, with rooms from 40dh; *Hôtel-Restaurant Salam* (☎ 04-83.07.62) which has adequate rooms for 60dh; *Auberge de Soleil Blue* (☎ 04-83.01.63), a step up, has good en suite rooms from 70dh; *Hôtel Madayeq* (☎ 04-

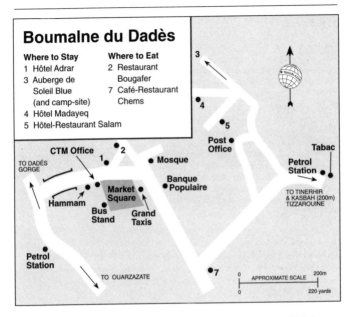

Boumaine du Dadès

Where to Stay
1 Hôtel Adrar
3 Auberge de Soleil Blue (and camp-site)
4 Hôtel Madayeq
5 Hôtel-Restaurant Salam

Where to Eat
2 Restaurant Bougafer
7 Café-Restaurant Chems

CTM Office
TO DADÈS GORGE
Mosque
Hammam
Market Square
Bus Stand
Grand Taxis
Post Office
Banque Populaire
Tabac
Petrol Station
TO TINERHIR & KASBAH (200m) TIZZAROUINE
Petrol Station
TO OUARZAZATE
APPROXIMATE SCALE
200m
0
0
220 yards

83.07.63), a large but unfriendly place with a bar and pool, which has en suite rooms from around 300dh; and **Kasbah Tizzarouine** (☎ 04-83.06.90), off avenue Mohammed V on the west side of town, which is the best place. Head here for beautiful rooms (some are carved into the rock) and attentive service for around the 300dh mark. **Campers** can pitch tents at Auberge de Soleil Blue or the Kasbah Tizzarouine.

Where to eat *Kasbah Tizzarouine* and *Hôtel Madayeq* have good restaurants serving Moroccan specialities; expect to pay between 70-100dh for a full meal, while *Café-Restaurants Chems*, just outside town, serves familiar Moroccan classics, tagines and couscous, of the highest quality. It's not expensive but cheaper still is the restaurant in *Hôtel Adrar* and *Restaurant Bougafer* which is similarly acceptable and inexpensive.

Transport There are several buses a day to Ouarzazate and from there to Marrakesh. Go to the CTM office by the bus stand. Grands taxis gather between the mosque and the covered market.

APPENDIX A: ARABIC, FRENCH AND BERBER

ARABIC

Basic words and phrases are given here but if you plan to take your Arabic beyond the 'hello' and 'goodbye' stage, you should take a phrasebook with you. Lonely Planet's *Moroccan Arabic Phrasebook* is recommended.

Pronunciation

Moroccan Arabic is a spoken language which is not often written; as a dialect of Modern Standard Arabic, which developed from the Arabic of the Qur'an, it is considered to have no proper written form. This makes writing Arabic words in Roman letters particularly difficult and inexact. Pronunciation is tricky for most Westerners but Moroccans do tend to try hard to understand anyone trying to speak Moroccan Arabic; they appreciate the effort.

The most difficult sound in Arabic is the **glottal stop** ('), which is produced by tightening the back of the throat as in a hiccup. Note also:

ai	as in 'eye'
ay	as in 'pay'
g	hard 'g', like 'go'
gh	low. rolled 'r'
kh	as above but harsher and shorter
q	like 'k'
r	high, rolled 'r'
zh	's' as in 'pleasure'

Pleasantries

Hello	*Salam a'laykum* (lit. peace be upon you)
(Response)	*Walaykum salam*
Goodbye	*M'a-ssalama*
Please	*'afakum*
Thank you	*Shokran*
How are you?	*Labas?*
I'm fine, thank you	*Labas, barak*
God willing!	*Inshallah!*
Excuse me	*Smeh leeya*

Basic conversations

I	*ana*
you	*nta/ntee*(m/f)
we	*hoona*
they	*hma*
why?	*'lash*
when?	*eemta*
open	*mehlool*
closed	*mesdood*
I don't speak much Arabic	*makan'refsh l'arbeeya*
Do you speak English?	*wash kat'ref negleezeeya*
Could you repeat that, please?	*ash gulltee?*
I don't understand	*mafhemtsh*
What's your name?	*asmeetek*
My name is...	*smeetee*

I'm from...	*ana men...*
I'm here on holiday	*zheet l Imaghreeb fe fel 'ohla*
I'm married	*ana mzhoowzh/a* (m/f)
I'm single	*ana mamzhoowzhsh/ash* (m/f)
How old are you?	*shhal f'merek?*
I'm...	*'andee...*

Problems and emergencies

Help!	*'ateqnee!*
Fire!	*l'afiya!*
thief!	*sheffar!*
help me	*'awennee 'afak*
I've been attacked	*thzhem 'leeya*
I've been raped	*thzhem ghtasabunee*
there's been an accident	*ooq'at kseeda*
please call the police/an ambulance	*'ayyet 'la lbolees/'la ssayyara del'as'af*
my.........was stolen	*tesreq leeya........dyalee*
I need to make a phone call	*wakha nsta'mel ttoleefoon*
I'm very sorry, forgive me	*smeh leeya*

Trekking terms

how many kilometres is the walk?	*shhal dyal lweqt kayn f had ddohra?*
I'm lost	*tweddert*
please show me on the map	*werri liya men l kharita 'afak*
col	*tizi*
compass	*bawsala*
lake	*daya*
map	*khareeta*
mountain	*zhbel/jbel*
path	*triq sgheer*
river	*wad*
summit	*ras*
trek	*temsha 'ls rezhleen* (v)
valley	*sehl*

Travel and directions

How do I get to..?	*keefesh ghadee nuwsul l..?*
Is it far?	*wash b'ad?*
opposite	*quddem*
next to	*hedda*
near to	*qreeb*
left	*leeser*
right/	*eemen*
straight on	*seer neeshan*

Shopping

Where can I buy..?	*fin ghadee neshree..?*
How much?	*bshhal?*
It's too expensive for me	*bezzaf'liya*
That's my final price!	*akheer ttaman dyalee heewa hada*
Is there a market?	*fin kayn ssooq*

Accommodation

hotel	*shee ootayl*
camp-site	*shee mukheyyem*
Please take me to a hotel	*wesselnee l shee ootayl 'afak*
Do you have any vacancies?	*wash kayn shee beet khawtya?*
We'd like to stay..nights	*ghadee ngles...*
full (no vacancies)	*'amer*

Food and drink

The menu, please	*'afak zheeblee lmeenoo*
Have you..?	*wash 'endkem..?*
What is in this?	*ash kayn f hada?*
The bill, please	*'afak zheeblee lhsab*
beer	*beera*
bread	*khobz*
breakfast	*ftur*
cheese	*frumazh*
coffee	*qehwa*
dinner	*'sha*
egg	*bayd*
fish	*hoht*
fruit	*fakeeya*
lunch	*ghda*
meat	*lhem*
milk	*hleeb*
salad	*shlada*
tea	*atay*
water	*lma*
wine	*shrab*
vegetables	*khdra*

Days and seasons

Monday	*nhar letneen*
Tuesday	*nhar ttla*
Wednesday	*nhar larb'*
Thursday	*nhar lekhmees*
Friday	*nhar zhzhhem'a*
Saturday	*nhar ssebt*
Sunday	*nhar lhedd*

January	*zhanveeyeh*
February	*fevreeyeh*
March	*mars*
April	*abreel*
May	*mayyoo*
June	*yoonyoo*
July	*yoolyooz*
August	*ghoosht*
September	*sebtamber*
October	*'ooktoober*
November	*noovamber*
December	*deesamber*

autumn	*khreef*
winter	*shta*
spring	*rbee'*
summer	*sseef*

Numbers

one	*wahed*
two	*zhoozh*
three	*tlata*
four	*reb'a*
five	*khamsa*
six	*setta*
seven	*seb'a*
eight	*tmenya*
nine	*tes'ud*
ten	*'ashra*
twenty	*'ashreen*
thirty	*tlateen*
forty	*reb'een*
fifty	*khamseen*
sixty	*setteen*
seventy	*seb'een*
eighty	*tmaneen*
ninety	*tes'een*
one hundred	*mya*
one thousand	*alf*

FRENCH

Pleasantries

Hello	*Bonjour*
Goodbye	*Au revoir*
Please	*S'il vous plaît*
Thank you	*Merci*
How are you?	*Comment allez-vous/comment ça va?* (formal/informal)
I'm fine, thank you	*bien, merci*
Excuse me	*Excusez-moi/pardon*

Basic conversations

I	*je*
you	*vous/tu* (formal/informal)
we	*nous*
they	*ils/elles* (m/f)
why?	*pourquoi?*
when?	*quand?*
Is there..?	*Est-ce qu'il y a..?*
open	*ouvert*
closed	*fermé*
I don't speak much French	*Je parle peu de français*
Do you speak English?	*Parlez-vous anglais*
Would you repeat that, please?	*Voulez-vous répéter, s'il vous plaît?*

I don't understand	*Je ne comprends pas*
What's your name?	*Quel est votre/ton* (formal/informal) *nom?*
My name is...	*Je m'appelle*
I'm from...	*J'habite à...*
I'm here on holiday	*Je suis ici en vacances*
I'm married	*Je suis marié(e)*
I'm single	*Je suis célibataire*
I have...children	*J'ai...enfants*
How old are you?	*Quel âge avez-vous/as-tu?* (to a child)
I'm...years old	*J'ai...ans*

Problems and emergencies

Help!	*Au secours!*
Fire!	*Au feu!*
Thief!	*Au velour!*
Can you help me?	*Pouvez-vous m'aider?*
I've been attacked	*On m'a attaqué*
I've been raped	*On m'a violée*
There's been an accident	*Il y a eu un accident*
Please call the police/an ambulance	*S'il vous plaît, appelez la police/une ambulance*
Someone's stolen...	*On m'a volé...*
I need to make a phone call	*Il faut que je donne un coup de téléphone*
I'm very sorry, officer	*Je suis vraiment désolé(e), monsieur l'agent*

Trekking terms

How many kilometres is the walk?	*La promenade fait combien de kilomètres?*
How long will it take?	*Ça prendra combien de temps?*
Can you show me where........is	*Pouvez-vous m'indiquer où est.........*
on the map?	*..sur la carte?*
circular trek	*boucle* (f)
col	*col* (m)
compass	*boussole* (f)
lake	*lac* (m)
map	*carte* (f)
mountain	*montagne* (f)
mountain guide	*guide de montagnes*
path	*chemin* (m)
river	*rivière* (f)
shelter	*abri* (m)
summit	*sommet* (m)
trek	*randonnée* (f)
valley	*vallée* (f)

Travel and directions

How do I get to..?	*Pour aller à..?*
Is it far?	*C'est loin?*
Is this the right way to..?	*C'est la bonne direction pour..?*
opposite	*en face de*
next to	*à côté dé*
near to	*près de*
left	*à gauche*

right · à droite
straight on · tout droit

Shopping
Where can I buy..? · *Où est-ce qu'on peut acheter..?*
How much? · *Combien?*
It's too expensive for me · *C'est trop cher pour moi*
Have you anything else? · *Vous n'avez rien d'autre?*
Is there a market? · *Est-ce qu'il y a un marché?*
Which day? · *Quel jour?*

Accommodation
hotel · *hôtel*
lodging · *gîte d'étape*
camp-site · *camping*
Do you have a list of accommodation? · *Est-ce que vous avez une liste des hôtels?*
Is there a hotel here? · *Il y a un hôtel ici?*
Do you have any vacancies? · *Vous avez des chambres?*
We'd like to stay...nights · *On voudrait rester...nuits*
full (no vacancies) · *complet*

Food and drink
Where can we eat? · *Où est-ce qu'on peut manger?*
The menu, please · *Le menu, s'il vous plaît*
Have you..? · *Avez-vous..?*
What is in this? · *Qu'est-ce qu'il y a dedans?*
more... · *encore de...*
The bill, please · *L'addition, s'il vous plaît*
beer · *bière* (f)
bread · *pain* (m)
breakfast · *petit déjeuner* (m)
cheese · *fromage* (m)
coffee · *café* (m)
dinner · *dîner* (m)
egg · *oeuf* (m)
fish · *poisson* (m)
fruit · *fruit* (m)
lunch · *déjeuner* (m)
meat · *viande* (f)
milk · *lait* (m)
salad · *salade* (m)
tea · *thé* (m)
water · *eau* (f)
wine · *vin* (m)
vegetables · *légumes* (m)

Days, months and seasons
Monday · *lundi*
Tuesday · *mardi*
Wednesday · *mercredi*
Thursday · *jeudi*

Friday	*vendredi*
Saturday	*samedi*
Sunday	*dimanche*
January	*janvier*
February	*février*
March	*mars*
April	*avril*
May	*mai*
June	*juin*
July	*juillet*
August	*août*
September	*septembre*
October	*octobre*
November	*novembre*
December	*décembre*
autumn	*l'automne*
winter	*l'hiver*
spring	*le printemps*
summer	*l'été*

Numbers

one	*un*
two	*deux*
three	*trois*
four	*quatre*
five	*cinq*
six	*six*
seven	*sept*
eight	*huit*
nine	*neuf*
ten	*dix*
twenty	*vingt*
thirty	*trente*
forty	*quarante*
fifty	*cinquante*
sixty	*soixante*
seventy	*soixante-dix*
eighty	*quatre-vingts*
ninety	*quatre-vingt-dix*
one hundred	*cent*
one thousand	*mille*

❏ Berber terms

These words which might be of particular use to trekkers are commonly understood between the three major Berber dialects spoken in the Atlas mountains. Since Berber is an oral language, these spellings are approximate.

col	*tizi*
food	*teremt*
gateway	*imi*
goodbye	*akayoon arbey*
hello	*la bas darik/darim* (m/f)
hello (in response)	*la bas*
lake	*aguelmann*
left	*fozzelmed*
mountain	*adrar*
mule	*asseerdon* (m)
no	*oho*
please	*barakalaufik*
right	*ffaseenik*
river	*assif*
thank you	*barakalaufik*
village	*douar*
water	*amen*
yes	*eyeh*

APPENDIX B: GLOSSARY

agadir	a large fortified communal granary
Alaouite	current ruling dynasty, founded in 1665
Almohad	dynasty which ruled from 1145 to 1248
Almoravid	dynasty which lasted from 1062 to 1145
attar	herbalist
azib	seasonal shelter for shepherds
bab	gate (often in city wall)
boucle	circular route or trek
brochette	kebab
burnous	hooded smock for men
caid	Berber leader or official
calèche	horse-drawn carriage
camion	lorry
caravanserai	lodgings for travellers on a caravan route
couscous	semolina steamed in a pot (a couscoussier) over a meat or vegetable stew
cuisinier	cook
dar	building or house
djeema	square or place
djinn	angel-like spirit appearing in human or animal form
ensemble artisanal	government-run craft market
erg	desert dunes
Fatima	daughter of the prophet
faux guide	false guide, conman
fêtes nationales	public holidays
gardien	refuge keeper, parking attendant
gare ferroviaire	train station
gare routière	bus station
gîte d'étape	lodging
glaoua	a plain, black and white High Atlas hanbel
grand taxi	taxi for up to six people, usually for longer journeys
haik	cloth worn by women to conceal themselves
hajj	pilgrimage to Mecca
hammam	communal steam bath
hanbels	carpet designed for domestic rather than ornamental purposes
harem	women of a Muslim household; their living quarters
harira	thick soup made with spices, chick peas, lamb and tomatoes
harissa	sauce made from chillies and garlic which is used to flavour most Moroccan dishes
Imam	religious leader
jallabah	large hooded smock with sleeves
jbel	mountain
jihad	holy war
kanun	Berber laws
kasbah	citadel, fortress
kif	marijuana

kilim	carpet
koubba	dome-shaped tomb of a Holy Man
ksar (pl *ksours*)	fortified village
kufic	stylised Arabic script often used in engravings
m'choui	whole lamb roasted slowly in a sealed clay oven
Maghreb	the 'land of the furthest West': Morocco, Algeria and Tunisia
marabout	holy man, his tomb
mashreq	eastern Arab world
medersa	university for religious study
Mellah	Jewish Quarter

❏ Map terms

Any word printed on Moroccan maps in Roman letters has been transcribed from Arabic or Berber dialects which are themselves rarely written. This leads to a lot of problems. Place names and words change from one map to another; some imagination is required to make sense of it all. To avoid confusion, all place names given in this guide are spelt as they are found on the main Moroccan maps (see p37). This glossary of words (Arabic and Berber) some of which appear on maps might also help to clear up some of the confusion.

adrar	mountain
afella	summit
aghbalou	water source
ain	water source
ait	sons of; tribe
almou	plateau
ararras	path
assif	river
azaghar	plateau
azib	summer shelter (for shepherds)
bab	gate
douar	village
ighzer	ravine
imi	river mouth
irhil	mountain massif
jbel	mountain
kasbah	fortified house or village
ksour	fortified village
marabout	shrine, tomb
oued	river
sidi	saint
taddart	house
taghia	gorge
tamda	lake
tizi	col

menzeh	summer pavilion
Merenid	dynasty in power between 1248 and 1465
merlons	squared battlements
minaret	mosque tower
mirhab	alcove in mosque which points to Mecca
mouflon	Barbary sheep
moussem	religious festival
muezzin	one who calls the faithful to prayer; the call to prayer
pastilla	sweet pigeon pie made with ligh pastry
petit taxi	taxi used for short, local trips
pisé	mud wedged between wooden boards for building
piste	dirt road
quatre-quatre	4WD vehicle
Ramadan	month during which Muslims fast from sunrise to sunset
ribat	fortified monastery
Saadian	dynasty which lasted from 1554 to 1669
Shahada	profession of faith
Sharia	Muslim law
sidi	saint, honoured person
souq	market
sufi	Muslim mystic or mystical brotherhood
tagine	earthenware pot with a chimney in which meat or vegetable stews are prepared; the stew
téléboutique	privately run payphone kiosk
tizi	col, mountain pass
vizier	highest officer under a Muslim leader
wadi	water-course, dry in summer
Wattasid	dynasty in power between 1465 and 1554
zakat	alms
zellij	geometrical mosaic pattern used in traditional décor

APPENDIX C: HEALTH

REDUCING THE RISKS OF GETTING ILL

Any journey will expose the traveller to a greater degree of risk than he or she might experience at home. Trekking, of course, creates its own dangers, as does travelling in a relatively poor country like Morocco. Disease is more prevalent, standards of hygiene are low and of medical treatment variable. But while it's important to be aware of the dangers, one should not be scared off a High Atlas trek. If you take your health seriously and act sensibly you will avoid any major problems. Thanks are due to Sir John Baird, former Surgeon General of the Ministry of Defence, for checking the accuracy of this section.

Before you arrive in Morocco
● Take out medical insurance (see p41).
● Have your inoculations in good time (see p41).
● Visit the dentist before you go.
● If you suffer from a long-term problem, such as diabetes, visit your doctor before departure and take plenty of medication with you. Ask your doctor for a letter explaining your condition and have it translated into French and, if possible, Arabic.
● Prepare medical and first-aid kits (see p32-3).
● Check that your equipment, particularly footwear, is adequate and comfortable (see p29-30).
● Ensure you are reasonably fit and healthy before you go.

In Morocco
● Drink plenty of purified, bottled or boiled water, well-known brands of soft drinks or hot drinks such as tea or coffee (see box on p242 for information about water purification).
● Avoid salad, ice-cream, rice and raw vegetables since these might have been prepared with contaminated water.
● Eat hot food which has just been cooked or fruit which you can peel yourself.
● Eat plenty of carbohydrates and protei, even if you're not hungry to keep your strength up.
● Follow the advice given below on Acute Mountain Sickness (AMS).
● Look after your feet (see below).
● Be very careful when mules pass you on the trail; stand on the mountain side of the path to make sure that if there's not enough room to pass, the mule gets knocked off the trail — not you.
● Don't hurry on the trail and avoid trekking in bad light.
● Avoid trekking alone.

HEALTH CARE IN THE ATLAS REGION

Standards of health care available in Morocco can vary considerably from one doctor or hospital to the next. In serious cases, contact your embassy or consulate for advice (see p68); it might be that your best course of action is to arrange a prompt flight home. There are hospitals in Azilal, Ouarzazate and Marrakesh. Most CAF huts have a first-aid kit and stretcher and all official mountain guides have had some basic training in first-aid. See p39 for information about mountain rescue services.

❏ Water purification

Never drink or even clean your teeth in water which hasn't been purified. A pure-looking mountain stream can be tempting to drink from, particularly when you watch your guide or *muleteer* take long, luxurious gulps, but the chances are it will have been polluted by bacteria from animals or higher human habitation.

● **Boiling** Despite the fact that water boils at a lower temperature at altitude, this is still one of the most effective ways to kill bugs. So tea, coffee, hot chocolate and soup are generally safe to drink. But it's not very practical to boil all the water you need to drink to prevent dehydration while trekking.

● **Chemical purification** Chlorine tablets do not kill all the bugs you need to dispose of; use iodine. Iodine can be applied to water in two forms: tincture or tablets. The first, tincture, is most widely used. Follow the instructions on the bottle carefully. Normally, you will need to let the iodised water stand for at least ten minutes before drinking it. Tablets are my preferred form of iodine. The fact that one tablet purifies one litre of water (and I carry a one-litre water bottle) makes it very easy to get the measurements right. Iodine is bad for you if drunk regularly over long periods. Pregnant women should avoid it completely.

● **Filtering** Portable filter pumps, which can be effective but very expensive, are only really useful if you plan to set up camp for long periods and so don't want to rely on iodised water. If you do buy one, make sure it has a chemical filtration stage otherwise it will simply take out the large dirt but leave the bugs.

ACUTE MOUNTAIN SICKNESS (AMS)

AMS is caused by the fact that, as you climb higher, the change in pressure allows less oxygen to reach your lungs, muscles and brain with each breath you take. It can be fatal.

The key point to remember is that **it's your rate of ascent rather than the altitude itself which causes AMS**. There is some debate about the height at which AMS becomes a threat but one should be aware of the risks over 2500m. Since most of the treks in this guide are over 2500m, and the highest peak is 4167m, trekkers should read this section carefully. Some people are more susceptible to AMS than others. Fitness appears to make no difference. In all cases, however, AMS is relatively easy to avoid.

Prevention

● **Don't exceed the recommended rate of ascent** Your body must have time to acclimatise to altitude. Take two or more days to reach 3000m (10,000ft) and spend subsequent nights at 300m (1000ft) higher than the previous night. It's also a good idea to sleep a little lower than the highest point reached that day. Spend a rest day after each 900m (3000ft) gained over 3000m (10,000ft).

● **Drink lots of fluids** Drink at least six litres of water each day. If your urine is dark, you need to drink more water.

● **Eat well** Keep eating plenty of carbohydrates even if you've lost your appetite.
● **Avoid alcohol and sedatives** Drinking at altitude can lead to dehydration.
● **Don't rush** Ascend steep inclines slowly, allowing yourself plenty of rests. The faster you gain height, the higher the chance of suffering AMS.
● **Look out for symptoms** Read the section below and look out for symptoms of AMS. Since one symptom is confusion and delirium, you should keep an eye on your fellow trekkers and they should do the same for you.
● **Diamox** This is a drug which can treat AMS. But you should consider taking it only if you have suffered from AMS before and you should consult your doctor first. Some doctors believe Diamox is dangerous because it hides symptoms of AMS. Don't take Diamox to prevent AMS, only to treat early symptoms which, if they develop, should make you descend anyway.

Symptoms and treatment
● **Mild AMS** Early signs of AMS include **headache, nausea, difficulty sleeping** and **dizziness**. If you experience these symptoms, and you can't attribute them with certainty to some other problem, **do not go any higher**. Rest until you feel better before moving higher or, if the symptoms persist, descend a few hundred metres.
● **Acute AMS** Symptoms of advanced AMS include **extreme tiredness, loss of co-ordination, delirium, headache, vomiting, cyanosis** (blue lips), **coughing attacks** producing pink or brown sputum, **bubbling breath, rapid heartbeats at rest** and eventual **coma**. The sufferer **must descend immediately**. Acute AMS can be fatal.

AIDS

HIV and AIDS (*SIDA* in French), while far from widespread, is on the increase in Morocco where public awareness is alarmingly low. Any exposure to blood or body fluids could be dangerous. Most visitors will be aware that unprotected sex or intravenous drug use might expose the individual to HIV but the disease can just as easily be passed on through piercing, vaccinations or even blood transfusions. If you need an injection, make sure you see the needle unwrapped. Better still, carry your own sterile needles (although be prepared for some fast-talking if a customs official finds them in your bag). Never refuse a transfusion through fear of contracting HIV; the better Moroccan hospitals screen blood and the chance of picking up the disease in this way is minimal.

BILHARZIA

Bilharzia worms are thought to be present in some still pools and slow-moving streams in the south and, perhaps, the low Atlas. The higher you go, the less chance of catching bilharzia worms. These worms, which grow in the snails which inhabit the edges of lakes and streams, bore into humans and live in their intestines. The effects can be painful and debilitating but there is a cure. Avoid bathing in any water which you think might harbour the worms; in particular avoid the edges. Since the worms often bore into the soles of feet, wear rafting sandals to paddle. Early symptoms include a rash where the worm entered and, later, a high fever. Later still, blood might appear in the urine. If left untreated the problems could recur for 30 years. It's difficult to judge how great a risk bilharzia might be in Morocco; I've bathed in still pools in the Atlas many times and I don't appear to have contracted the disease — *Inshallah!*

DIARRHOEA

Few travellers escape Morocco without a bout of 'the trots'. In the Atlas mountains, of course, where proper lavatories are few and far between, this can be a particularly unpleasant state of affairs. Diarrhoea is almost always caused by food poisoning or drinking dirty water (see box on water purification). Take great care over what you eat and drink and follow a strict personal hygiene régime to reduce your chances of getting ill. It's generally best to avoid taking treatments like 'Imodium' or 'Arret' which simply block up the bowels but don't treat the infection. These treatments are, however, gifts from Allah when it comes to long bus or train journeys. The three main ways to combat diarrhoea are to **rest**, **drink plenty of fluids** and **replace salts** with rehydration mixtures such as Dialoryte.

● **Amoebic dysentery** This can be rather more serious than travellers' diarrhoea. Symptoms include frequent and sometimes bloody diarrhoea which recurs in cycles every few days or so. It might be accompanied by vomiting and abdominal cramps. Seek medical advice where possible since the treatment is a dose of Tiniba.

● **Travellers' diarrhoea (bacterial)** This most common form of diarrhoea can be brought on simply by a change of diet. Symptoms are similar to those above but perhaps less pronounced. Bacterial diarrhoea will normally clear up on its own after a few days so take no treatment at first except rest, fluids and rehydration preparations. If symptoms persist try Norfloxacin.

● **Giardia** Giardia or Giardiasis is a particularly unpleasant form of diarrhoea caused by parasites in contaminated water. The effects might not appear for weeks after drinking bad water. Symptoms are a few loose stools everyday, nausea, abdominal pain and heinous wind. Flagyl is the recommended treatment.

CARE OF FEET, ANKLES AND KNEES

A simple blister or sprain could ruin your trek so take great care to look after your feet, ankles and knees.

● **Blisters** Prevention is better than cure so make sure your boots fit well and are worn in. Wear silk or anti-blister inner socks and wrap potential problem areas in zinc-oxide tape. Dust down your feet each morning and evening with anti-fungal foot powder and wash your feet regularly. Change your socks often and keep your feet dry. If a blister forms, either burst it with a needle sterilised over a flame or build a protective layer around it, perhaps using a product like Second Skin. If you do burst the blister, look out for infection and change the dressing frequently.

● **Sprains** Good boots will help. Watch where you walk, particularly when you're tired, and never trek in bad light. Don't carry too heavy a load and don't rush. If you do suffer a sprain, keep it cool, firmly bandaged and raised and rest for a while. A mountain stream would be the best place to cool the swelling.

● **Knee problems** On the descent bend your knees slightly to avoid jarring them. Use knee supports if you have had trouble before. Deep Heat or Tiger Balm might help.

INFECTIOUS HEPATITIS

There are two types of infectious hepatitis, A and B, and both are fairly common across North Africa.

  Hepatitis A is less serious. Symptoms include **stomach cramps**, **nausea**, **fatigue**, and **jaundice** (yellowness of the skin). Hepatitis A can be picked up from contaminated food, polluted water or bad sanitary hygiene. A gamma globulin injection prior to departure helps to prevent this disease.

Hepatitis B is more serious. It can be picked up in much the same way as AIDS: as a sexually transmitted disease or from contact with contaminated blood or body fluids through needles or a blood transfusion. The symptoms are the same but the incubation period is longer. There is a vaccine available.

> ❏ **Normal health in adults**
> **Body temperature:** 37°C or 98.4°F
> **Pulse rate:** 60-100 per minute
> **Breathing:** 12-20 breaths per minute

MALARIA

Malaria is uncommon in Morocco but it does occur in summer in the deep south and some coastal areas. Consult your doctor if you think you might visit the far south in summer but otherwise it should be enough simply to avoid getting bitten by mosquitoes. Use repellent and perhaps a mosquito net as well. Most bites are inflicted at dawn and dusk so wear socks, trousers and long-sleeved shirts at these times.

OTHER HEALTH PROBLEMS

● **Bedbugs** There's a slight chance you'll receive a call from these pesky fellows if you sleep on old, dirty bedding. Better to sleep in your sleeping-bag even in *gîtes* and lodges. Bedbugs leave rows of itchy red bites which are best soothed with cool antiseptic cream.

● **Dehydration** This can lead to salt loss and heat-stroke and can be very serious. Drink as much clean water as you can while trekking, even when you're not thirsty. Also, unless you suffer from blood pressure problems, add extra salt to your food. In the Atlas temperatures can soar and you will lose a lot of fluid through sweating. The best way to look for dehydration is to monitor your urine. The darker the urine, the more advanced the dehydration.

● **Exposure (hypothermia)** This is unlikely to be a problem to summer trekkers but in winter it is a very real danger to the ill-equipped. Caused by inadequate clothing and food, dehydration, exhaustion and altitude change, the early symptoms are low body temperature (below 34.5°C or 94°F), poor co-ordination, shivering and fatigue. As the condition deteriorates shivering ceases, co-ordination declines so walking becomes difficult, and there may be hallucinations. The pulse will slow; unconsciousness and then death follow shortly.

Find shelter in the early stages if possible. It is vital that body warmth be restored as quickly as possible so someone should strip and get into a sleeping bag with the naked patient. Put in hot water bottles (your drinking bottles will do). Pile extra bedding under and around them.

● **Frostbite** Again, this is likely to be a potential threat only at high altitude in winter. The first sign of frostbite is frostnip when the toes and fingers become very cold, numb, white and painful. Warm them gently against your body. Actual frostbite occurs when a body part becomes frozen. Warm the affected area in water heated to 40°C or 100°F and seek help.

● **Gynaecological problems** Women should be aware that altitude, dietary change, travel or strenuous exercise might make periods irregular or even stop them altogether. There is no cause for alarm.

● **Haemorrhoids** Constipation is fairly common on treks and can lead to haemorrhoids. If you've suffered from this problem in the past, bring remedies for both with you from home just in case.

● **Prickly heat** This is an uncomfortable itchy rash caused by sudden exposure to a hot climate and perspiration trapped under clothes for long periods. Bathe as often as possible and wear cool, loose clothing. Unscented or baby talcum powder will help.

● **Rabies** Rabies is common in North Africa so if you get bitten by any animal which you think might have rabies, seek the vaccine from a doctor as soon as you can. In theory the offending animal should be captured for observation. In practice, however, this will probably lead to your getting bitten again. There is an anti-rabies vaccine which is available for a fee from your doctor prior to departure. It isn't very effective but it does give you more time to get to a doctor for the antidote.

● **Snake bites** If you see a snake leave it alone and don't put your hands or feet into a hole or crevice where there might be one. The possibility of coming across one diminishes as you climb higher. Should you get bitten don't panic: more people die from shock than from snake bite and even venomous snakes are not so all the time. Don't cut or suck the wound. Immobilise the bitten limb and keep still to avoid spreading the poison. Identify the snake if you can but don't waste time trying to do so, since the right antivenene is likely to be available only at major hospitals which may take some time to reach. The type of bite received will usually have become apparent by the time you get there.

● **Sunburn and heat-stroke** There is a real chance of being struck down by heat-stroke in the Atlas. The sun can be frighteningly strong in Morocco and its effects can be greater at altitude. Heat-stroke can, in extreme cases, lead to death so this is something all trekkers must take seriously. Drink at least six litres of clean water a day to avoid dehydration, wear plenty of sunscreen and protect yourself from the sun with sunglasses, a shirt with a high collar and a wide-brimmed hat. Rest regularly in the shade. In a serious case, immediate treatment involves getting the patient out of the sun, stripping them and coating them in cool, wet towels. Make sure the patient drinks lots of water, perhaps with salt added, unless they have slipped into unconsciousness. Either way, if the situation gets as bad as this find medical help.

AFTER YOUR TREK

If you want to leave unused medicine to an appropriate recipient in Morocco make sure you find someone in a position of responsibility, perhaps the mayor of an Atlas village, rather than dispensing medical material to random people who you think might need it.

If you get ill after your trek it's important to tell your doctor where you've been.

INDEX

Trekking in the Dolomites *Henry Stedman*
256 pages, 52 trail maps, 13 town plans, 30 colour photos
ISBN 1 873756 34 8, *1st edition,* £10.99, US$17.95
The Dolomites region of northern Italy encompasses some of the most beautiful mountain scenery in Europe. This new guide features selected routes including Alta Via II, an East-West traverse and other trails. Places to stay, walking times and points of interest are included, plus detailed guides to Cortina, Bolzano, Bressanone and 10 other towns. Also includes full colour flora section.

Trekking in the Pyrenees *Douglas Streatfeild-James*
256 pages, 80 maps, 30 colour photos
ISBN 1 873756 21 6, *1st edition,* £10.95, US$16.95
All the main trails along the France-Spain border from the famous GR10 coast to coast hike and the most scenic sections of the GR11, to many shorter routes. 80 route maps include walking times and places to stay.
'Readily accessible, well-written and most readable...' **John Cleare** *'Very informative ..Take this one with you'.* **Country Walking**

The Inca Trail, Cuzco & Machu Picchu *Richard Danbury*
256 pages, 32 maps, 24 colour photos
ISBN 1 873756 29 1, *1st edition,* £9.99, US$16.95
The Inca Trail from Cuzco to Machu Picchu is South America's most popular hike. This practical guide includes 20 detailed trail maps, plans of eight Inca sites, plus guides to Cuzco and Machu Picchu.
'Danbury's research is thorough...you need this one'. **The Sunday Times** *'...difficult to put down...This book is essential.'* **International Travel News (USA)**

Trekking in the Everest Region *Jamie McGuinness*
256 pages, 38 maps, 20 colour photos
ISBN 1 873756 17 8, *3rd edition,* £9.95, US$15.95
Third edition of the guide to the world's most famous trekking region. Includes route guides, Kathmandu and getting to Nepal. Written by a professional trek leader.
'The pick of the guides to the area.' **Adventure Travel**

Trekking in Langtang, Helambu & Gosainkund
Jamie McGuinness, 256pp, 35 maps,14 colour photos
ISBN 1 873756 13 5, *1st edition,* £8.95, US$14.95
This third guide in the **Nepal Trekking series** covers the region north of Kathmandu. Comprehensive mapping, where to stay and where to eat along the trails. Written by a professional trek leader.

Trekking in the Annapurna Region *Bryn Thomas*
256 pages, 50 maps, 26 colour photos
ISBN 1 873756 27 5, *3rd edition,* £10.99, US$16.95
Fully revised third edition of the guide to the most popular walking region in the Himalaya.
'Good guides read like a novel and have you packing in no time. Two from Trailblazer Publications which fall into this category are Trekking in the Annapurna Region and Silk Route by Rail.' **Today**

Trekking in Ladakh *Charlie Loram*
256 pages, 70 maps, 24 colour photos
ISBN 1 873756 30 5, *2nd edition*, £10.99, US$18.95
Since Kashmir became off-limits, foreign visitors to India have been coming to this spectacular Himalayan region in ever-increasing numbers. Fully revised and extended 2nd edition of Charlie Loram's practical guide. Includes 70 detailed walking maps, a Leh city guide plus information on getting to Ladakh.

'*Extensive...and well researched*'. **Climber Magazine**
'*Were it not for this book we might still be blundering about...*'
The Independent on Sunday

❑ OTHER GUIDES FROM TRAILBLAZER PUBLICATIONS

For more information about Trailblazer and our expanding range of guides, for where to find your nearest stockist, for guidebook updates or for credit card mail order sales (post free worldwide) visit our Web site:

www.trailblazer-guides.com

ROUTE GUIDES FOR THE ADVENTUROUS TRAVELLER

Sahara Overland – a route & planning guide *Chris Scott*
544 pages, 45 maps, 280B&W & 26 colour photos
ISBN 1 873756 26 7, *1st edition*, £19.99, US$29.95
This new guide covers all aspects Saharan, from acquiring documentation to vehicle choice and preparation; from descriptions of the prehistoric art sites of the Libyan Fezzan to the ancient caravan cities of southern Mauritania. How to 'read' sand surfaces, guidance on choosing a reliable guide, using GPS – it's all here along with 35 detailed off-road itineraries covering over 16,000kms in nine countries, from Egypt's Western Desert to Mauritania's Atlantic shore – Morocco, Mauritania, Libya, Mali, Tunisia, Algeria, Niger, Chad, Egypt.
'As addictive as it is informative' **Global Adventure**
'THE essential desert companion for anyone planning a Saharan trip on either two wheels or four.' **Trailbike Magazine**

Tibet Overland – a route & planning guide
Kym McConnell, 224 pages, 16pp colour maps
ISBN 1 873756 41 0, *1st edition*, £11.99, US$19.95
Featuring 16pp of full colour mapping based on satellite photographs, this new book is a route and planning guide for mountain bikers and other road users in Tibet. Includes detailed information on over 6500km of overland routes across the world's highest and largest plateau. Includes the Lhasa-Kathmandu route and the route to Everest North Base Camp. Plus full details on equipment for mountain bikers and background information on Tibetan culture.

Istanbul to Cairo Overland *Henry Stedman*
320 pages, 44 maps, 23 colour photos
ISBN 1 873756 11 9, *1st edition*, £10.95, US$17.95
Where to stay, where to eat, what to see and all modes of overland transport on this route through Turkey, Syria, Lebanon, Jordan, Israel and Egypt. Arabic script for all hotels and place names.
'Useful and enjoyable to read'. **TNT Magazine**

Australia by Rail *Colin Taylor*
256 pages, 50 maps, 30 colour photos
ISBN 1 873756 40 2, *4th edition*, £11.99, US$19.95
Previously published as *Australia and New Zealand by Rail*, this guide has been re-researched and expanded to include 50 strip maps covering all rail routes in Australia plus new information for rail travellers.

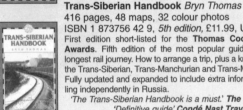

Trans-Siberian Handbook *Bryn Thomas*
416 pages, 48 maps, 32 colour photos
ISBN 1 873756 42 9, *5th edition*, £11.99, US$19.95
First edition short-listed for the **Thomas Cook Guide book Awards**. Fifth edition of the most popular guide to the world's longest rail journey. How to arrange a trip, plus a km-by-km guide to the Trans-Siberian, Trans-Manchurian and Trans-Mongolian routes. Fully updated and expanded to include extra information on travelling independently in Russia.
'The Trans-Siberian Handbook is a must.' **The Sunday Times**
'Definitive guide' **Condé Nast Traveler**